P9-EJJ-237

Richard Church

Richard Church's new book ranges far beyond the confines of the daily events of his life. It is the charting of an odyssey in search of spiritual fulfillment, so exciting and so startling in its depth and insight that the reader enjoys an experience that will remain with him always.

With uncompromising frankness and the disciplined simplicity of a poet, Richard Church shows his own striving—his own voyage home—towards maturity of understanding.

For twenty-four years he led the double life of office worker and artist with a growing compulsion to give literary form to his own glimpses of truth. The shyness of youth gave way to the needs of the artist, and *The Voyage Home* records the author's growing acquaintance with leading men of thought and letters in the past fifty years. He makes memorable appraisals of their qualities and of the mental climate of their times.

The Voyage Home springs from a poet's unwavering grasp of reality. Not only the fascination of the journey and the beauty of the writing make this a remarkable work, for Richard Church's manifold insistence on the importance of individual genius is also a warm reassurance in the present times.

for such a consideration for timing and rounded enunciation offered at once a clear-cut relationship with the values of verse, and the musical propriety of words, the medium of poetry.

The Voyage Home

RICHARD CHURCH

THE JOHN DAY COMPANY
NEW YORK

First American Edition 1966

Library of Congress Catalogue Card Number: 65-20731
Printed in Great Britain

To
C. A. C.
(the silversmith)

'The concept of earthly happiness is, after all, bound up with life in the home.'

– Clara Schumann, in a letter to Johannes Brahms.

CONTENTS

CHAPTER ONE

By Way of a Prologue

[1]

SOONER OR LATER we all turn homeward. A man who dies on foreign soil is judged to have had a sad end. To escape the possibility of such a fate, every human being is possessed by an instinctive urge to hurry home. I noticed this when I was a boy, working in the laboratory in the Custom House, beside Billingsgate Market. I walked over London Bridge twice a day, morning and evening, wedged in the solid phalanx of humanity moving into London City, and out of it again.

I noticed how that tide of trousered or skirted legs was sluggish in the morning, as it trickled towards offices and warehouses; how it rushed like the Severn Bore into London Bridge Station after the day's work, blown by a gale of furious purpose, the desire to get home.

I felt the impulse in my own blood. What was this urge, this primitive anxiety? Are men and women infected by some racial fear of the jungle, that drives them to seek the safety of the cave, even after several thousand years of the assurances of civilization? I remember now, half a century since the routine of those years in the laboratory, more vividly than I remember all other moods and events, this eagerness to get home to my rooms on Denmark Hill. The urge often made me break into a jog-trot over London Bridge, risking my life by edging out of the crush from the pavement to the gutter. Sometimes, I even had the illusion of rising above the heads of the crowd, and gliding like a seagull, levitated by my own frenzy.

It was as though I were expecting a visitor, some fabulous person, a dream-spirit, or a lover. But I knew that I should find my rooms as I had left them – empty: the breakfast cup and saucer in the sink, still to be washed; the volume of La Fontaine's *Fables* still open on the kitchen table, where I had been memorizing those lucid phrases, to improve my knowledge of French, before setting out every morning.

I knew, too, that as I put the key in the door, and entered my solitude, a cold, sinking sensation would seize me, like a stomach cramp, as once again the cheat of anticipation worked.

Yet in spite of this consciousness, and of my reasonable efforts to control its defeatist effects, I rushed home every day breathless with anticipation. In this I was but an individual in the mortal stampede. The same intent lit the eyes and set the mouths of those thousands leaning forward as they pressed on toward the flashing Bovril advertisement at the entrance to London Bridge Station Yard.

Not much farther along the Borough High Street stood the Tabard Inn, from which Chaucer's Canterbury pilgrims set out six hundred years earlier. I wish he had described their homecoming. Was the expression on their faces the same as that of those twentieth-century commuters, of whom I was one?

This vestigial habit is never quite lost. Indeed, as we grow, or shrink, into old age, the craving for home revives with redoubled force, the dominant of our second childhood. It is not a matter of cowardice, or timidity. People driven by the wanderlust, and those who are dare-devils always out in search of adventure in 'fresh woods and pastures new', come home from time to time, to look around at the familiar scene, and to recognise it with an emotional response that is awestricken, mystical. Even on our travels, the first thing we do on stopping for the night is to set up a simulacrum of home, temporary, but representative of and singular to our own selves: an altar to privacy.

The habit, the craving or instinct, cuts close and intimately into our lives. No outside directive, of politics, religion, or economic necessity, can wholly destroy it. A child in an orphanage will secrete a pathetic hiding-place, a mouse's nest, where he may be alone with his possessions, and thus assured of that universe.

There must be some cause, outside the reach and explanations of reason, for this homing instinct. It directs the centripetal movements of all organic life. The anemone in the sea is wholly conditioned by it, and remains anchored in its own lair. The pigeon released at the caprice of the fancier needs only to make a few circles in the foreign air, before orientating itself and winging direct for the cote.

The man who wrote of 'the kindred points of Heaven and home' was near the heart of this mystery, which controls us not only in our flight, but also in our moments of rest, especially if that rest be the immobility of pain, of suffering, of despair. As we crouch away from the world, seeking like the wounded plover to merge, unobservable, into our surroundings, we contrive even to make a home of that condition. The very attributes of our person, our clothes, the contents of our pockets and bags, become aspects and symbols of home: sufficient to reassure us, if we are in mortal fear, and to preserve our sense of identity and self-respect.

Where that recognition ceases, a potentiality for crime begins. The homing instinct is the fundamental impulse towards founding a civilization, for it works upon a nomadic people, pulls them to a standstill, and thus to agriculture and the building of houses, barns, and dedicated places where thanksgiving may be offered for the fruits of these first non-destructive labours.

Having thus made human society, and the moral structures that buttress it, the home-making instinct at the same time reacts against its own achievement, and turns to protect the individual from the resultant tyranny of society. It gives him, and more particularly, her, the impulse towards possessiveness, parental love, and the determination to hold, to shelter his own creations. He builds the home now not only against the elements, but also against his fellow creatures. Like the other elemental passions, it works in all we do and are, both for evil and for good.

But in speculating so generally about home, I have wandered too far from home. I intended to refer at once to an account of a recent homecoming. I see that it follows a journey so rich in contacts, sights, experiences both physical and mental, that I must come gradually to the return home. Sensation-mongers and melodramatists, people drunk on modernity and the post-war violences, will think nothing of my quiet itinerary through India and Ceylon, and of any professional pursuits there. I am not thinking of them either, for I am a sedentary person who responds slowly, perhaps belatedly, to changes, big upheavals. Home once more, and thankfully, I find myself still preparing to set out, this time in regurgitative motion, to appreciate, digest and absorb my experiences. That will take longer than four months, the time occupied by my original journey. I foresee obstructions. Preconceived ideas and prejudices loom like rocks out of the sea and on the roads. I shall have to steer round the one, remove the other, and probably lose my bearings in the process. Memory carries a defective compass, and the vagaries of the imagination are infinite, comparable to those of a kitten playing with a ball of wool. However, I am home again, and I thus have the illusion of safety, and of a fenced authority in my little world.

[2]

They are desperate people who cannot command one of these little worlds. Until I was recently in Calcutta, I had not been able to imagine what it was like to be homeless, though my old friend the poet W. H. Davies had talked about it to me vividly enough. He describes in his book, *The Autobiography of a Supertramp*, how he spent many years as a hobo in North America, and as a vagrant in London and the English countryside, living on his wits, a street-singer and peddler of shoelaces. His genius gave that life a Stevensonian glamour; but I observed that when he began to earn a little money from his writings, and was granted a Civil List Pension by Mr Asquith, he gave up sleeping in doss-houses, and settled in a cottage in the village of Weald, near Sevenoaks, lent him by Edward Thomas, a fellow-poet. There he made a home, so static and peaceful a place that butterflies settled on his pencil while he sat in the garden writing verses that still enchant poetry lovers with an ear for rhyme and a mind for lucidity.

At the beginning of this twentieth century, during the lull before the storm, the life of the vagrant was romanticized into a literary cult. Davies rode on the tide. Songs of the Open Road were fashionable in the manner of R.L.S. and Masefield. The composers of the period set them to music heard even after the mud and blood of Flanders had dried out. But it was not popular with the unhappy warriors who came home. They had seen enough of life 'under the canopy' as Coriolanus so bitterly called it when asked where he dwelt. All they wanted was a roof overhead and a hearth of their own, before which they might accumulate the fruits of privacy, including a wife and family, thus unconsciously setting about the rebuilding of a broken civilization. But it is easier to smash than to make, and that civilization has still to be restored. Gone down with it are many of its attributes, not all of them of lasting value, or appropriate to changed needs and conditions.

The provision of homes is always a major issue. It demands priority of attention from the statesman, the priest, the economist. All three have been in despair about it, since two world wars and universal revolution have bedevilled the constructive efforts of scientist, architect and craftsman. Subsidiary social and economic earthquakes, violent nationalism and other ideologies, not only have brought about a shortage of bricks and mortar; they also have attuned, or distuned, a younger generation to an indifference to home life. How significant it is that the young Russian hero, the world's first astronaut, the idol of his countrymen and symbol of their achievement in competitive science, should be described as 'living with his wife and two children in his two-roomed flat', and that no newspapers should comment on this irony.

But in the domestic circumstances of the world of the midtwentieth century, Major Gagarin may be considered fortunate to have even a two-room flat. By comparison with millions of displaced persons, he is certainly comfortably housed. I try to appreciate his content of mind, and even that of his wife, by recalling what I saw in Calcutta, a city of five million souls. I call them souls, to remind myself that thirty thousand of them are capable of that attribute, though driven from East Pakistan to squat on the pavements of Calcutta, waiting for something to be done for them.

They are to be seen in the very heart of the city, lying asleep, or dying, beneath filthy rags on the traffic islands, while the noonday flood of cars and lorries roars round them. There they lie, inert, immobile. Nobody even lifts the rag from a hidden face to find out if this be sleep or death.

Religion does not solve this problem. The Indian people are spiritual in a way that Europeans are not. Every moment of their lives, every gesture, habit, and reaction to circumstance, is conditioned by this consciousness which occupies the forefront of their minds: the dominance and superior importance of spiritual matters over the material concerns of everyday life. That may be why they accept physical suffering, other people's and their own, as of minor importance. Their indifference to this degradation of the homeless and hungry millions is terrifying to an observer from a modern Welfare State.

The President of India, Dr Radhakrishnan, a philosopher-statesman of noble character, said to me that this problem 'of poverty and population' was the principal anxiety of the Government. But I thought that the people in general were not thus concerned. They were not ashamed, nor desperate about it. They walked past these half-human derelicts, on their way to the temples of Siva, Krishna, or Buddha, wrapped in a sincere religious fervour of a kind found only in the few zealots among Western communities.

How can these conditions be reconciled by a rational observer? I saw the contrast even more shockingly presented up-country, at Budd-gaya, the place where Buddha is supposed to have sat under a tree and to have received Enlightenment. There stands the tree, not gigantic and not a banyan, backed by a garish altar. Behind them towers the *stupa* or temple, over-loaded with ornament and symbolical carving. It denies and reverses the principles and practice of the Buddha, just as the florid temples over the tomb of Saint Francis at Assisi deny his vow of poverty and the whole purpose of his mission.

Squatting round the *stupa* lay groups of Tibetan refugees. They were even more filthy and degraded than the refugees in Calcutta. In spite of the heat on that plain of Bihar, they wore their mat-like native garments and moccasins. The clothes clung to them rather as the protective accretions cling to a caddis-worm. The stench polluted even the holy air of the garden surrounding the temple. They sat delousing each other, until we appeared. Then they rushed at us, whining and crying, clawing at the car window. One old crone had dead eyes and a drooling mouth. She kept up a feeble moan, scratching at the windscreen with her nails. The children pushed her aside, to swarm round us as we walked to the temple, but she reappeared when we returned. Her claws were hardly larger than those of the begging children, who by now were screaming at us in a kind of mock fury.

In moods of despair, when we look out at this world-menace of 'poverty and population', and at the hostility of totalitarian governments to the privacy and dignity of the individual, we may wonder if the human race has had its day, and is now rushing to the brink. Will the end come soon, in a hydrogen holocaust, or shall mankind gradually crush itself under the pressure of population? Hitherto, we have never made weapons without using them. Either from prejudice, stupidity or urgency, the majority of people will not practise birth-control. So human life must either be exterminated soon, or degraded later.

Such cynical, fatalistic thoughts are too general to interest us for long. The particular event, here and now, offers more drama, though miniature. That is because it is personal, part of the individual's homecoming. What then is this controlling passion, that takes command as soon as consciousness dawns in the child's mind, and remains insistent throughout life, undeflected by the multitude of other desires and impulses that drag us aside on the journey? Even those mortals who are indifferent to a lodging on this earth, wanderers and Ishmaels who cannot find or accept a shelter within yet isolated from the community, are nevertheless driven on by this craving for 'a fine and private place', though their only domestication will be in the grave, their only settled property the 'entail of four planks'.

[3]

Certainly I was mastered by that craving, days before the moment came when I boarded the *Oriana* at Colombo. My wife and I had been on the move for four months, latterday wandering scholars, each with our offerings. I talked, and gave readings, at the universities. She, being a silversmith and jeweller, sought out the craftsmen who in India still work by hand at little benches shaped exactly like her own, which stands on a balcony in our living-room at home. This coincidence alone would have given her confidence, had she not discovered also that the Indian tools, and the handling of them, were familiar.

Our travels therefore had not been without interest. We had quartered the sub-continent, with the exception of Pakistan; met hundreds of hospitable people, from the Prime Minister and Vice-President down to the cleaner and sweeper (formerly called the Untouchables); visited temples and sculptured caverns; driven over semi-deserts and through the jungle; sweated in aquarian Trivandrum and shivered in Chandrigahr. I had talked publicly until I was voiceless, and my wife had filled her pocket sketch-book with formal designs. But now, engulfing all this excitement and experience, rose the longing to return home. It had begun to show itself during a bout of tropical sickness three weeks earlier, when we reached Ceylon. During our last four days, while we waited in Colombo, it became almost uncontrollable, and I gave my two final lectures at the Buddhist University in a condition of self-hypnotism, combating this craving.

I spoke to an audience of several hundred monks and young seminarists, and a scattering of picturesque folk invited by the Principal. The sun was going down after a hot day. His beams shone through the large, open auditorium, and threw horizontal shadows from the pillars supporting this ornate pavilion. They lay across the crowded floor, so deep in contrast to the livid fire of the sunset, that the people sitting in those shadows were almost extinguished, while those in sunlight burned like lamps, their saffron robes, their eyeballs, their shaven craniums, each bare shoulder and arm flashing up at me as though moulded in metal.

To add to the conflagration, a news-film unit trained its lights and cameras at the high rostrum where I sat beside my chairman, the Professor of Philosophy, a figure not unlike Pope Pius XII: very Roman, very severe, very formal. After some prayers and responses, a Buddhist litany in Sinhalese, I was introduced and began to talk, to the twirl of the cameras and the *obbligato* of voices and noises-off which combine with all lecturing in the Orient.

Speaking in public in any place outside Europe is exhausting work, because the lecturer is never alone with his audience. He has to collect and unify its attention in an environment of open doors and windows, a constant coming and going of cultural camp-followers, the rivalry of loud conversation, children at play, traffic blocks, sudden mysteries of political demonstrations, against the shout-throw of the lecture-room. In addition, there is the ceaseless hoicking of the hordes of crows, those scavengers of the East, who perch on the window-ledges and croak their disapproval of all that is being said from the dais.

The speaker has no need to be disconcerted, or to fear that he will never weld his listeners into a mass-personality (that desideratum of the orator). Indian audiences, once their attention is caught, are deaf to extraneous attraction. They lean forward, their eyes intent, their brows corrugated under the

B

pressure of seeming interest, quite unaware that the lecturer, if he be a pampered European, is suffering acutely from the effort to ignore the bursts of *joie-de-vivre* from the corridors, and the hubbub from the streets. This is indeed an *obbligato*, and not merely an accompaniment for it claims equality with the solo of the speaker.

During those two last lectures in Colombo, I shared my audience's imperviousness. But I was also distracted from my own voice, even from my own thoughts, under the compulsion of this desire that by now was dominant over mind and body. My limbs ached with the longing for home, and as I stood on that rostrum, high above my shadow-striped audience massive as rock below me, I found my consciousness splitting into halves, the one still dealing with the subject of my talk, still holding my audience together, while the other was carrying me out along one of those solid sunbeams, past the white *stupa* shining in the courtyard beyond, and to the harbour, and the ship reported to be steaming up towards Ceylon from Australia, on its way to pick me up and to carry me to my home.

[4]

This is not a matter easily to be dramatized and put to literary account. Like the authority of sleep, it claims everybody, from birth to death, and expresses itself only through other states of mind: fear, loneliness, maybe even cowardice, prejudice and ignorance. Can an emotion which employs such communicants be a worthy one? Is the house, the family enclosure, a relic of the childhood of civilization, when mankind's environment was always dangerous, an unexplored jungle? Communist peoples may see it that way, and thus find a reason for suppressing family life, and the home which is its centre.

But what is to replace it, and its infinite attributes, whose influence penetrates into a person's consciousness with a complex subtlety comparable to the minute veins and nerve threads that co-ordinate and control his body? I cannot conceive how a man would think, feel, act, who has no basis of home-craving. But as populations grow tumid, needing some kind of mass control, a totalitarian system that must override the individual and his privacy, we shall rear vast communities that may have no experience and no conception of home life. Will they still be human, as we know the humanity hitherto moulded by civilization? Will privacy be possible, or desired?

These questions, surely, weigh down our minds with dread, though maybe already generations are growing up to whom our fears are incomprehensible. They are already conditioned, and would dismiss my speculation as reactionary, sentimental, a by-blow of the superstitions of 'religion'.

The fox is a home-lover without being prompted by religion. Even the ant and bee, wholly reared in communistic societies, have this prejudice in favour of their own queen-mother, symbol of home. No political surgery will root out this urge from the bloodstream. I can write of it with an unshakable faith in its permanence, and its future influence on the conduct, habits, beliefs and hopes of individual men and women. It will therefore continue to emerge, especially in times and circumstances of crisis, as a force in the community of mankind, even when politics have been dissolved in a world federation, and there are no more nations, if such an outcome be possible.

CHAPTER TWO

Fate at the Telephone

[1]

MEANTIME, I REACHED HOME SAFELY, and have since been pondering on so commonplace an event: desultory thoughts, drifting in and out of the traffic of a busy professional life. We all have this serial activity of mind. Whether we become highly educated, specialized sophisticates in one or other walk of life, or whether we remain primitive and contentedly anonymous, this slow, ruminative, intermittent contemplation saturates our waking thoughts, and probably directs our dreams at night. It is hardly conscious, and only half-rational, but it keeps an authority over us as individuals, and ensures us the retreat into privacy, where we believe our sanctuary to lie, safe from molestation by politics, dogmas, and the increasing pressure of the traffic of the community.

I am not aware of having learned more about this ordinary experience of homecoming since I returned from India. I mentioned recently to an old friend, a surgeon, how indolently I had been puzzling my mind with this matter. 'Oh!' he said, 'it's just the desire to return to the womb: a birth trauma!'

But that lucid explanation really told me nothing. One of the many disappointments of the scientific labelling of things, and states of being, is that this statistical trick brings us no nearer the 'why', and the purpose.

The doctor's dismissal of the problem, however, set up a kind of obstinacy in me (he would call it a relapse into superstition), and I found my two-year ruminations crystallizing round more intimate, family memories. I realized that since writing an autobiographical diptych a decade ago, I had, in that task, purged myself of acute feeling about, almost even of any memories of, those early years of my life. The catharsis had left me the poorer, as though I had lost a limb, or an eye. For that book, in common with all autobiographies, had been of necessity almost solely concerned with the task of evoking recollections of home life, at a period of childhood and youth when home is an absolute, a universe. Never in later years is home so concrete, and this may be why it is comparatively easy to write about the beginning of our mortal journey from the cradle to the grave; but only comparatively easy.

Not many autobiographers are able to keep up the narrative after early middle life. Even Goethe, the greatest of all in this self-concerned literary practice, could not carry on the fluid portraiture beyond the point of his twenty-seventh year. He wrote the book in later life, working it up from his diaries over a period of twenty-four years, with a long break of seventeen years between 1813 and 1830. So in its latter stages it was a swan-song, knowingly inconclusive. He ends it abruptly with the agonized cry: 'Child! child! no more! The coursers of time, lashed, as it were, by invisible spirits, hurry on the light car of our destiny, and all that we can do is with calm courage to hold the reins firmly, and to guide the wheels, now to the left, now to the right, avoiding a stone here, or a precipice there. Who can tell whither he is being borne, seeing he hardly remembers whence he has come?'

That is the outcry, the final demand, of one of the giants of modern Europe. The orthodox answer, by a devotee of any religion, is 'Home'. That answer, unlike the surgeon's, covers both ends of the mystery of our earthly journey.

Thinking about Goethe's relinquishing of *Poetry and Truth*, I suddenly realized that my own chronology had been almost identical. I had written the books late in life, during my sixties, and had rounded off the narrative where I reached the age of twenty-seven, contenting myself, in the effort to build a shapely structure, by making the diptych portray an individual's conception of the first two decades of the twentieth century, with a puerile rooting in the eighteen-nineties.

I asked myself if this arithmetical coincidence could be due

to some rhythm common to all human life? Most masterpieces
in this form have been similarly conditioned. Joseph Conrad's
A Personal Record, W. H. Hudson's *Far Away and Long Ago*,
Frank Kendon's exquisite *The Small Years*, John Clare's
Personal Sketches, W. H. Davies's *Autobiography of a Supertramp*
all end abruptly on the threshold of adult life. It is as though the
midday sun withers the blossom.

There is an obvious, practical explanation for these premature endings. The difficulty becomes an impossibility when
the record of middle and later life brings the autobiographer to
portraying people who are still alive when he is writing. Of
necessity, for the vitality and interest of his story, he will need
to picture those people who have intimately entered, or left, his
life: and could not some of those relationships be sacred, or
even disgraceful? Is the sanctity of marriage to be exposed, or
the equally sacred experience of an illicit affair hitherto sensibly
concealed? What of the reservations and disguises imperative
in the writer's professional and business activities? Suppose
him to have developed into a public figure in the political world,
or in any other sphere where far-reaching responsibilities
command him to secrecy?

Rousseau, in his immortal *Confessions*, ignored these pro-
hibitions by being a charming cad, so oblivious of other people's
feelings that he might be called a madman. Richard Wagner
was more flagrantly a monster of genius, Benvenuto Cellini
just a Renaissance ruffian, living in an age of social depravity,
drunk on the newly-decanted wine of the Classics, too strong
for medieval stomachs.

To try to carry on with one's life-story into its mature and
autumnal stages is to risk being classed with that unlikeable
company. Even venturing on the personal history with a hope
of using it, to illustrate the theme of this strange rhythm of
universal homecoming, is to risk producing a series of subter-
fuges, evasions and distortions. Literary parricide, for example,
is a crime that few autobiographers have dared to commit.
Edmund Gosse stopped just short of it. Had Dickens openly
written an autobiography (instead of disguising it in *David*

Copperfield) he would have been even more reluctant than Gosse. Yet many writers, as they mature, see their fathers as poor figures in the family group, recognizing with chagrin their own male inadequacy in the finer and more fruitfully sensitive articulations of home life. It may be that adequate fatherhood, unlike motherhood, is a rarely fulfilled function. With the birds and the beasts, a man's biological tendency is to leave the rearing of his young to the mother, and to react possessively and protectively only in moments of danger. That, in general, is his function: to maintain a fence and patrol round the domestic lair.

It is not positive enough to be approved by the introspective temperament usual in an autobiographer. I found this to be so in myself, and I have realized that accordingly I did less than justice to my own father in my portrait of him. I exaggerated his foibles, and was too distant to appreciate that the paternal instinct has its own peculiar powers, less freely and less constantly demonstrated than those of the mother, which remain spiritually umbilical long after the parturition.

But less than justice; more than justice: what is justice to an artist who is struggling to load every moment of consciousness, every ingredient of self-expression, with the glowing stuff of life, the pulse of sympathies as infinite and as subtle as the fountain of all love? Justice is static; it sits in judgment; and human justice pretends to, by means of law, by means of philosophy.

The artist does not function that way. Even when ruled by an austere style, he is on the move, he is making a gesture. And this is an emotional process, springing out of love, or its counterpart, hate. He has to forgive himself for these impulses, and to seek self-discipline in another way, through the aesthetic demands of the medium he works in, as musician, poet, sculptor, painter. He is rarely just; but he brings something to life again: it may be his own father.

I think of that fatherhood now, as I recall where I left the record of my own life at the moment when I stood beside the bed in a little box of a house in the high street of the village of

Limpsfield in Surrey. I took a first-born daughter in my arms, and after a sensation of profound nothingness, was suddenly penetrated by an illusion of sound, a gathering and crescendo of new music. I listened in awe, still standing dumbfounded beside the figure of the young mother.

I had come up from downstairs pen in hand, abruptly summoned from work, the labour at a long dramatic epic, the merging by ambitious youthful intention of two incompatible literary forms. And there, I remember, my record ended with the bewildered request from the 'voice from the bed', to 'Put your pen down.' And my own last words were in wonder 'at the mysterious identity between death and birth', because in the course of those slow-treading moments, I suddenly saw myself similarly holding a dying mother in my arms, ten years previously, almost to the day.

[2]

The rest of that year, 1920, passed slowly and serenely: a period of close domestic privacy, unbroken even by my daily travel to and from the Custom House. I told none of my colleagues of the birth of my daughter. One of them, the elderly chemist who had given me, some years previously, duodecimo editions in diamond-point type of Milton and Wordsworth, came to me one day and openly asked me if there had been 'an addition to my family'. I saw that he was disturbed: he wanted to confide something to me, to relieve his own feelings. I knew that he was living with a young woman, for my wife and I had visited him soon after our marriage. I knew that his wife had been in a lunatic asylum for many years. What I did not know was that he too had become a father for the first time, and was worried about the social situation, and his burden of years.

I repelled him, I lied abruptly and completely. Even now, I cannot understand why I did so. It was not I who had cause for embarrassment. The poor fellow looked at me searchingly for a long moment, then said, 'Oh, I see,' turned and walked out of the laboratory. From that time, until I left the Custom House at the end of the year, he never approached me again, except over official work. I had lost a good friend, and deserved the loss.

Maybe I was still unable to realize the responsibility of this first experience of fatherhood, and could not publicly recognize it until I had learned what it meant, what it was to demand of me. A kind of guilt silenced me, driving me during those first months to a secretiveness. It was as though I had stolen something.

Further, my wife, while working as an analyst in the Laboratory for three years, had been on friendly terms with all the staff, one of four women among about thirty men. I could not reconcile this open, social background, with the deep, intimate atmosphere of shared parenthood. Terrible memories, only half conscious, were revived. The sensuous tenderness with which I had nursed my dying mother still made me vulnerable to all things connected with a woman's body: her sex, her suffering, her fecundity. The act of childbirth demonstrated them all too openly for my prematurely initiated nerves. I must cover this up. I must not let the world know.

That may have been an additional cause of my lying to this generous colleague. I did not learn until later why he had been so eager to share something with me. When the news went round the staff that he was the father of a daughter, I was so remorseful that my dumbness increased: too late then to speak. I could not ask his pardon, or congratulate him. I still have the miniature books he gave me, long after the emotions have died away. Only the shame remains in my mind, a stain almost faded out of the pattern of my experience.

Life at home, however, was less furtive. The spring and summer moved slowly over that exquisite Surrey landscape, which lay unshadowed by war. Life in our little late-Georgian box of a house moved on, draped in flowers and honey from the garden. The bee-keeper and his pretty wife were still with us, and also that wife's Pleyel pianoforte, to ensure a running accompaniment of Bach and Debussy, Chopin and *The Beggar's*

Opera, Fauré's and Schubert's songs, to the nuzzlings of the infant at the breast, and the dancing of the napkins on the clothes-line in the yard leading to the garden.

The pen, which I had not put down during that nativity scene, was at work all through the year on the grandiose scheme of an epic poem *The Deluge*, the story of Noah and the re-generation of the human race. When it was finished, and laboriously typed on a fourth-hand machine somewhat senile in its alphabet, I took it to Roger Ingpen at his publishing house in York Buildings, Adelphi.

It was a tremendous conception, born in that fruitful year. The theme was carried along on a structure of Wagnerian 'song-motives', which recurred again and again among the many metrical forms, blank verse, hexameter, octosyllabics, by which I told the story of Ararat and the Cities of the Plain. As I carried the typescript up Fleet Street one October afternoon, on my way from Billingsgate to the Adelphi, I felt the nerves and muscles of my arm tingling from the magnetic influence of this mountain of verse. I stopped outside the gateway to King's College, opposite St Mary-le-Strand, and compared my present self, parent of both a daughter and this world-shaking epic, with the youth who seven years earlier gate-crashed into Professor Israel Gollancz's evening classes for schoolteachers, and carried off the prize offered by him for a sonnet written in the style of Milton. I told myself, confidently, that this epic, though seeded from the Old Testament, was no pastiche of *Paradise Lost*. The prim little church of St Mary-le-Strand made no response to my self-assurance. The traffic thundered by, and a student hurrying out of the courtyard of Somerset House brushed past me, supremely indifferent in his act of *lèse-majesté*, and nearly swept my satchel into the gutter.

This jolt brought me back to practical considerations, and I moved on towards Charing Cross, turned up John Street and found Roger Ingpen standing on the doorstep of his tiny premises, just about to lock up and depart. With him was a young man of extremely handsome features. Ingpen, parchment-grey in face, and vague in manner, introduced this companion as his nephew, Richard de la Mare. The presence of this Apollo restrained my fervour, and somewhat haltingly I broke the news to the generous publisher of my previous book of verse that I had brought him an epic poem.

The bowed shoulders drooped a little lower, and the junior partner, son of a famous poet and therefore familiar with the breed, stared impassively past me, with just a gleam of restiveness as though about to say that he had a train to catch.

Roger Ingpen sighed, unlocked the door, and held out his hand. I put the typescript of *The Deluge* into it, and I could have sworn that the weight jerked the whole of that fragile human frame into a forward stumble that almost precipitated him into my arms. He smiled wanly, and the papyrus skin of his cheeks wrinkled up with a crackling motion. 'It will be safe there,' he whispered, for his voice was as ghostly as his physique. 'We'll be glad to read it, won't we, Richard?'

There was no reply from Richard de la Mare, for he had vanished. Roger Ingpen appeared not to notice his disappearance. He invited me to accompany him to the Underground Station beside the public gardens where once stood the blacking factory, the purgatory scene of Charles Dickens's boyhood.

We talked of other poets of my own period, most of them survivors from the battlefields of Flanders. I singled out Robert Graves, but Ingpen would have none of him. This surprised me, because I had founded my enthusiastic interest in Graves's poetry not only on his technical precision, but also on his pungent individuality. I have never lost that enthusiasm, nor have I lost any opportunity to praise his work in public, either by reading it to audiences, or reviewing it in the press. During the second world war, the editor of *The Fortnightly Review* invited me to write a series of essays on contemporary poets whose work I thought likely to survive. Of the eight I chose, Graves was one. When the essays appeared in book-form, under the title *Eight for Immortality*, one or two critics were petulant because I had included him. His turn to be taken up by the literary fashion-mongers had not yet come.

What surprised me about Ingpen's blindness to the quince-like flavour of Graves's poetry was its lack of consonance with his relish for Shelley's. He was the editor of the massive ten-volume Julian Edition of *Shelley*, a life-time's work. Here was another nonconformist to literary orthodoxy, a creature of passionately expressed personal views on all things under the sun and moon, self-exiled from his native land. Perhaps Roger Ingpen's fragile frame could not sustain the impact of another such uncompromising genius.

I did not meet Robert Graves until some thirty years later, when his elder half-brother Richard brought him to lunch with me at the Savile Club. Richard Graves and I had been friendly for many years, since the day he showed me a photograph of his daughter Diana, and I had been deeply moved by the beauty of those stilled features.

Robert, the poet, did not share that grace. I found myself silenced by his gruffness of speech, and the rugged, battered physique that emanated a sense of weight. Conversation failed, and I was concerned only for the elder brother's vain efforts to keep the luncheon party alive. I told myself afterwards that Robert Graves might be an artist who cannot believe that praise of his work is merited, or enthusiasm for it sincere. There is, among writers especially, a kind of literary masochism which seems almost to prefer abuse to praise, using it as a stimulant and a challenge; as the nightingale is said to press her bosom against a thorn in order to produce that immortal song which 'found a path through the sad heart of Ruth' still to be heard today, and in that respect comparable to Robert Graves's severely disciplined lyrical muse.

[3]

Some few weeks later Roger Ingpen invited me to call for him at York Buildings, and I stayed in Town after leaving the Custom House at four o'clock, filling in the time by lingering in the bookshop kept by John Wilson near the City approach to Southwark Bridge. He was later to take charge of the world-famous bookshop founded by the brothers Bumpus, and to ensure a concise fame by being the first to publish the poetry of Andrew Young, the Scottish minister and naturalist.

My free reading that afternoon in John Wilson's shop was half-hearted. A sense of foreboding prevented me from concentrating my attention on the shelves of riches before which I stood unsteadily, my legs and stomach, as in all times of crisis, trembling as from a recurrence of that dire physical disability which had darkened my childhood. That is why I cannot now remember what I read that autumn day in 1920, as dusk gathered in the shop, and the two assistants hovered near, hinting by mimed gestures that they wanted to close for the day.

I was, by that time, chilly and hungry, and I walked westward against the tide of humanity at the rush hour, as it surged out of the City towards the railway termini and the bus stops.

I found Ingpen waiting for me on Adelphi Terrace. He was standing against the balustrade, day-dreaming above the sooty foliage of the trees in the Embankment Gardens below. A breeze from the Thames was lifting occasional leaves from the planes, and casting them up to the pavement of the Terrace, where they subsided with a little crackling sound, or scratched along the ground for a yard or two. The figure of the waiting scholar-publisher was so frail that he might well have been sent scuttling off with the autumn leaves.

He smiled wanly at me, mothlike in the dusk, and was about to usher me into the Savage Club (housed at that time in the stately Adam terrace), when he stopped, meditated behind a wrinkled brow, and asked me to go back first to York Buildings. 'It's early yet for a meal,' he said; 'Besides . . .' There he paused, and nervously fingered his lips. But he could not bring himself to say what I dreaded he intended to say. 'Yes,' he resumed, 'there's something which will interest you.'

He had stopped walking as he broached this new theme, and the consequent lack of resistance to the wind almost caused him to be whisked away. But he breasted the opposition and we weathered John Street safely, to reach the little office in York Buildings.

Ingpen fumbled in his pockets for the doorkey, muttering in perplexity over this material problem. I stood shivering, for the walk from Billingsgate, the sense of pending defeat, and the emptiness of a weak stomach, combined to reduce my power of resistance.

Ingpen switched on a light, and I followed him into an inner and even smaller room. Furtively looking round, he opened a drawer in his writing-desk, lifted the paper lining and took out a hidden key. With this, he unlocked the drawer above, and reverently lifted up a package wrapped in a woollen scarf.

He paused again, muttered something to himself, and shut the door between the two rooms. Then he pulled down a dusty blind over a still dustier window which looked out on a blank wall. After those precautions, he unwound the scarf, and revealed a cardboard box, originally filled with writing paper.

It now contained a notebook, on a bed of tissue. The note-book was black, rusted and stained. I noticed that as Ingpen lifted it out of the box, his hands trembled. So did his voice, as he whispered, 'Take it in your hands. It will be something to remember. It is a privilege. I would not invite many people, you know.'

Then his voice dropped to a sub-whisper: 'This is the note-book found on Shelley's body after he was drowned. There are several, but this one – oh, dear!' He turned aside, overcome by strong feelings, and there I stood with the impossible treasure in my hands. I opened it, and saw the pages impregnated by sea-water just a century ago, in 1822. I believe I recognized stanzas from *The Revolt of Islam*. Margins here and there, round the loose and often illegible handwriting, were decorated with little drawings: faces, doodlings, scraps of blossom.

'It belongs to the family,' he said, having recovered his emotional balance. 'Careful! Don't drop it!'

Perhaps I had been swaying, equally overcome. Thankfully, though with the reluctance of one confronted with too-muchness, I handed Shelley's notebook back to his biographer and editor. I hadn't a word to say. I wanted to sit down, to breathe more freely; but both chairs in the office were occupied by piles of books. So I leaned weakly against the desk, while my host slowly wrapped up the treasure and locked it away.

There was a long pause, as after a church service, then Ingpen took up an all too familiar parcel from his desk. 'I'm afraid,' he said, looking from right to left and left to right, 'that this is beyond our resources. You see, the length . . .'

Then he went on. 'But you need to do much more work on it. Most ambitious! Well worth having attempted. No need to be discouraged. But long poems today – well, you might as well walk down the Strand in a suit of armour.'

I thanked him. I had no kind of sensation except a doggedness, as though I were butting my way against a blizzard. I did not confess that I had spent a year writing this massive epic drama, uninterrupted even by the birth of a daughter, and the subsequent domestic realities.

We did not refer to the matter over dinner: a sturdy English dinner of steak-pie and claret. I appreciated the vintage of the wine, for my nine years in the Government Laboratory, where all import and export alcoholic drink was tested – and tasted – had educated my palate.

Ingpen was a gentle person, with a quiet humour and shrewdness firmly anchoring an elusive and distrait character. He had just mastered a difficult situation without hurting my vanity or my confidence. In a day or two, I found I could be grateful to him for his tact. More gradually, the realization of two failures came down upon me, two failures within a few months.

I had spoiled a friendship with an older man who needed a confidant at a difficult moment in his life. That was a failure of character. I had spent a year on a task altogether beyond my scope, both educationally and intellectually. The one failure was due to cowardice, the other to folly.

This truth slowly spread over the sky of my mind, like a storm-cloud ominous with threat. It darkened my days, and I went to work day by day, pondering over this so constantly that I bemused myself, and could hardly be conscious of what was happening in the actual world. Humiliation is a powerful medicine. It is a sort of spiritual antibiotic, bred on decadent tissue.

I recalled the resilience with which nine years earlier, at the age of eighteen, I recovered from my mother's death and found myself on fire with the determination to strike out for immortality along with those poets in whose orchards I had been gorging with no restraint, or regard for my mental and physical digestion.

I found, to my further distress, that I was connecting this disillusionment with the fact of fatherhood. The failure as a writer, and as a scholar, must be due to dissipation of vitality. The Roman Church had discovered celibacy to be the only condition for a dedicated priest. Was it not the same for the poet, a creature even higher in the ascendency from mortal to godhead? So I believed, led on by the aesthetic theories of the Romantics, Coleridge in the *Biographia Literaria*, Wordsworth in his Prefaces, Shelley in his prose pieces, and Francis Thompson in his fantastic essay on Shelley. That is a small sample of the diet on which I fed my feverish imagination during the years of adolescence and early manhood; a time when I could have profited, no doubt, from the more balanced menu of a university, the diet-sheets prescribed by an experienced tutor. I had fed alone, over-indulged by my elders and colleagues in the Laboratory and the Custom House. I realized, now, that I had been a spoilt child in a large family, or a kind of village prodigy. The real beginning had yet to be made.

Then, suddenly, out of the middle of this leaden cloud, there came the lightning flash. One day I was sitting in the Tea Laboratory, hopelessly, mechanically repeating the job of entering particulars of samples into the large leatherbound registers, later to record there the results of the tests. This was the background motion against which I had danced among the Parnassians for nine years, unaware of the danger latent in gradualness.

But that day the realization came. It was part of the larger awakening which I have already described. Here I sat, as I was likely to sit for the rest of my career in the Civil Service, chained to this job because I had been fool enough as a youth to believe that I could do without the material things and ambitions, being assured of a vocation among the elect in the arts. Now I had thrown out another anchor to moor myself in this backwater; for parenthood must prevent me from taking any belated risks, which ought to have been hazarded years before.

My only excuse in playing for safety, and such a petty safety, had been that I was taking the hazards, proper to youth, in another field. I was staking my whole fortune of temperament and intelligence on that untamable horse, Pegasus. But that fiery creature was still galloping free, and I had not done much towards making a bridle to subdue him, a bridle of self-education and discipline.

I sat day-dreaming about my rooms on Champion Hill, where I worked in the early morning and through the evenings, reading and note-taking, trying clumsily to piece together the fragments of knowledge gathered from this haphazard process. At that time, during the first four years of my service in the Government Laboratory, I had at least the solitude necessary for a person with a vocation. That was now gone, and I had still to find a routine which would combine study with the attention owed to family life.

This reverie among the test-tubes and condensers, the miniature roar of the muffle-furnace and the tinkling of fluids in flasks over bunsen burners, was interrupted by the further door being flung open and a voice calling from the corridor:

'Algy: wanted on the phone!'

I was nicknamed Algy because of my habit of drinking a glass of fresh water every morning as soon as I arrived in the Laboratory. I did this to counteract the fatigue which drugged me after the rush over London Bridge, and the nervous apprehension that preceded the day's work in the disciplinary atmosphere of the Custom House. 'Freshwater Algae' was inevitably abbreviated.

c

A private call on the official telephone was forbidden. Even the person daring to ring up a member of the staff was disapproved, except under circumstances of extreme crisis and gravity. I woke from my despairing daydream, therefore, in alarm, to hurry guiltily through the Tea Laboratory, across the corridor, into the main Imports Laboratory, to the telephone, a dusty early model fixed to the wall. Inquisitive glances like arrows flashed over me.

A woman's voice inquired about my identity. Satisfied on this, she said that Mr Wolfe's secretary wished to speak to me. My mystification deepened. Then a breezy male voice said that Mr Wolfe would like to see me, and would I present myself that afternoon at 4.30? The speaker seemed surprised when I replied that I did not know where the rendezvous was, nor who Mr Wolfe might be.

'Good Lord,' I heard the secretary exclaim; 'Why, Mr Humbert Wolfe, of course! This is the Ministry of Labour. Come to Montague House, opposite the Cenotaph in Whitehall.'

From the tone of this instruction, I was sure that he assumed me to be a dim-witted yokel, pitchfork in hand among the dungheaps. I fancy that I felt like one when I stood at the lodge-gate of the headquarters of the Ministry of Labour, on the opposite side of the road to the Treasury and the entrance to Downing Street.

The building was a palace, with turrets and a mansard roof in the French manner. Beneath the plane trees in the garden were clustered wartime huts, now shabby and carpeted round about with fallen leaves. This autumnal dressing even littered the paved way to the main entrance, and the susurration accompanied me to the threshold of the Ministry, with a sound of foreboding, as though I were wading through the Dantesque approaches to another world.

That world, by comparison with the fishy surroundings of the Custom House, was a magnificent one. The entrance hall was wide, paved with coloured marble, flanked by mahogany doors at floor level. The staircase rose to a landing where recesses housed great vases on pedestals, then parted in right and left curves up to the salon floor.

I stared in awe, until accosted by a one-legged man in a dull blue uniform. When I said that I was to see Mr Wolfe he at once showed a friendly, deferential interest, and invited me to follow him.

It was a syncopated progress, for we had to ascend that grand, marble staircase, past the statues, the Greek vases, the gilded columns and acanthus leaves. The messenger could only surmount this glory sideways, for his wooden leg was but a passenger, which had to be helped up after the living anatomy to the next step. The effect on me was like that of a person who stutters. I found myself almost overcome by an inclination to follow suit. But I conquered it, and demurely, with downcast eyes, rose step by step up the red carpet in the middle of the wide marble treads. By the time we reached the first floor, after this crablike ascent, I was breathless with physical sympathy for this poor war-victim who so cheerfully passed me on to another messenger wholly in possession of his limbs. The second man proved, however, also to be damaged, for he spoke only in a hoarse croak, and could not turn his head to left or right without the accompaniment of the rest of his body. I began to wonder if I had come by mistake to a war reliquary hospital, and I inquired again for this Mr Wolfe, who wished to see me.

The messenger made a sound which I construed into 'Expecting you', and he led me along the lofty corridor to the right, and knocked at a door of highly-polished mahogany, with gold-lace finger-plates and a carved golden knob. Beside it was a similar door. Both led to rooms at the back of the palace, as I discovered when I entered a small but lofty office with cupids painted on the ceiling. One urchin was cut in two, through his rosy bottom, by a partition wall.

Against this wall sat a Civil Servant of about my own age, a dark, smart fellow whose voice I recognized. It was he who had assumed that I was a yokel with straw in my hair. He looked at me now with an eye that obviously confirmed his first impression, formed over the telephone. He was justified, for I was wearing a rough tweed suit made for me by a friendly haberdasher who undertook tailoring on the side. It cost thirty shillings, and had already served me through two winters. Though the sleeves were some three or four inches too long, I had not cared to expostulate, for fear of hurting the feelings of the little man, who had some distant connection with my father. All that I remember of him now is that he professed a religion called Christadelphian, which made him unfailingly cheerful. Whenever I asked after his permanently ailing wife, he beamed with benevolence and replied: 'Oh, amongst the middlings, you know, amongst the middlings!'

I therefore wore the suit with the sleeves turned up at the cuffs, exposing a striped lining which after two years had been neutralized to my eye, by grime. No doubt strangers must still have been startled.

Further to increase the rustic effect, I wore at that period of my life short side-whiskers, and a hair style in the manner of the French Symbolists. Even the social upheavals begun by the first world war had not quite destroyed the age-old custom by which people dressed according to their place and occupation: the baker in his paper hat, the lady in her silks, the maid in her cotton dress, the rustic in his smock, the artist in his velvet coat, and flowing tie and hair.

The secretary was far from hostile. He offered me a seat and a cigarette, explaining that 'the Chief' had someone there, and was likely to be engaged for another ten minutes.

'Frightful life,' he said. 'Never knows when he'll be caught.'

This sounded as though Mr Wolfe might be a burglar, but his secretary explained further that life in this new Ministry of Labour was a living hell, everybody working at full pelt from morning until late afternoon and often well into the evening while Parliament was sitting, or some labour crisis was hovering over the community. I learned that Mr Wolfe was a great swell, a Principal Assistant-Secretary, and the bright genius of the Ministry, British Representative at the International Labour Office of the League of Nations.

I nodded reverently, and did not betray my ignorance of all these titles and classifications, so remote from that *cul de sac*, the technical little world of the Government Laboratory, and especially the Custom House branch of it, where thirty solitaries laboured in Dickensian oddity.

The flow of information went on, while I turned my attention from a study of the office to the scene through the almost denuded plane trees, to the roofs of more huts below, and the Victoria Embankment, the moaning trams, and the familiar Thames beyond. Half an hour must have passed, before the inner door opened, and paused halfway with a figure still hidden behind it except for one hand on the further knob. I heard a high-pitched, chanting Oxford accent, saying:

'Do come back, do, and explain just as briefly what you feel ought to be done!'

The secretary winked at me. 'That's how he behaves!' he whispered stagily.

Then the whole man appeared; but I was so conditioned for exalted rank by this time that I hardly dared to look up.

'Do come in. So sorry,' the piercing Oxford voice explained. 'People *insist* on telling me how to run the country, as though I were Prime Minister instead of a wretched anonymous Civil Servant slaving as much against his will as I can see you do!'

This was my first experience of Humbert Wolfe's astonishing gift for judging character, at lightning speed. I looked up, as he led me into his room and gestured to the deep armchair beside his double desk. It was huge, but dwarfed by its position in the large room, whose walls were lined with elaborately ornamented bookshelves, each with a little valance of scalloped red and gold leather. Most of the shelves were empty, except for the group behind the desk. This was filled with a dull line of official publications and codes, and a majority of volumes in gaily coloured dustcovers.

The dimensions of the room, its vast bay window, the books, the deep carpet, the long curtains, and, dominating all, the picturesque figure of the man who had invited me there, combined to give me the illusion of stepping into a novel by

Meredith or Disraeli. Indeed, Humbert Wolfe was an instant reminder of the latter: the handsome Jewish features, the dandified costume, the lock of hair and the powerful mouth, the protruding nose and the strange eyes with deep-brown irises surrounded by a thin ring of grey, all held me spellbound.

Whether or not Mr Wolfe appreciated the effect which his person made upon me, I suspect that he took my amazement as a compliment, for he was uncommonly friendly, and broke through my shyness with calculated impudence.

'I like the little side-whiskers! What are they protesting against? Do you hate your job?'

I accepted this, for there was neither condescension nor malice in his opening gambit. I glanced up, and he saw the amusement in my eyes. He too smiled, and tossed back the lock of hair with a hand which I noticed to be surprisingly powerful, with spatulate fingers. I had no time to reply.

'It's a pretty coincidence, you know. I have seen poems of yours here and there, in *The Nation*, and the *Spectator*. You are already exalted, and deserve it. Don't congratulate me, for I've not reached those heights – yet. But we shall see! I am as determined a creature as you are. What a deceptive mildness you cultivate, my dear fellow.'

Speech poured out of him as from a hydrant, while he sat back in his chair and stared out of the window, punctuating the flood of words with that gesture of the hand to the tumbling lock of hair. At the same time, and this was miraculous, I was aware of my whole person, physical and mental, being taken to pieces and ruthlessly scrutinized. After I had been complimented, and told that I was in the same poetic category as Wordsworth, Mr Wolfe confessed that he too had aspirations outside the Civil Service. He opened a top drawer with his left hand and took out a manuscript. He was about to read, when the door opened and the secretary's head peered round it. Humbert Wolfe frowned, and waited, the powerful teeth bared in a snarl of disgust.

'Call from the Private Office. Minister wants you before he goes down to the House.'

Humbert's voice rose two tones, which made the affectations more marked:

'Tell him I'm not a nursemaid—' but the door was shut again. Then he read a poem to me, impressive in its rhyming skill. I was, by now, incapable of appreciating more. I was drowning in this man's vitality. So I said nothing. He appeared not to mind, and put the manuscript back in the drawer, saying as he did so, 'I sat next to a charming woman at dinner recently, and we talked poetry. Your name cropped up, I think from me, and she knew you, told me you were rotting quietly away in Billingsgate.'

He got up, resignedly, murmuring about obeying his political taskmaster. Then suddenly, as he was at the farther door leading to the corridor, he said, 'Would you like to join my Department? You'll have to work hard, you know. But you'll find some interesting people. There's a Treasury ruling against transferring staff from one Ministry to another, a wartime regulation, but that's beside the point. Think it over and—'

'I'll come,' I said. I believe I shouted, fearing that he would be gone before the words had left my mouth. He smiled again, and the lupine teeth flashed. Then he disappeared, leaving me to retreat alone from the inner chamber to the ante-room and the secretary.

'That means he'll be here until about seven o'clock tonight,' I was told. 'Then a dinner with Hugh Walpole. He'll kill himself in the end.'

I sat down again, to recover, though by now I was worrying about trains, and getting home late.

'This was the Duke of Buccleuch's town house,' the Secretary explained, 'the most expensive building in London at that time; every ceiling triple-layered, and insulated with sea-shells, all the doors rosewood.'

I had mistaken them for mahogany! Instinctively I marked myself down one point in poetic perception; a humiliating acknowledgment.

'The Chief's room in there was the Duke's library. You saw the bookshelves?'

I nodded. I also got up, thanked the friendly fellow, and explained that I lived twenty miles out, in Surrey, and was worried about being late, as 'my family' would be wondering what had become of me.

'What! You married?' he cried, as though this were an improbable condition in the creature whom he saw retreating nervously to the door, clutching an attaché case that contained a sample bottle of red wine, and an opened tin of baked beans, samples that had been analysed and were now 'to be disposed of', as the instructions in the Code Books put it. The two samples were separated from each other, and safely wedged, by one of the several volumes of Birkbeck Hill's edition of Boswell's life of Johnson, a work which I had almost been learning by heart, including the copious notes, over the past three months.

As I hurried along the gloomy and characterless Victoria Street towards the railway station, I suddenly recollected that I should have gone to tea with W. H. Davies at 14 Great Russell Street, according to my weekly habit. I was both alarmed and relieved. I should have to write and explain to him, for he was prone to disastrous interpretations of minor failings and accidents. The relief was because I would not be expected home early that evening.

Even so, the thought of home was more than a thought; it was a consuming passion, a hunger that drove me headlong down Victoria Street, though I knew that I should have to wait twenty minutes for the next train to Oxted. But I had no means of self-control; nor reason, nor common sense. I ran into Victoria Station breathless, hot and sweating though the early evening air of autumn was chilly. But I was one with thousands of other workers, all of them hastening like lemmings, driven by this suicidal craving to rush home.

CHAPTER THREE

' *And passing rich—* '

[1]

MY TRANSLATION TO WHITEHALL altered the temperature of my life. It carried me out of the nursery, and a protective routine, to a world of wide human traffic. It was an experience which I ought to have encountered six years earlier, at the outbreak of war. I had tried then, and failed because of the stomach malady lingering from childhood. Instead, as the initial part of my plan to enlist, I had married on a salary of £65 which had been steadily growing by increments of £5 a year.

That plan had failed, leaving me committed to responsibilities which I had no training or ability to fulfil. I had no conception whatever how to make money, and fundamentally no interest or appetite for doing so. I had been reared in a household run on this naïve principle, an economic system based on a way of life compounded of New Testament mythology and the picturesque, utopian socialism of the William Morris, Robert Blatchford, John Burns amalgam that was infusing the liberalism at the turn of the century. Money was something necessary but hardly mentionable. A concern for it was a step towards evil thoughts and uncharitable passions. In some devious way I even connected arithmetic with this dubious ingredient of daily life.

So here I was now, suddenly jolted by my new workday environment, and by the hard facts of marriage and parenthood, out of my childlike unconsciousness of the significance of money. I was not unhappy, and not as yet frightened, because of this abrupt confrontation. Here we lived, in a pretty though box-like cottage in Limpsfield High Street, with a fruitful garden maintained by my Wiltshire-born colleague, who also shared the rent of £30 a year. In 1920 the village was still rural and quiet. I realized that blessing, because during 1919 I had spent three months in bed, in a room whose window faced the street, with the walls of the house rising from the narrow pavement, not even a paling or strip of private ground intervening.

What more could I need, in this halcyon ménage? I was not the only one, however. There were three of us to consider.

[2]

This urgent persuasion added to the disturbance of mind and nerves caused by the problems confronting me in my new work in the Ministry of Labour. I found myself posted to a department called the Joint Substitution Board, housed in one of the asbestos huts in the forecourt of Montague House, the Duke of Buccleuch's former palace.

I spent my official day interviewing officers as they were demobilized from the fighting services. They came in their hundreds, their thousands, and my job was to send those with the necessary qualifications to fill temporary posts in Government Departments; surveyors, lawyers, architects, accountants, clerks. It was like trying to bottle Niagara in a pint pot.

My lack of experience made me identify myself with these 'temporary gentlemen'. I found that most of them were real gentlemen, clean from the furnace of war, and expecting to find civil life equally purged of its ancient impurities. Only a minority of them had the professional qualifications to fit them into that life. And all too many of them were married men with young families.

I listened to their stories, their hopes and demands, and I felt my small reserve of vitality dripping away in eleemosynary sympathy, so useless that it was an insult to these men returning to a Britain 'fit for heroes to live in', as Lloyd George proposed.

Every morning, before the interviewing began, I studied and learned by heart the lists of vacancies, so that I should at once be able to direct a square peg into a square hole. But that was a rare achievement. More often I had to act the part of comforter, making false hopes a plausible antidote to the gradually encroaching despair. I saw the same men again and again, and noted, without daring to show my observation, how week by week they grew shabbier and shabbier, their whole personalities, physical, mental and moral, slowly dissolving into bewilderment and despair.

The darkness of spirit affected me too, the custodian at the gate of this hell. I could not free myself from a sense of guilt. It poisoned my habitual delight in life. Even the woods of Titsey, and the open commonland above Limpsfield Village, where the nightingale and nightjar haunted, were smeared by this sulphuric consciousness of a vast and inevitable betrayal. In my innocence I cursed the politicians who had promised what neither they, nor anyone else, could perform at that stage of economic evolution after the first world war. Here were these millions of young and middle-aged men, already cheated out of five years of civilized life, released at last and joyously expecting to come home again, or to set up homes for the first time, with family life a reality.

That was the hope. At the beginning I could see how these demobilized officers took it for granted. It was what they had fought for. They were educated men, professional men, who had interrupted their careers to go into the trenches. Now they expected to come back to sanity. They did not see, at that time, how the heat of war had melted the joints in the fabric of civilization.

The assumption of the Government, and indeed of the whole community, was that the confusion would be only temporary, that society would regain an equilibrium and that meanwhile the benevolent and grateful civilians would see to it that the ex-soldiers be eased back with sympathy into an economic way of life supported on the newly-painted pillars of the four freedoms.

Day after day, month after month, I sat in the box-office of this theatre of despair. The job reduced me to silence. A dull, angry sense of confusion replaced the guilt which was my first re-action to this new job in Whitehall. I had not lost the vision which lit my world that morning in boyhood when I stood at the foot of my brother's bed and, opening his copy of Keats's poems, read the verses beginning 'I stood tiptoe upon a little hill', and felt the axis of the round world tilt a little nearer to the zenith, amid a blaze of celestial fire. But something had erupted, as an opaque and broken foreground, between me and that glory.

I wrote no poetry. I was humbled; I had nothing to say, confronted by this enormous problem of moral responsibility. I had the illusion of my broken toys dropping from my hands.

That being so, what was now my purpose? Here I stood, over the threshold of adult life, wholly unequipped in the matter of formal education and credentials, suddenly jostled into awareness of a double responsibility; as head of a family, and as a citizen in a world-wide community whose politics and economies were beyond my understanding. What was I to do? What was my duty?

[3]

These questions beat about in my mind like an insane ringing of bells. The din bemused me by day and haunted me by night. My state of mind was like that of the poet William Cowper, during his period of guilt. His were due to a fear of the horrifying, primitive God of the Calvinists. Mine were more immediate. I forced myself to read the political and economic articles in *The Nation* and the *Spectator*, journals which had been publishing my poems from time to time during the past two years. But my mind was as obtuse in this effort as it had been during my schooldays when I tried to battle with arithmetic, algebra and geometry at Dulwich Hamlet Elementary School. The shadow of the cane, still overhanging from the Victorian age, deepened the darkness, bringing remembered fears to present-day humiliations. What greater torture is there than recognizing one's own ignorance and inability in the face of new and rigorous experience?

This sense of failure could not last. The summer of 1921 was long and powerful. The wines it produced were of prime vintage. So too it assuaged the sharpness of my mental and emotional comings and goings during that first year of parenthood and contact with the needs of the ex-soldier.

East Surrey flourished like a girl under the embraces of an ardent and skilful bridegroom. The woods of Titsey, flowing down the southern slope of the Downs, were dark with a passion that brooded over the teeming life within. We took our infant up there, weekend after weekend under the strangely impressive sunshine.

The glades running at stages east and west through the woods were explored, one by one. No other humans walked there, on the leaf-carpets, among the bushes of deadly nightshade and the canopies of old-man's-beard. One Sunday afternoon I saw a huge dog-fox sitting on his haunches ahead, in the middle of the glade. He stared at us as we approached, and did not move until we were near enough to look into his red, baleful eyes. I saw his lip wrinkle, exposing a white canine. Then he levered himself up, contemptuously, and louped off, flashing in and out of the tree-shadows, into the darkness where an elder bush hid the boles of a group of larches that broke the ranks of the beech trees.

More frequently we went over Limpsfield Common to the Weald beyond. It was farther south, and that was always an attraction, a deep racial lure no doubt for all creatures living in the Northern Hemisphere. The sun beat down, day after day, ripening the universe, cauterizing the war-wounds of western Europe.

On a later Sunday, at the beginning of September, we trundled the pram, laden with the twelve-month infant, a huge picnic basket, tins for botanical samples, my precious copy of Palgrave's *Golden Treasury*, and Bonnier's *Name this Flower*, along the gypsy lanes, to come to midday rest in a stooked cornfield near Cowden. There we spread the rug on the bristly stubble, and set to on the cold chicken, the tomatoes and lettuce, the rolls and butter and the bottled beer. Then my wife wandered off to search for wild flowers, and I settled down with the child in my arms and Palgrave in my hands, my back against a stook. Soon, like the spirit of autumn seen by John Keats, I was 'on a half-reaped furrow sound asleep, drowsed with the fume of poppies', certainly half-sunk in the herbage that seems to rise overnight after the harvesters have left the reaped corn to dry, during that interim period which the combine-harvester has closed for ever, with no more stooks for ardent poets and protective young fathers to lean against, symbols as classical as the Greek Anthology, or the nostalgic landscapes of Constable and Samuel Palmer.

My protectiveness, however, was in abeyance during my short nap. Several half-dreams later, something roused me. It may have been the chortling of the child. I opened my eyes to a world of blinding light and saw that she had crawled off my lap and was leaning out beyond the rug, grasping at a huge snake. It was reared up, like a swan's neck, staring at her as she reached out her arms to embrace it.

I was still dazed with sleep, in the state between legend and actuality. I saw the Original Serpent, at his first mischief. 'No!' I shouted suddenly, struggling to burst the fetters of this horrible magic that bound my limbs and constrained my lungs.

The harmless grass-snake dropped his curious stance, wriggled through his whole length of some three feet, and rustled away through the stubble.

Beads of sweat broke out on my forehead and upper lip. The child sat staring with unabated interest at the spot where imagined Death and Old Damnation had threatened her. She was quite rebellious when I snatched her up in my arms and walked away, my heart throbbing with reaction after that confrontation with fear.

But the fear subsided. It could not exist in this world of harvest-home. I wandered off along the cool half-shadow of the headland beside the copse, calling the vagrant botanist. But there being no answer, my voice retreated into a whisper close to the infant's ear, shaping sounds as formal as its tiny convolutions. And the form they took made them memorable, so that when the family was together again, and my arm relieved of its burden, I was able to write down what I had been crooning to my year-old daughter.

> Under this hayrick lies
> All my heart's treasure.
> The impermanent skies
> Pass at their leisure,
> And the flowers of the noon
> Prepare to fade soon,
> The bird-music dies.
> Oh bitter heart's treasure,
> To anchor me so
> To this woman, my lover,
> While the skies fade above her
> And the earth dies below.

The song had no direct relation to the recent incident between the child and the slow-worm, and I was aware of something absent; of some forcing of the emotional content of the lyric. Am I so anchored, I asked myself; and there was no answer. Perhaps there the bitterness lay.

Puzzling over this, dutifully and with a sense of guilt that reduced me to silence all the long way home over Limpsfield Common and down into the sheltered village, I suddenly realized that the many months of silence, since I began work at the Ministry of Labour, were broken. My life once more had a meaning and a sense of direction, with creative energy restored.

CHAPTER FOUR

Concerned with Incomes

[I]

WHILE I WAS WORKING in the Government Laboratory, my acquaintance with writers had been limited to the few enthusiastic amateurs in the Custom House, and latterly to Clifford Bax and W. H. Davies in the wider world beyond. Both these poets, wholly dissimilar in person, taste, background, offered me affectionate friendship. I responded half incredulously because these two men were the first I had ever met who did not have to earn a living. Davies had a small Civil List pension and very few wants. Bax was independent with a large private income; so large that a broken marriage and other emotional commitments did not prevent him from living luxuriously in a studio in Kensington, maintaining a country house in Gloucestershire (where he ran a literary cricket-team), and going off periodically to Europe and the Far East to collect poetic honey.

Wealth had not stifled his simplicity of heart, nor made him suspicious of his fellow-men. He was unworldly by nature and upbringing, and this bias had been given an additional push by his study first of Plotinus's heady teachings, and then by his espousal of Buddhism and a belief in reincarnation. This made him somewhat foreign to his own western world, which works in a more energetic and practical way than he was able to appreciate. But his wealth protected him; maybe to his further disadvantage. Had he been forced to earn his living, his talents might have been more vigorously used.

He made some mark, however, especially as a poetic dramatist with his one-act plays, and the full-length *Rose without a Thorn* which was a commercial success. Not much attention has been given to his best work, a long narrative poem, *The Traveller's Tale*, published in 1921 by Basil Blackwell in Oxford. It embodies in seven stages of reincarnation the life-series of a soul on earth, beginning away back in pre-historic ages, and recurring through known periods of civilization: the Egyptian, the Greek, the Renaissance, the Elizabethan, accumulating in these experiences of suffering, the ever growing intuition that (as Bax sings in the epilogue)

> Love, the true love that seeks for nought,
> The love that Christ and Buddha brought,
> Comes, like a wind, we know not whence,
> But comes not from the world of sense.

Bax put that faith into practice. He was therefore an easy prey for harpies, long-suffering and generous in spite of his own volatile and flinching character. But he had good friends too, men and women who took him at his true worth, and not because of his wealth.

One Whitsun weekend he came down to stay with me at Limpsfield, and we spent three days wandering about in the small park round the Leveson-Gower dower-house, whose entrance gate was opposite my cottage in the High Street. The last afternoon was prematurely hot. The Maytime sun brought the foliage almost audibly to fullness. A tide of umbels rose under the hedgerows and over the meadows, spilling its almond-like perfume until the air was sickly-sweet.

Bax and I sat near an ancient oak, watching, as we talked, the traffic of wild bees moving in and out of a hole in the hollow trunk, their panniers heavy with yellow pollen. We were discussing Plato's 'Banquet'. He had brought me a set of the dialogues in the Loeb Classics series, and we were planning my course through this wealth of reading.

Then, with great shyness, he remarked that I must be having considerable economic problems now that I was responsible for a family. I was so embarrassed that I could not reply. Whereupon he apologized, but pursued the matter with more

D

resolution than I had ever known in him. He looked at me almost with severity, spoke of my fragile appearance, poor health, and undoubted promise as a poet. He said that he regarded it as his duty to do something toward the fulfilment of that promise. It would be very little, he said, because he was having post-matrimonial difficulties at the moment. He proposed to put £60 a year into my bank until such time as I was able to do without this help.

'But I have no bank,' I exclaimed, too dumbfounded either to accept or refuse the offer, or to thank him for it.

He seemed to be incredulous, but after pondering for some minutes, while the bees came staggering home with their contributions to the common deposit account in the vaults of the oak tree, he said that he would arrange with his own banker to get into touch with the manager of the Oxted branch of Lloyds Bank, who would then supply me with a cheque-book and instruct me how to use a bank. He predicted that before long I should begin to make money as a writer, for he sensed staying-power, provided I stood up for myself and guarded my health.

These qualifications puzzled me, and I was inclined to be indignant. They sounded too much like the advice which used to be poured over my obstinate head by senior members of the Laboratory staff, that I must be *sensible* and practical, in a tough world that had little use for poetry, and none for those who practised it. Such advice came oddly from this Platonist, out of a cloud of personal affluence. However, I smothered my pride, and somewhat belatedly, with all the agonies of a receiver confronted with a giver, thanked him. We said no more, and after a long, embarrassed silence, got up and strolled back to the cottage down the mossy drive, the mercenary hum of the wild bees diminishing at each step.

[2]

A week or two later I received a letter from the local bank

manager, asking me to call, and the following day I knocked at the closed door of Lloyds Bank, opposite Oxted Station, after I left the train at five o'clock. I had never before been into a bank, except once when I was a schoolboy, and the Headmaster sent me with an envelope to the bank in Dulwich Village, a gloomy pseudo-Gothic building near the gates of the Old College. I presume the envelope contained the Headmaster's salary.

The door of Lloyds Bank was opened by the manager himself, and I saw no other staff. There was hardly room for more, the premises being no larger than the coal-office next door. They were indeed so homely that I quickly overcame all misgivings. It was obvious that here was no institution battening on the greed and avarice of mankind. The manager was a most straightforward man, and I felt somewhat ashamed of myself for having expected to meet someone half Shylock, half Judas Iscariot. He talked to me about thrift, the advantages of having a bank account and the disadvantages of over-drawing on it. He even showed an interest in my literary activities, and was patently impressed by the fact that a rich client had so decisively put his money on a dark horse. The encounter was altogether human, even friendly, and as I walked home to Limpsfield village, cheque-book in pocket, I told myself that probably I was unnecessarily apprehensive whenever I entered shops, post offices, and any other in-stitutions connected with money, book-keeping, registers and statistics. But I have never quite cured myself of this neurosis. Even when I go into a post office to buy a stamp, I do so with a kind of reluctance, physical and nervous, rooted in a past hidden deeper than I can comprehend.

Bax's qualification about my health, and 'standing up for myself' still rankled a little.

[3]

A few weeks later, when summer had flung open all doors,

W. H. Davies came down for a few days, to escape from his grubby double-room in Great Russell Street, of which he was so proud. He often explained to me, gravely but with a slight gleam of self-consciousness in his large, eloquent eyes, that 'no gentleman in the land' was more fortunate than he, because he had his own private quarters, and no woman to dictate to him. Then he would add, maliciously, that this was a primary necessity for a poet: freedom from dominance of women, especially what he called 'educated ladies', who were more fatal than serpents.

During his visit, that summer of 1921, my wife and I had occasion to go out one afternoon, Davies staying as baby-watcher. We left him squatting on the rug in the tiny Regency period sitting-room, in front of the armchair into which the baby had been secured with the nursery harness. Two hours later, we returned, to find him still there, haggard and exhausted, but benevolent. 'D'you know,' he said to me, but pointedly including the young mother, 'this young Turk knows I'm an old Welsh poet [he pronounced it 'pawt'], and she's determined to put a stop to it. She's kept me busy, I can tell you! As fast as I pick up that rattle, she throws it out again. Up, down – up, down; it's gone on like that all the afternoon. And I reckoned to work on a poem [pawm] while I was on the watch. Not a line done, look you.'

He got up stiffly, his wooden leg creaking like the timbers of a sailing ship luffing to the wind.

I thought this was a good moment to tell him what Clifford Bax had done towards compensating a young poet for the handicap of fatherhood and marriage. Davies listened gravely, as he filled his pipe with strong shag (the baby having been removed). As the door closed behind the two handicaps, he puffed away in silent satisfaction for a few moments, nearly asphyxiating me; then he beamed with pleasure.

'D'you know, that's a good thing. It's what you need, I've always said.' He thought about it for a while, and became conspiratorial, with a nod towards the door recently closed behind the family: 'Now don't you let her know about this, my boy. It never does to encourage them. The more you give, the more they'll want. It's their nature, especially when they've got little ones. It's instinct. You can't blame them. But a poet has to guard against it, or he'd be silenced. I've seen it happen.'

He then gave me instances from among his friends, many of them well-known writers who had shown no sign of being silenced by matrimony and paternity. I knew, however, that if I pointed out this inconsistency, Davies would say that these poor Benedicks who had betrayed their vocation as poets may have gone on writing but that their efforts were but a tinkling of cymbals, a feeble sounding of brass. I remembered that at our first meeting in 1918, towards the end of the war, he aired this obsession about 'educated ladies'. Nothing would persuade him to lose one of his unique collection of persecution manias. I knew that he believed me to be a doomed soul, too frail to surmount the perils of marriage combined with the ardours of a poet's career.

My friendship with Davies was punctuated with these displays of oddity. They endeared him to me, as they did to his other friends. They must have been in the mind of Augustus John when he made the subtle pencil portrait which he gave to the poet. It sums up the cunning peasant-like quiddities of character which directed Davies's reactions to events and people. He would have been less original without them.

One hot day that week, while I was on annual leave from the Laboratory, Davies and I went for a walk over Limpsfield Common, to call on the painter Lewis Fry (cousin of Roger Fry). I knew that Davies would enjoy looking at Fry's large collection of water-colours painted by members of the Norwich School. Fry's Quaker grandfather, a Tuke, had been a banker in Norwich at the beginning of the nineteenth-century when the Cromes, the Cotmans, Peter de Wint, David Cox were in full spate. The banker bought heavily, and his collection had passed down, much of it in portfolios and therefore as fresh in colour as on the day of inspiration, to this quiet, asthmatic country gentleman and amateur, Lewis Fry, who had sought me out and set up a most neighbourly acquaintance; flattering from a

cultured man so much older than myself. I was invited to go up
to his studio in the large house on the southern slope of the
Common, overlooking the wide Wealden landscape, to browse
over the portfolios, or the superb *Liber Studiorum* of Turner,
god of my boyhood. Cotman's affinity to Wordsworth showed
itself to me during those sessions; slow procedures accompanied by desultory conversation with my host, between the
bouts of asthmatic agony which he dispelled temporarily with
an inhaler like an old-fashioned hair-spray, a small bottle with
an atomizer and a rubber bulb.

Fry was out that morning, so Davies and I returned slowly to
the head of the village, after many halts while he hitched up the
wooden leg, or marked what he was telling me by means of a bit
of mime, which could only be done after hanging his famous
stick by its crook-handle, either over his arm or in the join of his
waistcoat. By one clump of hawthorn trees set in a lake of
bracken, we paused for a longer while to locate a nightingale
whose daytime song came pouring over our ear-drums almost
offensively. At last we saw the bird, and stood watching its
whole body given to the purposes of music, shaking and
pulsing on the branch, in danger of apoplexy.

I took a sly glance at Davies, and marvelled at the complete
absorption of the human lyrist in the technique of the singer
whom he had celebrated so often, with 'the moon's white
beams across her throat'. His large brown eyes, slightly
kippered through a lifetime of contact with strong tobacco-
smoke, were suffused with joyous tears. His pipe was removed
from his mouth and cold in his hand, leaving his lips free to an
expressive tenderness, each touching the other but about to
part for speech, or some exclamation of joy, or worship.

'My word!' he breathed. 'My word!'

This, and more minor delays, brought us to the top of the
village, just as the church clock struck twelve noon.

The effect on Davies was instant. He pulled up sharp on his
live leg, using his stick as a brake. An expression of utmost
alarm was directed reproachfully at me. 'What's wrong?' I
demanded, somewhat impatiently because I was tired after

being on my feet for most of the morning. Hunger, too, made me weak and irritable, acting like a drug on my muscles and nerves.

'You heard that?' he demanded angrily. 'It's twelve o'clock and here we are out in the public street!'

He was gravely alarmed. The gypsy face was flushed, and his eyes rolled, like those of a doe confronted with a tiger.

Fortunately, we were opposite a steep footpath to the right, up between rocky ground and a copse. It led to an old beer-house. I steered him adroitly to this haven, and he gradually recovered his equanimity, beaming in front of a tankard as he explained the cause of his disturbance.

'You see,' he said, 'I'm a very kind man; and it shows in my face. All children see it. They are very cute that way.'

He paused for refreshment.

'Now all schools come out at twelve o'clock. It's the same all over this country, and in my country, Wales. That means if I get caught by all the children as they come out into the public streets, I shall be ruined. You see, they look at me and immediately expect to be given a halfpenny. But even with my increased pension I can't afford that. You can't explain to children, so that's why I have to take care never to be out of doors at twelve o'clock. We'll wait here until they have all gone up the street.'

We made that drink last for twenty minutes, and I curbed the pangs of hunger with an arrow-root biscuit. When we ventured out, the merciless predators from the village school had all rushed home. The High Street was clear, and the old poet's income secure.

CHAPTER FIVE

A Larger University

[1]

LIKE PHYSICAL HUNGER, hunger of the mind also put me into a feverish state. The mere absorption of book-knowledge was not enough appeasement. Unless I was gaining in creative experience by the practice of writing verse, I had a feeling of starvation. Anxiety gnawed at my flesh and bones. Bouts of sickness laid me low, coming unexpectedly and causing great inconvenience. I might be in the train, or at work on the registers in the Laboratory. Suddenly a consciousness of having produced no verse for days, even for weeks, would halt my work on the job in hand. A wave of fear and despair would flood my intestines and stomach, driving me to the nearest water-closet, to be convulsed by a spasm of diarrhoea and vomiting. This release was always followed by cold weakness, prelude to peace of mind and a gradual build-up of hope, even of ecstasy and vision, a condition too exalted to be borne without a means of expressing it.

Such was the usual cycle of combined mental and physical experience, closing fully in the final relief of writing. The verse was a catharsis. I had yet to learn the art of poetry, the discipline that should make it superior to and directive of my personal feelings.

My state of mind during that first year at the Ministry of Labour was therefore almost pathological. Self-confidence was shattered. Contact with the returned and angry soldiers made me ashamed of having been a civilian *malgré moi*. I could see, with painful certainty, that these men who had been through the horrors and filth of the Front Line were permanently cut off from the rest of us. They were a brotherhood of death. They had learned something we could never comprehend, nor they communicate. Years later, some words spoken to me by Edmund Blunden, author of *Undertones of War*, recalled the sense of isolation. 'The trouble with me,' he said, 'is that I stopped living in 1916.' It was a grim statement, and, thank God, Blunden's subsequent career and achievement have given it the lie.

Another saying, by another poet, Herbert Read, also many years after my vision of that brotherhood of death, carried me back to those dark and sterile days of my apprenticeship in the Ministry of Labour. 'One thing the war taught me,' said Herbert Read: '—it gave me the ability to recognize a coward.'

These two soldier poets have made permanent contributions, in verse and prose, to the literature of war. They spoke to me with authority. I was guilt-stricken by both, though they spoke as friends, reminiscential and perhaps only self-contemplative. I wonder if either of them observed the spasm of dismay which shook me? Cowardice? I moved the word round in the theatre of my conscience, examining it and applying it to my own character. Who is not a coward in some degree, or under certain strains, physical, moral, emotional? Is it a state which we can learn to control, by doctrine or discipline? Or is it so primitive that it can undermine all the superstructures of civilization, the codes and conventions, the laws and decencies, by which we brace ourselves to communal responsibility and interdependence?

I remember that I studied Herbert Read covertly as he spoke, seeking to find in the bony face, the grey almost cold eyes, the sparse figure, some key to the secret of courage. I had read his short prose piece 'In Retreat', the account in well cadenced prose of his wartime experience as commander of a company cut off during one of the major recoils of the Allied armies in Flanders and Northern France; an experience that was recognized with a D.S.O. and an M.C.

I found no answer. Maybe we were doomed henceforth to speak different languages, the soldier and the civilian, though sharing the labours and disciplines of the same art, and abhorring as well as loving many things and values in common. The currency of aesthetics was not enough. A terrible dichotomy had arisen; and it was likely to split the whole of human society. My friendship with Blunden and Read, whose work I have so freely appreciated, has endured for some forty years, but it has stopped short at that barrier. Shall I ever know the price they paid by leaving home, the one for his knowledge of the other side of death, the other for his terrible faculty of inquisition? There is no answer, though the inquiry concerns the two halves of the divided family of mankind.

[2]

My removal from Billingsgate to Whitehall set in motion a chain of events that speeded up my life. I moved from a tributary into a main stream. Clifford Bax began the process soon after the birth of my daughter. He invited the young family to Arundel, where his mother lived in a tall house near the castle, tended by a staff of elderly servants who treated her like a Holy Relic. They whispered reverently in her presence, or when mentioning her. She was a devout Catholic, tall like her son, gentle and authoritative. Old silver, gracious period furniture, deep curtains, and a long-established domestic ritual surrounded her, and protected her 'from the contagion of the world's slow stain'. That is how she impressed our young, naïve minds at that first meeting. As I sat talking to her, facing the long Georgian windows of her drawing-room, Clifford hovering attentively near her, I found my impression overlaid by a memory of the huge Chelsea studio in Tite Street, on that first day of the twentieth century when my brother and I, credulous urchins, went to receive an aquarium, a gift from the housekeeper.

My horizons had widened a little, and slowly, during the intervening two decades. Now the process was accelerating, and the increased range made me aware of my poor sight, in those eyes of the mind and character, for whose improvement the oculist and optician are so hard to find.

I was at peace in that drawing-room. The young mother and infant had been discreetly spirited away, for nursery purposes, and with them a certain embarrassment which I could not explain, even to myself. Old Mrs Bax was interested, however, and suggested that on the morrow we should all go in the car to see the newly unearthed Roman villa at Fittleworth. This expedition would have been wholly enjoyable, had not the baby howled savagely all the way to the site. Mrs Bax at last took the child on her lap, and at once it quietened down, to lie gazing up at the queenly hat, feather boa, and long pale face, with unabating curiosity. Clifford and I were at last enabled to renew a conversation about Shelley and Platonism, a kind of serial theme among our mutual interests. I noticed that his mother glanced not quite approvingly from time to time at her son, as the facets of Shelley's all too explicit philosophy were aired by us.

The next day the elder son, Arnold Bax the composer, came and stayed over the weekend, for his mother's birthday. He was shorter, more incisive than Clifford, inclined to be nervously irritable, rapid in speech, sharp in gesture. He showed an aloof interest in the literary affairs so important to Clifford and me, but shrank with distaste from the evidences of my family life. He talked willingly and with enormous vitality about music, quizzing me for my interest in Schumann. 'Dangerous! Dangerous!' he said; 'The wrong sort of romanticism.' I recalled this, many years later, when talking with Arthur Bliss (who succeeded Bax as Master of the Queen's Musick), one day at the Savile Club. 'The emotions of a schoolgirl!' he exclaimed, testily, after I had again proclaimed the nobility of Schumann's character, and his exploratory work in developing the potentialities of the iron-frame pianoforte, pioneering which he shared with Liszt and Chopin.

I was too awestricken to dispute with Arnold Bax. He was the first composer I had met, and I had known his work for the past ten years, introduced to it by my brother, who as an adolescent discovered a passionate interest in what may be called the impressionist composers, Bax and Bliss amongst them. Names that we learn in boyhood keep an aura of sanctity for the rest of our lives. So while I sat with Arnold Bax in the drawing-room of his mother's house in Arundel, he at the grand piano and I beside him, drawn up close as though I were to turn the pages of the music score, I saw him as a figure of myth rather than flesh and blood.

His playing strengthened that illusion. It was massive, a composer's utilization of the pianoforte, his thumbs translating the deeper strings and woodwind. But it was also dexterous, for he had studied under Tobias Matthay, the teacher whose expert engineering theories produced the technique of York Bowen, Myra Hess and many other English concert pianists.

Bax filled the drawing-room, the house, the streets of Arundel, with his transcription from the orchestral score of Wagner's *Rheingold*, and Debussy's *Pelléas* and *Mélisande*. The thunderous atmospherics rolled and reverberated from the walls of the Duke of Norfolk's castle. 'You must not wake the baby, Arnold dear,' said his mother during a pause between his exposition and his increasingly excited argument.

I found this a dramatic plea, for Mrs Bax had previously told me how distressed and puzzled she was by his desertion of wife and children and refusal even to see them. But he obeyed her, and brought me back to earth with him.

We did not meet again until some years had passed, when he wrote to me after I had written in the press about his tone-poem *Tintagel*. I went to see him at Harriet Cohen's flat, and found him less resilient, with the irritability increased under the abrasions of fame. Like most composers, he was inclined to treat writers as beings in a lower order of creative employment. I suspect they have not needed Schopenhauer's sanction for this belief. The universality of their medium, with none of the restrictions of language, and possessing a freedom from utility and idea (the other and heavier facets of language), are sufficient authority for the musician's claim. But this has its dangers too, for even Beethoven, yes, and even Bach and Mozart, were human.

[3]

All through those early years in Whitehall, I was still influenced by the personality of my brother Jack, who had dominated my childhood benevolently but austerely. Now we had reached manhood, however, his health weakened while mine improved. As a boy, he never ailed, and was able to take scholarships from elementary to secondary schools, and to the Goldsmiths' College at New Cross where he trained to be a teacher.

He was always a mysterious character: a boy who walked alone, finding out by himself with fastidious and almost disdainful insight the means of self-expression for his melancholy, sardonic spirit. His tenderness was almost pathological. His whole body and mind recoiled from the crudities of daily life, like exposed nerves.

Such friction was bound to wear him down. In his late twenties the effects became apparent. He grew less authoritative, more hesitant. He withdrew into himself, and not even his marriage to the fellow student with whom he fell in love at first sight and with absolute finality – almost terrifying to behold – could draw him out of this retreat. His interest in music followed this almost physical mysticism. Only in his water-colour painting did he release his lighter moods, the joy in light, in spaciousness, which made him so endeared to us, to his friends, to the worshipping colleagues amongst his fellow teachers, and particularly to the passing generations of school-boys who came to him like moths round a candle-flame.

But the flame began to flicker. Maybe his occupation as a teacher for some years in the Church School of St Peter's, Vauxhall, called out the disease latent in his constitution. The Victorian building, the slum-born children, the environment of poverty, our Northern poverty festering in semi-darkness, cold

and ugliness, must have worked poisonously upon his nerves
and lungs. The beauty of his hands became more marked,
month by month: pallid, transparent, the filbert nails fastidi-
ously cared for. The great nose, and the shell-like ears also took
on a keener pronunciation. The dark brown silky hair receded a
little, and this added to the austerity of his features, as also did
the darkening of the heavy upper eyelids.

He walked gently, as though to counteract the obduracy of
the pavements, the necessary mounting of kerbstones, and the
easing down off them again. He seemed to stoop a little, or
rather to draw an invisible shawl around his shoulders to keep
the cold world out.

Yet with all this instinctive self-protectiveness that commanded his general stance more and more noticeably, his eyes
never lost their fire. They smouldered in their caverns, breaking
out from time to time into flame, at the breath of some enthusiasm, stirred by thought, by passing circumstance that
kindled his humour, or provoked him to anger.

Since my marriage, of which he did not approve, he had
relinquished his monitorship over me and my development. It
was replaced by an increase of the old affection; marked by a
small gift, a book usually, or approval of a verse which I had
written. He spent time increasingly alone, in the little back
study-sitting room behind the larger front room in the Peckham
house where the Victorian poetess Eliza Cook once lived. The
window looked down over a long, narrow garden studded with
apple trees, marked along the western wall by a thick bed of
lilies of the valley, the foliage sombre and smoky after the
spring flowering. At the end of the garden some poplar trees
mourned all through the leafy period, making the summer
melancholy, dropping their twigs and faded leaves over a
derelict greenhouse.

Into this retreat, my brother confided his music, stuff for the
pianoforte ferreted out by him from I know not where, lesser
composers of the nineteenth century, Stephen Heller, Cornelius
Gurlitt, Niels Gade, Robert Volkmann, John Field who
'invented' the nocturne, for Chopin to perfect it. Jack's

inclination led him, as his physique deteriorated, towards the more atmospheric composers: Delius, Fauré, Macdowell, Debussy and Ravel, Liadov and Scriabin. He had a gift for improvising in this manner, remote elegiac explorations, formal but poignant, to which I sat listening, brewing my own fantasy meanwhile, half-impatient of the remoteness and the renunciation. Moments of fear touched me too, for my short-sighted eyes had the illusion of his disappearing into this twilight, and I wanted to drag him back into the rough and tumble.

I went less often after I removed to Limpsfield from London; but we corresponded, and his letters carried the astringent personality, releasing more humour than was permitted in his conversation. We were not far apart during our working hours, I at Whitehall, he at Vauxhall. We lunched together once a week at the restaurant in the basement of the Tate Gallery. It was an unfrequented place in the nineteen-twenties, like the rooms above it, and this sense of being out of the mainstream of con-temporary life, in the lull and pause of a backwater, was congenial to my brother. The public eye and interest had not yet been drawn towards a study of painting and sculpture. The B.B.C. was still in its puerile years, feeling its way towards an educational policy, which included aesthetic awareness, under the directive genius of Mary Somerville. Picture galleries and museums were places of rendezvous for courting couples, or frustrated hermits.

Jack and I did not have long sessions together, for most of the luncheon hour was spent coming and going. Eager to see him, I would snatch a minute or two from office time, and half run, half walk, past the Houses of Parliament and Victoria Gardens, alongside the Thames, to look out ahead as I approached the Tate Gallery, sometimes to see him appearing from the end of Vauxhall Bridge by the Breakers' Yard, or across the road past the Military Hospital. There he came, at that measured pace, as though carrying something fragile, his head steady, held a little forward. Maybe that head was the fragile object. Often as I saw him coming, I recalled the incident on the first day of the century, now over twenty years ago, when he carried the empty aquarium safely over Battersea Bridge, impeded by my dragging anxiously at his coat-tail.

We met in silence, or to the family whistle, a robin-like and wistful tune of three notes. He always inquired after my baby daughter, and I after his wife; then silence, as we entered the Gallery and made for the basement. There we sat, consuming a chaste, institutional luncheon, surrounded by the gay, mannered festival scenes done in tempera on the walls of the restaurant by Rex Whistler. This decoration, so lively and malicious, was the first commission given to the young artist, and it set him on the path to fame. Week after week my brother and I studied Whistler's comedy, while we swallowed our meat and tepid vegetables, our suet pudding and golden syrup, before going upstairs to spend a few minutes before familiar masterpieces.

Now, forty years later, I forget the perfunctory conversations we held. All I remember is the atmosphere which surrounded him: the authority of his quiet presence, the slight figure, the deliberate and almost reluctant movements of head, body, limbs; the glances from those brown eyes under the canopy of the heavy lids; the emotional appeal, the craving, that they signalled, from behind the discipline, the stoicism by which he commanded himself to silence. Even now I am not surprised by the shyness with which I habitually confronted him. I seemed to be a chatterer by comparison, and recognized the fact even while I was spilling my news, or my confidences: gossip about the Ministry, my colleagues, my affairs at home in Limpsfield (but this always guardedly for fear of a rebuff); or penetrating confessions about my more real adventures among books, the reading and the writing that were encroaching increasingly upon my time, attention and vitality. 'Don't follow your own kind too much,' he said one day as we left the Gallery and stood for a few moments looking over the parapet at the bridge-end by the Hovis bakery. The weather must have been rough, for seagulls were wheeling over the river, flashing pallidly against a leaden sky.

Jack coughed a little, for the air was autumnal. Instantly, I saw and heard our mother in that cough. I looked at him, but he was staring up at the gulls, his eyes moist after the slight strain of the coughing. He frowned.

'No,' he continued, unaware that a coldness, of premonition, had frozen my mind. I heard as from a distance: something was being snatched away. 'You'll topple over with too much Shelley, too much Keats. That was a good start. But you've got to study your opposites: Dryden, Byron. These are men of the world, and you need that ballast. Good-bye.'

He left me waiting for a bus back to Whitehall, and I watched him walking over the bridge, back to the horrors of the slum school. The gulls planed above the water, over the parapet, and round the concentrated figure, moving slowly but surely, diminishing into the distance. His hands were in his pockets. He had turned up his overcoat collar.

[4]

A few weeks after I began my new life at the Ministry of Labour in the front garden of Montague House, Whitehall, I was visited by a strange figure. He butted into my room one morning just after I had interviewed the son of Colonel Cody, the famous 'Buffalo Bill' of the American circus world. This young man, neat and charming, had fought in the British Army, but as he was of American nationality I could not place him in one of the temporary posts in a Civil Service department. He had been to see me several times, and I sent him along for interviews, until instructed to do so no more.

The intruder, unannounced, peered round the door, his head surprisingly near the top of it. The elevation of that head was increased by a cloud of fine fiery hair that appeared to hover or flicker over it at the caprice of the draught raised by the opening of the door. 'Are you Dicky Church?' said a loud, cheerful

E

voice. I was too astonished to reply, and my reticence was taken as an invitation, for the whole man entered, and threw a shapeless hat at the seat of the chair recently vacated by Cody Junior. It was thrown too forcibly, and passed on to skid along the floor.

By this time I had studied the stranger. He stood over six feet. His face was mobile, with a long upper lip and an indented nose. His eyes were greenish, and restless. The features were over-ridden by that conflagration of hair, which fluttered in perpetual motion. The cause of this was obvious at first sight. The man was a furnace of nervous passion. Every movement, every word he spoke, indicated this possession. His hair was kept in motion from the heat engendered by the personality within that leonine skull. 'Our chief, Humbert, told me you had joined us. I'm to see that you don't get run over. So come out to lunch. What?'

I had not even ventured to reply. This appeared to surprise him, even to anger him. He frowned, threw out an arm in a convulsive gesture that almost wrenched it from his body.

'Nonsense! Let them wait! Half an hour more or less; poof! Where's your hat?'

He stooped to pick up his own, and swept several files off my table to the floor, where he left them. I rescued them, then reached for my hat, and began to stammer something, a few incoherent sounds of politeness – but he burst out again.

'I'm Flint. Frank Flint; as good a poet as you are. Ever heard of me?'

I hadn't; for at that stage in my literary life I was still living among the masters of earlier centuries. I had not even found much enthusiasm for the Georgian Group. But I knew that this man's name was not among that set; nor did his appearance suggest anything so pastoral. He must have read my thoughts. A derisive but good-natured grin disturbed those oddly composed features. He slapped me on the back so forcibly that I was propelled out into the narrow corridor of the hut.

'Of course you haven't! Who has?' An agony of self-questioning brought him to a halt. 'No! No!' he almost shouted. 'No silver spoon in my mouth. Gutter-born, gutter-bred! Oh God! Forget it, man, forget it.'

He calmed down, and took my arm as we left the gateway of Montague House and turned up Whitehall.

'Lunch is on me,' he said. 'We'll go to the Corner House; nearest place. So big you can eat unnoticed, one of the mob.'

For the rest of the way up Whitehall, this unrestrainable companion poured out further explanatory particles of information about himself and his affiliations. I learned that he was one of a group formed in 1916 to attack the citadel of the Georgian poets, and to besiege them where they lay entrenched in the anthologies edited by Edward Marsh and published by Harold Monro at the Poetry Bookshop in Devonshire Street, off the Theobalds Road. I was surprised, even after half an hour's acquaintance, that this inflammatory creature could be contained within any group. I saw him as an active volcano of emotions, likely to overrun everything static in his neighbourhood.

This impression was confirmed by what happened as soon as we were seated at a conspicuous table in the middle of the huge general restaurant at the Corner House by Charing Cross Station. My host immediately relapsed into despair. No one served us, and this lack of consideration for his unique person and vocation reminded him of the humble origins, already hinted at so long ago, at the beginning of the eternal half-hour since first we met.

A waitress appeared, and Flint controlled himself while we ordered our meal. He broke out again when she had gone. He stared savagely at me, stretched himself back in his chair, ran his two hands through his hair and thereby stirred the flames to greater fury.

'I've had enough! I'm going to put an end to this. It's the only way out. Good-bye, my boy.'

He made to get up, but with just that delay in the action that made me suspect a touch of theatrical effect. 'It'll waste a good lunch,' I said quietly. 'Better stay now you've ordered it.'

I thought he was going to strike me. Customers at near-by

tables stopped eating and stared at us, indignant at being embarrassed. They may have thought my companion was drunk.

He wasn't. He was truly in despair, the victim of his own temperamental imagination. To my horror he put his head between his hands on the table and wept.

I was at a loss what to do. Our neighbours hurriedly resumed their meals, or retreated behind newspapers. I waited, and was about to say something consoling, when the waitress appeared. She glanced at Flint over the tray. 'Now, duck,' she said. 'Move your head. Here's your dinner. That'll cheer you up.'

Flint obeyed, quite unself-consciously. The storm had passed, and he looked at the waitress like a child at its mother. He didn't even thank her. He took it all for granted; and so did she.

We celebrated his recovery with half a bottle of claret, the first wine I had tasted since I left the Laboratory two months earlier. Flint talked comparatively calmly while we consumed our food. I learned about a childhood of extreme poverty in a large family, the shock and degradation of watching the furniture being taken out of the home by brokers' men. I could see that Flint's wounds were still bleeding. This extravagant self-pity was the result. So were the recoil, the loud and aggressive histrionics.

The man behind all this was undamaged. At least, it appeared so to me, at our first uncomfortable meeting. I listened to him, and my heart warmed, as I recognized the courage, the ability, which had carried him out of that setting, the dark, greasy Victorian slum, to a responsible post (he was in charge of Foreign Statistics in the Ministry), and to recognition amongst the most fastidious and exclusive group of poets in England and America at that time.

I had two or three more luncheon sessions with Flint in the following weeks of late winter at the beginning of 1921. It was a stormy experience, but stimulating. I learned about the group, called the Imagists, its rather vague technical ideals, which aimed at eliminating from verse all abstractions, all expressions of ideas, and to permit only symbolical images. This seemed to be labouring the obvious, a high-faluting way of restating the principle which John Keats propounded to Shelley when he advised him 'to load every rift with ore'. But I did not dare to say so. I had never before met so emphatic a character as F. S. Flint, even among the highly individualized men who used to gather round me in the Custom House Luncheon Club: Irish poets, assertive young intellectuals from the provinces, sceptical budding scientists.

Flint was a creature from another planet, a seismic planet. Later, when he gave me a copy of his book called *Otherworld*, published in 1918, I observed the title instantly to tell myself how doubly appropriate it was, first to the intention of the author, secondly to my conception of him. I noticed also that the book was dedicated to someone named Herbert Read, and I wondered who this could be. I was soon to learn.

Meanwhile, I read Flint's provocative Preface to his poems, and I studied the poems also, wondering what was original in the argument in the former, and the example in the latter. I found in the Preface a prophetic statement with which I disagreed, though now I suspect there may be much truth in it. He said: 'I have kept three propositions before me: the first being that poetry is a quality of all artistic writing, independent of form; the second that rhyme and metre are artificial and external additions to poetry and that, as the various changes that could be rung upon them were worked out, they grew more and more insipid, until they have become contemptible and encumbering; and the third that the artistic form of the future is prose, with cadence – a more strongly accented variety of prose in the oldest English tradition – for lyrical expression.'

The prophecy lies in that third statement; and literary fashion over the half-century since it was uttered has tended to fulfil it. What puzzled me was the contradiction between the first and second statements, since writing that is 'artistic' must have an artifice in its composition, inherent and not external. Flint's violent temperament overrode logic, and I suspect that his theory of poetry was special pleading, to cover his impatience with the discipline demanded by tradition, in verse-forms or any other art. It prevented him also from large creative purpose. His lyrical outbursts were momentary, to fall back into the darkness of self-pity that was so painfully evident in his person and his social behaviour. Nevertheless, that temperament was so powerful that it sent his lyrical rockets soaring up, to burst often with impressive beauty. When, for instance, I read his poem called 'Swan', I marvelled at the miracle that could bring such a clear, cool lyric out of the matrix of London slums, the degradation of his childhood, the ugliness and resentment out of which he struggled, only to be crippled in the effort. I realize now that I recalled this miracle, but subconsciously, when I created the character of Mouncer, the poet from Camden Town, in my novel *The Porch*, a study in that stoicism which was an imperative philosophy for all self-educating aspirants from the lower-middle and working classes in those dark days at the beginning of the twentieth century, when 'the satanic mills' of the industrial age were grinding at their loudest.

Flint never found serenity. He went on belabouring the past long after it was dead. Even in this poem in free verse, with its echoes of Mallarmé and Debussy (a period piece today), the bitterness lingers.

O Swan,
My eyes watch you through the sallows,
Wounded by your cruel beauty . . .
O white splendour,
You have hurt me.

You do not heed us;
Our music crashes through the stillness;
Our shouts crack in the evening;
We gather round your pool:
The cygnets twist their swart heads
And their crimson beaks, and listen;
But you do not heed them;
You do not heed us.

Your yellow feet move
Through the clear, cold water;
Your belly rests upon your belly,
Soft, cool, caressing;
Your beak meets your beak;
Your necks repeat the figures
Two, three, eight and zero.

O twi-shaped, O triple nature,
Bird, fish and serpent,
Do you plunge your head
To lose your torment?
Does your beauty tire you?

The wind moves the leaves to a sweet sound;
It bends the sedge and the sallows;
The tulips sway and the iris;
But it brings to you the peace of curdled waters,
Where you are no longer.

Humbert Wolfe must have recognized the quality of
potential poise and judgment hidden in the depths of the
character that produced such lyrical manifests. He conjured
Flint into the Ministry of Labour, on an established grade, and
put him in the least dreary department of Intelligence and
Statistics, under another man of temperament, John Hilton,
who would understand his fiery demon, and harness it reasonably to a stable career, while encouraging the poetry spumed
from its nostrils. Here, in some degree, Flint found a home,
where he had the opportunity and security to be sure of himself.
But it came too late. He never lost his resentment of the miseries
of his childhood. In the later years of his service in Whitehall,
and in his retirement, he dropped away from the circle of
literary friends capable of recognizing, on equal terms, his
perennially unfulfilled promise as a poet. I met him once or
twice in later years. The fire had died into fumes. Flint had in-
flated himself into a saloon-bar orator, a layer-down of the law

on all subjects, at any time of the day, other than closing-hours.

[5]

Within a few weeks of our first meeting, Flint announced that he was taking me along to meet Herbert Read, whose name was now known to me as an inhabitant of *Otherworld*. Amongst other heroes of the Imagist group, Read was the one most vociferously and frequently referred to by my latterday Virgil. I learned of his distinguished war record, his powerful personality and his dogged scholarship, his post in the Treasury as Private Secretary to R. R. Scott, the Permanent Secretary and Head of the British Civil Service. 'Terrific fellow, Read! Dark horse! Great future before him!' shouted Flint, with a gesture of his arm that took in the whole of the Horse Guards Parade, which we were crossing after leaving Downing Street, on our way from Montague House to a rendezvous in Soho.

I remember little of that first meeting, because I was overcome with shyness, that distressing disease of self-conceit and uncertainty, so common in young humans, and also in young animals. Even the manners of an adolescent cat may be affected by it. But I was in my twenty-ninth year, and had no excuse for retaining these unlovely symptoms which play such havoc with the smooth working of society, and torture the individual into a condition almost of imbecility. People who spend their early years alone are susceptible to this shyness, which fails to cover suspicion, lack of standards of comparison, poverty of debating power, and the egoism that so frequently goes with self-education. We are all princes or princesses when there is no one else around.

My state of mind may have been aggravated by the extreme reserve, in manner and personality, of this man about whose ability and achievement I had heard so much. He looked at me out of a bony skull, gave me a faint gleam of recognition, and relapsed into silence; if it could be called relapse, with no word spoken. Flint's voice filled the vacuum, and Herbert Read listened, occasionally contributing one of those eye-gleams that made me think of a winter dawn below a leaden sky, with a thin break of silver on the eastern horizon.

I liked this undemonstrative stranger. The very sparseness of his figure and features gave me a feeling of discipline, of quiet resolution. He seemed to be surrounded by cleanliness, of mind and body. What attracted me, of course, was the familiarity of his type, if it can be called a type. Here was a person of the same kind as my brother Jack: austere but, I should suspect, latently passionate, concerned ruthlessly with the aesthetics of life, and merciless to any clumsy or crass fool who should violate his principles, built up half by instinct and half by a relentless will-power.

Such was my immediate reaction to this man, of my own age, who had already done so much, and gone so far, towards the building of a career, and a character openly significant of that career.

That introduction to Herbert Read led to more. Within a few weeks I met other members of that group, the Imagists, all of them distinctive individuals, and none of them slavishly surrendered to the theories of art which they held in common.

The rendezvous was an Italian restaurant called The Commercio in Frith Street, Soho, almost opposite the house in which William Hazlitt died in 1830. In the parallel Greek Street, the young de Quincey had found shelter in the room of the girl who saved him from destitution, afterwards to disappear and leave him to an emotional deprivation that almost affected his sanity. The disreputable neighbourhood of Soho was at least rich in literary reputation. Also in Greek Street stood the mansion, at the corner of Soho Square, where the young Beckford lived, the millionaire sybarite author of *Vathek*, a crownpiece to the cult of Orientalism which dominated the whole of Europe during the eighteenth century, affecting even the insular Dr Johnson, who probably caught it from Oliver Goldsmith, the imitator of Montesquieu.

Now we moderns proposed to add a new chapter to the

literary history of Soho. We had an upper room, overlooking
the Street, at The Commercio, and were usually waited on by
the daughter of the proprietors, an elderly couple from Milan.
They seldom smiled. Nor did the pale, handsome daughter,
whose madonna-like beauty of heavy-lidded, downcast eyes,
full mouth and chin, was a demurely living model of an Andrea
del Sarto portrait, haunted by a touch of sedate melancholy
singularly in keeping with the temper of our small company of
purists.

For I was accepted amongst them, though I had little to say,
and no fully intellectualized principles of art to contribute to the
canon. By this time, after working for fifteen years in the
manipulation of language, clumsily and without the initial
discipline of a study of Greek and Latin, I had established a
personal code. It might be called a prejudice. I rejected subtle
divisions and nomenclatures. I would have no antinomy of
classicism and *romanticism*.

I saw art as I saw religion, from a non-conformist point of
view. Both these vast fields of consciousness were, for me,
prospects of worship, of adoration, before the living manifest
of nature, and of the Christ who first touched my eyes when I
was a child of ten years, one winter morning at sunrise, in a
sanatorium at Broadstairs, out of the sun rising above the
frosted landscape and the sea-mist. Revelation, revelation, all
through my days, with its certain uncertainty, its divine cheat,
its short cuts at the expense of solid hard work, its agonizing
assurances of an authority which could never be proved, or
produced in evidence against the claims and disciplines of
authority, especially academic authority: such was my method.

So the talk of the Imagists, their scorn for so much of the
poetry of the nineteenth century, and the neo-Georgians who
were the lingering autumnal foliage of it, meant nothing to me.
Nor was I impressed by the constant references to the French
poets who, under Mallarmé, turned in disgust from the
materialism of the Second Empire and its equally sordid aftermath, the Third Republic, to an esoteric game with verbal
symbols rather than with sane meaning and the whole birth-

right of poetry as a legislature towards the improvement of human society. I heard much about Jules Laforgue, Rimbaud, Verlaine, and I read with some excitement Arthur Symons's book on the French Symbolists. But the only one of them who penetrated into my curiously constructed world of art was Verlaine, with his music *'toute sonore encore de vos derniers baisers'*, whatever that might mean.

It meant much, always more than could be rationalized, or fitted into the schoolbooks of art, and the dogmatizing of university dons. The aesthetic experience hinted at in this line from Verlaine's sonnet was for me equivalent with the religious encounter which overtook Saul on the road to Damascus. Both are mysterious, the aesthetic and the religious overtakings, and I can no more explain them now, forty years later, than I could in my twenties. Only recently, after I had said something sharply critical of F. R. Leavis, who has spent his professional life conducting a kind of cloistral revolution within the Faculty of English at Cambridge, I was answered equally sharply by John Freeman, editor of the *New Statesman*, 'But at least he has taught us to study the text!'

Study the text! How flat-footed that sounds! And I would suggest that even studying the text (an admonition which labours the obvious) does not justify the student in coming to foolish conclusions, such as that *Our Mutual Friend* is Dickens's greatest work, or that D. H. Lawrence in comparison with his contemporary novelists and poets was almost superhuman.

What is so dangerous about these schoolroom zealots (so often belated in their discoveries), is that they fit their students with a reach-me-down insolence and absolutism, before sending them out into the academic world, at home and abroad, to spread the virus of this disease: obtuseness and over-certainty. I realized this when I encountered two such misguided literary missionaries, one in the university of Münster, Germany, and the other in that of Madras, in South India.

[6]

During the early months of 1921, a year of interminable summer, plans were laid for establishing the quarterly magazine *The Criterion*. Both in purpose and personnel it exceeded the bounds of the Imagist theory: but in principle it was of the same disposition. It was to stand for austerity in critical judgment and in creative execution. It would admit emotionalism only under the duress of a discipline not so much academic (though that was acknowledged) as philosophical. Later, this philosophical control took a religious turn, under the influence of the founder and Editor of *The Criterion*.

T. S. Eliot was a young man then, still working, I think, in the Foreign Department of Lloyds Bank. Indeed, we were all earning a living outside the literary profession. Not many writers, especially creative writers, are able to do otherwise during the early years of their careers. Amongst the people who sat round the table in that upper room of The Commercio restaurant, waited on by the del Sarto madonna, not one of us was a free-lance writer. Eliot was still in a bank; Herbert Read, F. S. Flint and I were Civil Servants; J. B. Trend was a don at Christ's College, Cambridge, teaching Spanish; Bonamy Dobrée had given up his commission in the regular army and was about to go to the chair of English in Cairo University; Alec Randall was a young diplomat in the Foreign Office. One was to come in later, and unexpected, who, after demobilization, went on to the staff of *The Times Literary Supplement* and thus qualified for full-time professionalism in our economically unreliable craft.

I think I had met T. S. Eliot before that occasion, but my recollection begins from that night. It was quite unforgettable. Something big was in the air, an excitement, a sense of challenge and a preliminary recruitment. Thus keyed up with the others, I put aside my obstinate individualism (the result of my upbringing) and took on the temper of the team, though conscious even then that I fell short of its austerity. I realized, too, the nature of Eliot's personality: its nervous intensity, its deliberate reserve cultivated to counteract the influence and naïvetés of his American childhood and youth.

I studied him that night, because he was so patently the central figure in this gathering of young enthusiasts. He sat there, quiet and calm, under the limelight of our attention. Opposite him, the monolithic Herbert Read communicated from his fastness by means of an occasional monosyllable dropped from 'his granite lip'. The others offered more normal contributions, and the policy, proposed format, editorial dispositions, took shape in the air. Nobody made notes. No minutes were taken down. Finances were not mentioned.

Amid all this activity I remained silent. I had no experience as a journalist, or as a literary critic. I knew nothing about the technique of running a newspaper or a magazine. I sat, there, back to the wall, obscured by Flint's close barrage of waving arms and verbal artillery. I was glad of this protection; never before had I felt myself to be so inadequate. I suppose a freshman at Oxford or Cambridge, translated from the minor triumphs as head of his school, must feel as I felt that night in this company of scholars, writers, and warriors.

What overawed me was their certainty, the emphasis with which they debated the problems involved in the birth of *The Criterion*. I realized what these men had won from their rougher lives at university and in the trenches. How dramatically their environment and training compared with mine, the gentle, protective and isolated maternalism of the lower middle class, the lack of debate with its thrust and counter-thrust, the lack too of impersonal criticism and resultant intellectual detachment.

I observed these differences, concentrating on them so closely that I lost the threads of the arguments over *The Criterion*, and indeed I was willing to leave all that business to the rest of the company, while I sorted out these new impressions, and depressions, which threatened to overwhelm a mind and personality still unhardened to act with authority, still untrained to administrative conduct.

That night, I suspect, was for me the first stage in a process of disillusionment of the *folie de grandeur* which so often poisons the early life of the person whose lively intelligence is drawing him up out of humble social beginnings, with their suffocating cosiness, or their physical degradation. Some of us never outgrow these early warpings, and we carry chips on our shoulders all the way from the cradle to the grave. It is a disease of the underprivileged, and whole societies can suffer from it, as we see in the conduct of the decolonialized governments and peoples in Africa and Asia today. It takes a long time, through many generations, to become an aristocrat; that is, a person of firm self-discipline while wielding power, of humility in authority, and of nonchalance in the ceremonies of office.

Though I was only dimly conscious of these matters while I sat shrunken into myself that night in 1921, I believe now that I was drawn to that awareness by the presence of T. S. Eliot, and his silent control of the proceedings, during the birthpangs of *The Criterion*. His voice was soft, with no trace of its American origin. The accent indeed was old-fashioned, in the Edwardian mode of such English precisionists as Max Beerbohm and Osbert Sitwell, every syllable enunciated as though it were a gem to be rubbed with rouge and a velvet duster before being suspended on a necklace of gold. I found it delightful; for such a consideration for timing and rounded enunciation offered at once a clear-cut relationship with the values of verse, and the musical propriety of words, the medium of poetry.

Even though there was a cutting edge to this voice, a hint of merciless satire, I found myself instantly attracted to the personality which it expressed. I have never lost that attraction, though the necessities of my own work in poetry have made me insufficiently appreciative, especially in those early days, of Eliot's achievement. But there I have been in a very small minority, as Bonamy Dobrée pointed out rather sinisterly a few years ago when I went up to Leeds to lecture during his Professorship of English there.

I have never been able to understand this lack in my response, and probably I have worried myself into exaggerating it. I share Eliot's temperamental attitude towards the demands and function of the art of poetry, both in society and as a discipline in the life of the individual. But I have distrusted the Montparnasse influence in his verse and doctrine, his sponsoring, even out of loyalty, of the writings of Ezra Pound. The dreadful self-consciousness of so many *déraciné* Americans, aping the hyper-civilized European decadents, has always given me the sensation of being in the presence of death, of flowers withered because the plant has been torn from its taproot in a native soil. Even the novels of Henry James have for me this desiccated atrophy: unsimple and pretentious.

But latterly these manifestations, in a world whose values are increasingly internationalized and given an American bias, are no longer thought to be decadent. Even such writing as that of the late Gertrude Stein is taken seriously. That, however, is a long way from Mr Eliot's poetry, its world-wide acclaim, and my failure to appreciate it to that degree.

I think he has been aware of this, for friends are ever ready to carry adverse criticism to its victims. He has never shown such awareness, never offered me anything but that characteristic, quiet courtesy, and on one occasion, during my period of twilight of the soul, he took me in a hansom-cab one night from Soho to Sloane Square, to talk to me of my troubles, and shyly but authoritatively to offer advice and encouragement. Such gifts can never be forgotten. Further, a year later, in 1928, after I had been experimenting in writing *vers libres*, somewhat belatedly perhaps in the manner of the Imagists, Eliot took the work and published the book with his firm, then called Faber and Gwyer. The copyright of the book, *Mood without Measure*, was subsequently bought, first by Dents and later by Heinemanns.

[7]

The evening grew late, and I was beginning to feel restive because I had arranged to sleep at my brother's home, when the still active committee of poets was disturbed by a newcomer. The door opened, and a tall man stalked in, with an air almost of hostility. He approached, towered over the table, and announced himself as though he were presenting a police warrant:

'Aldington!'

Silence fell, for several seconds. Some of our members must have known of preceding drama, for I sensed a combination of embarrassment and curiosity. I saw Read's eyes take on a glassy stare, an opacity that curtained off his thoughts and feelings. Eliot was leaning forward a little, his bent head turned, with an upward, quizzical glance at Richard Aldington, aware of his defiance and what must lie behind it.

'I am leaving,' said Richard Aldington. It was an unhappy voice, touched with a perpetual anger. I remember wondering instantly if Byron might have shown the same symptoms of a habit of grievance. There was a Byronic suggestion of nobility also in Aldington's figure. He was a handsome man, bold and authoritative.

I was eager to go, and somewhat heavy and dazed after a dinner of oxtail and a session at the cheap Chianti supplied by The Commercio *en carafe*. But I could not leave while Aldington stood there, holding up the editorial proceedings, and threatening, by a sort of animal, magnetic propulsion, to dare us to criticize, or interfere with, his proposal 'to leave'.

'I'm on my way to Paris,' he said. 'I've done with this country.' He waited for protests, but none came. We were all silent, and I saw Eliot slowly nod his head, several times, by way of reluctant understanding.

'But you'll be hearing from me. Be sure of that!'

Flint leaned back, flung up an arm and grasped Aldington

by the sleeve. Wine had made him mellow. 'Dear fellow,' he said, thickly. 'Dear fellow! You mustn't, mustn't go. Your career! A French scholar like you? Not another in England like you. Not even myself!'

Aldington looked at him as though he might be a tree waving in the wind. Flint's arm dropped away and he subsided into a muttering defeat.

'Well, good luck to you all,' said Aldington. Flint shifted his chair and nearly crushed me against the wall.

'Bring a glass; join us, Richard!' he cried. 'Waitress, a glass!' But the young madonna did not appear, and Aldington ignored the invitation. Slowly he turned, and walked out as magisterially as he had come in.

A minute passed while the power of his presence died away. Even then nothing was said. Only some days later did I learn from Flint that Aldington, after the failure of his wartime marriage with the American poetress Hilda Doolittle (who wrote under the initials 'H.D.', to the prescription of the Imagist dogma), had lived with a charming woman, a painter, in a cottage near Newbury. There he had accumulated a library of French literature, and at his early age was already being spoken of as the future Editor of *The Times Literary Supplement*, selected by Bruce Richmond to succeed him in due course.

But now Aldington, chased by some fury or demon in his character, had thrown all that away, left his lover, deserted his home and his library, to join the colony of self-exiles, the perpetual and ever-changing set of refugees to be found in the cafés of Montmartre and Montparnasse in Paris.

He was quickly to emerge out of the welter of impossible causes, and rootless, despairing aesthetic fashions. His novels *Death of a Hero*, and *The Colonel's Daughter* had a worldwide success. His long poem *A Dream in the Luxembourg*, a latterday idyll on the Left Bank, meanwhile sustained the reputation already won in the smaller literary world. Even in these robust works, however, there nestled the serpent of discontent and destructive anger. He might be called the forerunner of the Angry Young Men, raising in the nineteen-twenties an outcry

F

against the older generation, the politicians who had manœuvred mankind into the first world war, against all mothers for having produced sons, against all women for being women, and against life and human society for their contribution towards his distrust of himself and his talent.

This Byronic attitude was not uncommon in that decade, so often miscalled gay. The civilization of Western Europe had been split down the middle by war, and all kinds of hidden powers released: the sullen resentments of the wage-earners, the triumph of the machine predicted by Samuel Butler in *Erewhon*, the will of the majority still uneducated, still primitive in its desires and taste.

Aldington saw all this happening round him, and made the mistake of believing it to be happening only in Britain. He was to be quickly disillusioned, and his disgust fed other misgivings founded deeper in his character, partly temperamental, partly conditioned by an unstable and tragic childhood. Even his name was an assumption. All conspired to make him a rogue elephant, heavy-treading and dangerous, and as he grew older this tendency increased, tearing down his own successful career, alienating many friends, exiling him from his English homeland, and forcing him in the last years of his life to write a series of biographical books that sought to destroy the reputations of such friends as D. H. Lawrence, the bookseller Orioli, and Norman Douglas the author of *South Wind*; from which he roamed farther to drag down the public monuments put up by history to the figures of Wellington and Lawrence of Arabia.

This was done with telling effect, for he had a scholar's precision and no small literary skill. The legend of T. E. Lawrence has been permanently damaged, and this may please generations that are suspicious of heroes and hero-worship, an inevitable reaction after the rampaging of Hitler and Mussolini. But a people without heroes is a people with no intermediary between itself and its own blind strength, a strength as indifferent as the ocean, as wanton as the hurricane.

What puzzles me, as I look back on Aldington's life, and his pathetic death in loneliness and obscurity in Montpellier, where

he lived after a second marriage had collapsed, was my subsequent friendship with him from the time he returned to
Europe in 1946, until the end in 1962.

The success of his war novels wafted him off to America, and
he spent many years writing film scripts in Hollywood. Those
were years of affluence, and he was able to live opulently. I
know one or two lame dogs whom he helped over stiles. One of
them was a Lancashire dramatist and novelist named Halcott
Glover, always a near failure; a charming character but
crushingly garrulous, a weakness that seeped, by osmotic
pressure, into his writings. Aldington, that so-called impatient
choleric, put up with this, and entertained Glover over long
periods again and again, especially when the old man was
nearing his end, but still talking. I saw that final stage of a long-
standing hospitality when, in 1947, I went to stay with Aldington at a villa in Le Lavandou, near St-Tropez, to convalesce after
a couple of operations. Glover was there, very feeble, so for
some six weeks Aldington's villa, standing up a valley in a
thicket of winter-blooming mimosa, was more a nursing-home
than a literary household. There Aldington, approaching his
own professional autumn, showed an aspect of his personality
that, alas, rarely appeared in his books. He was benign, considerate, restrained.

One early winter day he and I escaped from the oracular sick-
room, and carried a picnic basket, packed by my wife who has
an art in that medium, up to the rolling *causse* behind the
Corniche. When we got to the rising ground and the irregular
footpath among the fragrant flowering bushes, my wife had to
take the basket, while Aldington hoisted me from one stone
slab to the next, supplying the muscle that my still-gelatinous
legs had lost. We thus got up high enough to look north-
eastward, where the distant Alpes Maritimes shone, a silver
chain glittering between the eggshell-blue winter sky, and the
sombre green scrub; the olive, the cistus, lavender and rose-
mary, the skeletons of asphodel and the more earthly floral
beauties familiar to English eyes.

As we opened the picnic basket, we heard from across the

valley the sudden outbreak of the angelus bell at twelve noon. It floated over the silence, a miniature agitation that thinned out and faded back into loneliness: our loneliness. We stopped eating, awed into silence. Aldington chuckled.

'Old Halcott Glover would have had something to say about that.' He filled our glasses with wine bought by the litre from an Italian peasant small-farming on these French hills. Our hearts warmed to the old, widowed dramatist slowly dying down there in the villa. Perhaps, as time passes, Aldington's faculty for putting his finger on the weak spots, as he did at that moment when the angelus surprised us, may prove to be benevolent also in the books whose savagery ruined his own reputation rather than that of his victims. Writers are often the slaves of their own pens, which make them caper like Til Eulenspiegel when he took up the bewitched broom.

Now Aldington is gone, I think of him with sadness. He was a man incapable of finding his way home. That is a terrible fate.

CHAPTER SIX

The Advance to Professionalism

[1]

IT WAS NEARLY MIDNIGHT when I reached my brother's home. I found him waiting up for me, still busy on drawings for the building of a gramophone which was to throw the sound up from a concealed trumpet out of the open top of the cabinet. He was working by the light of a table lamp in the back of the L-shaped sitting-room, where his pianoforte stood under a burden of albums and music manuscript sheets.

I was conscience-stricken, and imagined myself to be accused of inconsiderateness by the other members of the household, his parents-in-law down below, his wife at the top of the lofty house. Jack looked ghostly by the close lamplight. Concentration, with its excitement, had drained the lifeblood from his face, and I noticed how much thinner his cheeks were, how pale and rigidly set the lips. His hair clung limply to his skull, and added to the impression of fatigue.

'Late!' he said, smiling grimly. 'All in bed! I've got the acoustics right now. I made a false start and had to take the innards out again. You'll be able to hear it next time you come.'

He recollected something.

'I was told to give you some hot milk. The old lady always thinks you're at death's door. Nothing wrong now, is there?'

He looked at me searchingly, as I waved away the half-accusation. I could have turned it back against him, but I was too weary to admit any more emotion. I had to tell him something of the evening's events, however, if only to break through his detachment. As I watched him there, in the silence of the night against the faint shapes of the poplar trees at the end of the garden, I was reminded of the inquisitive glance he gave me

77

years before, on the night when at the age of seven I was fitted with a pair of spectacles, and looked out on a crisp, incisive universe for the first time in my myopic life. 'Is it any different?' he had demanded.

I wanted to tell him now about this farther stage in that difference, and of the invisible university into which I had been accepted. But though my mind was in turmoil, my body was exhausted. I had been up since five o'clock that morning, to put in an hour's reading before breakfast and the train journey to Town from Oxted. The day's work at the Ministry, taxing to my still untrained and not deeply interested intelligence, had been followed by an hour at St Paul's Cathedral, to be enraptured by the choral singing, while I killed time until the meeting in Soho. This coming and going, east and west between the City and Soho, whipped along by fervour and an enthusiasm eagerly on the look-out for evidences on which to feed, was only the preliminary to the experience in that upper room at The Commercio, my enrolment in a group, a brotherhood, such as I had never known before. Even on that first night, I was timid. I suspected a trap. I might have been a Catholic novice at his preliminary prostration. The faith was not in question; indeed, it was the preservation of my ever-growing faith, my free worship of the minute-by-minute stuff of life, my joy even in the miseries of physical pain and the deflating pressure of domestic routine, that I was jealous to protect. I feared this dogma of *The Criterion* team. I could not believe that it could contain one half the glories that I demanded from life, and that I found under the direction of my self-selected masters, and the authority of that Burning Bush by whose light I was making my way homeward.

That was a full day, and I could give or take no more. I sat there passively, while Jack talked. I was not even in a condition to be surprised, still less to be alarmed, by his midnight animation. He told me that we should be able to meet no more for lunchtime sessions at the Tate Gallery, no more for organ-recitals in St Peter's, Vauxhall, to an audience of ragged urchins and the patrons of Kennington doss-houses.

I learned that he had been feeling 'tired', and had applied successfully for removal to a school nearer home. He was about to start work at an elementary school just round the corner, an airy L.C.C. building halfway up the hill, overlooking the flat land eastward to the Thames. It would be as good as a sanatorium, Jack said.

'A sanatorium?' I echoed, from the hollow of my fears.

'Well, you know what I mean,' he answered, testily. 'Not a good record, our family. You, and Mother. I take after the old man, strong as a horse, but one can't be too careful. Besides, I'm sick of that squalor in Vauxhall. I haven't even the support of a religion, like those eunuchs in the Church House. But they were very good to me. Lent me the organ whenever I wanted it, so long as there wasn't a service on.'

I had never known him speak so violently against the Anglo-Catholic priests, who from a celibate community ran that riverside parish, their reward not of this world. Perhaps some newcomer among them, young and righteous, had tried to convert my elusive brother, whose unspoken but sceptical tolerance must have been disconcerting, within the fold.

'Nice and secular,' added Jack. 'And no travelling on those hellish trams. I shall almost be living over the shop. I can do with more time to myself.'

I was not too tired to compare this change in his life, with that in my own: he, retreating farther into solitude; I for the first time joining what might almost be called a community. Would this pull us farther apart? Marriage had already begun the process, especially my marriage some two years after his. Reticences, avoidances, were widening like the waters between two ships slightly off course from each other. Neither of us, perhaps, had noticed it before. But at that hour of night I was weary and devitalized, open to misgivings and the cold touch of omens.

I wanted to reach out to my brother to reassure myself by feeling him with my hand, as a reminder of the past, the idyll of our childhood, its secrets and discoveries, its isolation in the beginning of time, its approximation to what we were striving after now, in midstream: a stable and secure home, with harmony unbroken and incalculable perfection fulfilled.

But I dared not lift my hand. Jack had always been beyond my reach, and now I saw him farther removed from me. Was I beginning to criticize him for some weakness, some gradual falling away from the versatile power which had burned within him, a beacon to my childhood? Or was the change in me, the effect of being cast out into a wider contact with people of larger equipment and assurance, not only in society but in the arts which Jack and I had discovered so innocently, so naïvely, rather as Robinson Crusoe discovered the footprints in the sand?

We said no more. Jack saw me to the guest-room, stood for a few moments at the foot of the bed, studying me.

'Don't overdo it,' he said. Then with a nod of emphasis to his last word, he closed the door with quiet precision, and I was left alone, lost in the crowd of impressions still milling about in my mind, on their way to the exits of sleep.

[2]

Clifford Bax, as an amateur astrologer, had predicted that my life, hitherto sheltered, would in the near future be changed, both in scope and pace. He said that it would be good for my development as a writer. I could have assured him that this was a safe bet, for up to 1921, from the time I started writing in 1911, I had worked solely by the book, making my own laws as I went along. I met W. H. Davies and Bax in 1918, and Humbert Wolfe in 1920. It was a limited literary acquaintance, too perfunctory and infrequent in its contacts, to be of much influence. I was so exuberant, so prolific in pouring out verse – sometimes several poems a day – that these colleagues could not have realized how sketchy, how home-made, was my equipment. Only to Davies, as one equally naïve, did I confess that I still carried in my pocket two tiny black-covered notebooks, one for French words, the other for English, newly discovered day by day in my progress.

Humbert Wolfe was too remote, and too officially exalted, for me to lay bare my primitive mental armoury to him. I had yet to discover the generous and indeed helplessly susceptible heart living hidden behind Humbert's façade of audacity, impudence and razor-like wit. These weapons made him not only to appear formidable, but also to be formidable. As the tools of a quick and practical Jewish intelligence, they had carried him to the fore in his career in the Civil Service. During the first world war he became private secretary to Lloyd George at the Ministry of Munitions. That must have been a good training in bluff, chicane, and the manipulation of human nature. It was Greek helping Greek. Humbert once told me that he knew only one man 'who was a hundred per cent wicked'. It was Lloyd George. He said the reason for this was that the Welsh Wizard had a mind and imagination that functioned from minute to minute, moving with an inspired power of extemporization as each necessity arose, either practical towards events, or psychological towards men and women. But after that moment, all was forgotten, promises and commitments obliterated from his memory, his conscience left treacherously virgin.

Perhaps Humbert had adopted some of the devices of that Old Conjuror. He seemed to be too clever by half, and that may be why he was suspect among many colleagues of his own high rank in the Civil Service. Edward Marsh, and Harold Nicolson, two eminent Civil Servants also active in the world of letters, would have nothing to do with Wolfe's facile verse, which during the nineteen-twenties was being poured out in volume after volume, to be popularly acclaimed with a circulation of over eight thousand copies: a miraculous range for books of verse put out by a young writer at a period when the wartime boom had collapsed, and publishers were reassuming their habitual shyness when approached by poets.

By working with Humbert, and particularly working under him, I discovered the real man. I was able to assess his ability as an administrator, his astonishingly mature political sense in dealing with Ministers and Parliamentary Secretaries on the one hand, and Trade Union and Employers' Union officials on the other. I saw his genius for handling irreconcilable groups and individuals in committee, for deflating pompous fools and hitting the more dangerous Goliaths neatly between the eyes with the pebbles of his deadly wit.

Even in his kindness this wit flashed out; and it could sting. I remember one Saturday morning I was wearing a tweed coat and flannel bags. I had a knapsack over my shoulder, for I intended to break my train journey home and to walk over the Downs and through Titsey Woods.

As I entered the flowery iron gates of Montague House I felt a tap on my shoulder. Turning my eyes, I saw an agate knob, at the end of an ebony stick. Turning further, I saw Humbert Wolfe dressed up to the nines: a huge bow tie, a heliotrope hat and overcoat to match. A whimsical, half-pained smile played about the muscular mouth, and the goat-like eyes glittered.

'My dear Richard,' said the high-toned voice, with exquisite affectation, 'why *will* you come to the office in fancy dress?'

I must have looked at him gravely, for he immediately changed his mood, put a hand on my arm, and said, 'No! Forgive me! But you mustn't!' We walked in together, up the musical comedy staircase, past the saluting messenger, to part on the first floor, Humbert to disappear into the former ducal library, I to ascend another stage to my room above.

One day in 1921 trouble arose in the Ministry of Labour. Confidential information about some forthcoming Order in Council had leaked out to the Press. The Minister, an ex-school-teacher named Macnamara, was a tall, horse-faced man with a large mouthful of teeth, and the booming voice of a bully. He had little respect for his permanent staff, and was apt to disclaim them, and criticize them in public, where they had no means of answering back.

On this occasion he summoned the Permanent Secretary, the Under-Secretary, and the heads of all departments into the Private Office. Having seated them all round the wall, he tossed his head so that one could imagine the rattling of harness.

'Now, gentlemen,' he snorted, 'I am going to ask you categorically, one by one, if you know anything about this gross breach of official confidence. I hope you realize that the position of the Government has been gravely imperilled?'

With that, he began the round of this Unholy Communion, offering the formula to each, beginning with the Permanent Secretary, who replied with impeccable suavity. One or two of the Assistant Secretaries went red about the gills, partly from fear, partly from a sense of outrage which they were not self-disciplined enough to conceal. The stoicism which is the code of the British Civil Service should have drilled them never to show emotion.

As the inquisition proceeded, gradually drawing nearer to Humbert Wolfe, who had come in last and seated himself at the end, near the door, he lounged more and more languidly, so far as the small chair permitted, and made much play with a pale hand in failing to hide an attack of yawning. He looked most picturesque amongst his orthodox and sombre colleagues. His bow-tie stuck out, flamboyant and aggressive. His little side-whiskers added to a natural resemblance to Disraeli.

The Minister, still pompous and unaware of the hostility aroused by this schoolroom technique, at last approached Humbert, but before he could utter the now dreary formula, Humbert, half recumbent, rolled his eloquent eyes to heaven, and drawled: 'It's no use asking me, Minister. My private secretary *never* lets me see important papers!'

Symptoms of apoplexy amongst the staff, one or two of whom pretended to be outraged by this audacious and dis-ownable fellow, put an end to the inquisition.

Three years later, in 1924, during the short insecure life of Britain's first Labour Government, another record was created by the Ministry of Labour being given a woman Minister. She was Margaret Bondfield, who had come into politics the hard way, through Trade Union office. She was a kindly soul, who reminded me of old Peggotty, David Copperfield's nurse. But she was nervous in Whitehall, anxious perhaps not to let down the feminist side, as the first of her sex to hold ministerial rank. She kept the permanent staff on their toes, especially over the incessant flood of questions in the House on labour matters. Two members, I think they were Independent Liberals, Geoffrey Mander, and Pringle, kept up a daily bombardment. Mander was a genuine philanthropist, fighting through all his parliamentary life for the rights and just treatment of the individual.

One day Miss Bondfield kept her staff round her right through the morning, and at two o'clock Humbert staggered across Horse Guards Parade and into the Athenaeum to find that the last lunches were being cleared away in the long Coffee Room. One lingerer, a colleague of equal rank in another ministry, said to Humbert as he passed, 'Well, Humbert, and how is Maggie getting on?'

Humbert did not stop. At the distance of some few paces he turned his head vaguely towards his interlocutor, and cried, with an acid clarity, 'Oh, she's still *virago intacta*!'

[3]

This was the complex character who had butted into my remote, monastic life, to lift me out and drop me into the seething world of Whitehall at the moment when the Welfare State was being born, with Beveridge as midwife, under conditions prepared by the Liberal Government over a period of ten years before the 1914–18 war.

Everything was new in the newest of the ministries, whose chief function in those first after-war years was to re-establish the fluid population, as soon as possible, to family life, regular work, and the privacy and sanctity of home. There was no other way of assuaging the fever, the disillusion, the unrest, which threatened to perpetuate the horror and degradation begun amongst the mud, blood and lice of the battlefields of Flanders.

Hitherto, my conception of the Civil Service was Trollopian.

I had entered it naïvely, partly under compulsion from my father, partly because I knew of no other way of earning a living without having to give my whole attention to the matter. I have already described how I proposed to myself (and thought myself shrewd and worldly-wise in doing so) that I would be content with the humblest rank so long as it was permanent and guaranteed to give me the opportunity to practise my life-work, as a poet. I saw nothing immoral in this purpose, and when, many years later, I gave this motive to a character in a novel called *The Porch*, I was startled to read a review, by George Orwell, which was heavily reprobatory.

However, the official maelstrom of Whitehall gave me no time to brood over these miniature first causes by which I followed in my father's footsteps and became a minor Civil Servant. I had not been many months in the Joint Substitution Board, before I was swept closer (no doubt under Humbert Wolfe's benevolent influence) to the centre, to find myself in a small department, known as Intelligence and Statistics, under the leadership of John Hilton, formerly an engineer who had taken up social welfare work in the Garfield Foundation. He entered the Civil Service by the unorthodox route, over the war-wrecked convention of the competitive examination system. He was a Lancashire man and, on the basis of his native dialect, had built up a powerful speaking voice that later was to carry him to wide popularity as a broadcaster, giving advice to work-folk on all matters relating to their jobs: legal, technical, and in their relation to the Acts of Parliament which the Ministry of Labour at that time was putting through the House of Commons, like sausages through a machine.

It was in connection with this relationship that I was soon to find myself occupied; but first, I was given a mass of incredibly dull literature to study: blue books, Acts of Parliament, huge Code Books, and works on social reform by the pundits who were the theorists guiding the post-war Governments towards a new 'Jerusalem in England's green and pleasant land'.

At that time, forty-odd years ago, I looked down at all this new activity, and the study which it had forced upon me, with reluctance and boredom. I was far above it, isolated in 'a coign of the cliff', where I had determined to establish myself after trespassing on the slopes of Parnassus. I believed that I had left the world of lower middle-class stolidity and preoccupation with grocery and the petty statistics of daily life. My only principle of economics and money matters (the main theme of politics and governmental activity) was never to fall into debt. This was an ideal for a saint; but I had compromised my claim to sanctity by getting married and entering into parenthood, an experience which at that stage in my life made me appreciate the wisdom of the Catholic Church in imposing celibacy on its clergy.

The study of those dreary official books was suggested by my Principal Officer, in charge of the tiny department called 'Intelligence', to which I was now assigned. The immediate change was from the front garden to the back garden of the ducal palace, Montague House. But the huts were identical, exactly like those with which the dry bed of the lake in St James's Park had been filled.

My first interview with this Principal Officer was reassuring to a shy, bewildered and unwilling novice. The Head of the Intelligence Department was a young man, slim, handsome, with a clean-cut, bony physiognomy. He was loosely clad, with an old but well-fitting suit, a soft shirt and careless tie. He might have been a painter, or a musician. In fact, he was a dramatist, who wrote his plays under the pseudonym of C. K. Munro. At that time, when I first met him, he was just about to emerge into public notice through the Stage Society and the enthusiastic patronage of Bernard Shaw, who acclaimed his play *The Rumour* as a masterpiece of sociological drama. So it was, and still is: timeless in its exposure of international politics and the death-dealing chicane and downright fraud with which they are misconducted.

He sat bolt upright at his desk in the utility roomlet of the hut, with an attractive expression of permanent surprise commanding his features. After the usual preliminary inquiries about my previous service, as from an officer to a ranker, he asked me what papers I read. This rather touched my vanity. I expected so intelligent a person (which his physical attributes indicated) to see at once, from my build, what sort of creature I was. I replied rather haughtily: 'I don't read the daily papers. I depend on *The Nation*, and the *Spectator*.'

This, of course, at once betrayed me. The touchiness, uncertainty, over-weening ambition of the self-educating individual were laid bare. This emotional self-defensiveness was an occupational disease half a century ago. No doubt, in a remoulded society where educational opportunity is free for all, and barriers between the quarter-deck and the forecastle have been removed, these pathetic evidences of chip-on-the-shoulder are disappearing. I have recognized in undergraduates at Oxbridge during the nineteen-fifties and later an easy self-assurance, a disregard of self, that make me look back on my own early development with dismay.

C. K. Munro, perhaps because he was a dramatist and able to look into other people's natures, showed no such dismay. He stared steadily, out of a pair of innocent blue eyes, then said, 'I see!'

That was the beginning of a long association, and gradual establishment of a valuable friendship. For several weeks I was put into solitary confinement during office hours, to be seconded after that studious probation to a team of three or four whose job was to prepare a daily brief for the Minister, of all matters relating to Labour throughout Great Britain. I enjoyed this, because any form of composition and use of words has always acted on me like wine. I feel the warmth coursing through my veins, counteracting the heaviness of flesh and bones, and the obstinacy and repetitiveness of material things.

The team read the metropolitan and provincial newspapers during the morning and dictated to stenographers afterwards. This distillation was then collated and further reduced, under the editorship of an Assistant Principal, the final quintessence being laid on the Minister's desk next morning – twenty-four hours too late. Surely, all news likely to concern the Minister was picked up by him, through his political pores, while it was hot in the press? So I thought as I ploughed through the dreary columns, morning after morning. But I was still living in the unreal world of Platonic concepts, and I expected all legislators to be of the calibre of those supermen whom we meet in the pages of *The Republic*.

One such Minister – I think it was Steel-Maitland – must have arrived at Montague House, for I had not been working for more than a few months on this assignment when the news-sheet was abolished. For the next two years I worked with another team, compiling a Dictionary of Occupations, upon material supplied by the Information Officers in contact with industry and work-people all over the country. This work, like that of précis-writing for the Minister, was good technical training for a young writer. It taught me verbal concision and precision, a fundamental virtue in a poet. The necessary impersonality and objective accuracy were health-giving antidotes to the flamboyance and self-concern with which most young poets set off on the career which in the long run must consume them, as the moth is consumed by its passion for the candle-flame, and the mystic by his desire to confront God face to face.

Further, my delight in dictionaries was given a practical outlet, and I learned, by imitation, the value of lucid definition. That was why, some twelve years later, I welcomed the new dictionary compiled by Henry Wyld, the Merton Professor at Oxford. I like to have a dictionary in every room in my home, so that physical inertia shall never prevent me from looking up a word when I meet it for the first time, maybe in the pages of Gibbon, or in a review by Raymond Mortimer. But Wyld's *Universal Dictionary* I keep at hand on the reference shelf by my work-table.

That physical inertia! What a curse it is, curbing our efforts from the cradle to the grave! What can it be? Is it part of the mathematical character of the whole universe, whereby stars and constellations are reluctant to change their orbits, atoms to release their energy, men and molluscs to break out from their habits and environments? Yet only by throwing off their cosmic impediment are we able to move out to wider conscious-ness, more celestial courses, lifting the articulations of this common humanity one move nearer to the gestures of the gods, and so to harmony and unity, on the way home.

I remember how this reluctance of limb and internal organs dragged at me in childhood, youth and early manhood. For a time, I subdued it, but now in old age here it comes again, in a more ingratiating but no less treacherous guise, slowing down the processes of mind, the capacity for wonder and worship, by which alone man is able to approach the meaning of things, and the reality of his lodgment in this world.

[4]

One Saturday forenoon in the spring of 1922, I was pruning a closed rose-arbour from the inside, assisted by the infant daughter aged two. The morning was lyrical with March sunshine. Warmth fell from the air, and the soil could almost be heard responding to it, crocuses and aconites lifting up their voices over a chorus of dandelions.

The child was content, and so was I. I looked at her from time to time, breaking off from my pruning to suck a scratched finger, or to wipe away the sweat running down my spectacles.

For once, the demon of literary hunger was not gnawing at my vitals. I was content neither to read nor write that day: a rare condition which I contemplated with surprise even while enjoying it. I realized that I was beginning to slow down from the first mad rush of youthful ambition. I saw farther ahead, and the length of the journey cooled my ardour.

I had been a Civil Servant for thirteen years, and not for one day had I taken the career seriously. Bemused – and that is the right word – by my sense of vocation as a poet, I went regularly to the Laboratory, and later to the Ministry, like Lady Macbeth candle in hand. She was occupied with murder, I with language, and I am not sure who of us was the more besotted.

G

The remumeration as well as the duties was unrewarding. When I married in 1915 my salary was £65 a year. Increments and war-bonuses over seven years had brought it up to about £160. Something must be done to augment this income now that I had a house and family to support. The cost of living was steadily rising. For the first time in my life I began to think of economics seriously.

Even so, on that golden morning I let these problems slip from me, along with the heavier but joyful burden of my function as a writer. At that moment, the only necessity was to look, to smell, to listen, as the tide of new life came surging through the northern world, waking primitive cravings, age-old instincts, carrying away all the structures and obligations of civilization.

I felt the urge in my blood, and I looked at my daughter, to see the same power touching her. She was brooding over objects collected from the garden: buds of wildflowers, a few pebbles. She murmured over them like a witch incanting, and a power of concentration, unself-conscious, held her rigid. I stood over the small figure, longing to share my sensuous excitement, and to compare it with her more mysterious pre-occupation with the stones which she had gathered and the springtime buds already wilting under her warm hands.

She must have forgotten my presence. The sunlight through the bare boughs of the rose-arbour threw lances of trembling light over and around her, adding more to the illusion of ritual. Here was something beyond my capacity to understand, and to use in my trade of word-mongering. I watched the singleness of purpose, feline and merciless. Could this be the reservoir of all creative genius: the giving of the whole self in the moment of making something out of what we mistakenly call nothing?

What is this 'nothing'? It was filling the universe around me as I watched my daughter, where she sat poised like a wickedly demure Buddha, in the calm centre of this tornado raging over the sky, through the soil, and along the corridors of my imagination.

The spell was broken by a cheery whistle. It was the family whistle, the three notes on which my brother had composed his nostalgic little piece for the pianoforte. It came from my father's lips.

I felt a change in the temperature of that springtime day, and I shivered. My hand trembled as I closed and locked the secateurs. I stepped over my daughter, who was still spellbound under her own magic won from the stones and the flower-buds. She had not heard what I had heard.

There he stood, outside the back door of the little house. He wore a novel headgear, half helmet, half cap, and a pair of goggles dangled from one shoulder. Instantly, I knew from his assumed easy posture what had happened. My wife had opened the front door, and because of long-standing antipathies and quarrels, had curtly told him to go through and find me. I interpreted thus the jaunty way he brought up a hand to shade his eyes while he peered down the garden, pretending he could not see me.

Again the old, affectionate whistle, before he dropped this bit of play-acting, due to nervous irritation; his response to any kind of opposition or criticism.

'Ah, there you are, my boy!' he said, going through the gestures of seeing me for the first time. 'And the *babby*! Ah, the *babby*! Bless you, bless you both. May she see her old grandfather; may she? Is that allowed?'

These last words were accompanied by a sly, malicious glance backward at the house, and by implication at the child's mother, who had concealed herself indoors.

Whether or not the infant remembered this infrequent visitor, she looked up now and smiled at him, her chubby face suffused with kindness. She held up a dandelion to welcome him, and he took it from her, leaning over her, his grey eyes glittering as his head bowed through a shaft of sunlight. For a second I had the impression that he was moved to tears by this recognition from his only grandchild. Again I shivered, and was ashamed of myself. A vast complex of old entanglements, misunderstandings, moments of anger and even childhood hatred, put out the light of the sun, and drove the innocence from my Limpsfield garden.

'Not unwelcome, am I? Not unwelcome, my boy?'

He looked at me plaintively, and I saw that he was in trouble, a condition that normally he would never admit. Things must always be right for him. My brother and I had been taught that in childhood. Battersea and Dulwich, scenes of that childhood, were still bright in memory under the sun of Father's optimism and protestations of well-wishing.

Something serious must have happened to make him doubt his own benevolence. The chill closed round me more icily. I had to counterbalance the hostility with which he had been received. But how to do so without betraying newer loyalties?

'I don't understand,' I lied. 'Are you on tour again?'

For once, the open road, his lasting love, had to take second place. He let the dandelion fall from his fingers to the child's hair. She put up her hand and retrieved it, staring at him with puzzled attention.

'Her mother and I have decided to part,' he said, nodding toward the house, with this unwilling reference to my wife. I heard the news without surprise; but I wanted to ask him, with some bitterness, why he had ever let himself in for this entanglement, so soon after my mother's death. It had involved me too, and I was permanently caught. But I could not say so. It would have been to acknowledge misgivings that as yet were hardly rising to consciousness in my bewildered mind, round which the hard facts of daily life were closing.

'You both made a mistake,' was my compromise. 'You had nothing in common.'

He looked at me appealingly, eager to meet me halfway.

'No, poor girl,' he said: but that did not ring true. The implacable and uncomprehending boy that lay too near the surface was fully exposed as, for once, he tried to be unselfconsciously sincere. Suddenly I felt guilty, and I knew it was a weakness I could not afford, during so complicated a domestic crisis. I stood between two loyalties, both of them dutiful rather than ardent; the one born in my bones, the other legally affixed. I had no counter motive to help my conscience to dismiss them. Even the thought of doing so had roused this sensation of guilt.

The child, meanwhile, had decided that her grandfather was a desirable companion. She drew herself up and clung to his leg, looking up at him with an abandonment hardly to be distinguished from adoration. He picked her up, balanced her skilfully on his arm, and plucked at her rosy cheek. Here was something concrete, that he could understand; a means of escape too. But my resentment at feeling guilty made me cruel. I pulled him back from that exit.

'Does this mean that you are separating?'

He had lost interest, but he answered me, 'Oh, yes. We've arranged all that. I'm making her an allowance. Found some nice lodgings too, with a comfortable woman; good motherly sort; makes quite a fuss of me!'

I looked at him a little more coolly, self-accusations somewhat assuaged.

'Oh, I see. So you won't be homeless.'

He was hurt.

'No need to say that, my boy. I find friends wherever I go. That's my nature. Think no evil, see no evil, do no evil.'

I almost broke out again, to accuse him of having left me behind in the mess of his making. But I said nothing. I did not even remind him that with his ex-wife's daughter married to his younger son, he was still not quite free of his domestic embarrassments. I did not learn what he felt about it, for the embodiment of that problem appeared at the back door, to call across the little courtyard: 'You had better come in and have some coffee.'

I was in the mood to take exception to the ungraciousness of that, but again I restrained myself. It may have been due to moral immaturity and cowardice, but I did not dare to acknowledge this. I must reserve my confidence for what lay ahead, when I should break the news after my father had gone. For I knew that he would leave this job to me.

The prospect of this ordeal made me somewhat distrait as I

bade him good-bye. There had been no outbreak, during the drinking of coffee, but the tension and veiled but visible hostility had reduced me to a state of cold perspiration, and that special kind of boredom which is the forerunner of terror in the presence of violent conduct, either of tongue or hand. To witness a murder must be not only horrifying, but wearisome, because it is an irrelevant interruption of the exquisite processes of civilization, and the subtle drama of the mind. Violence has more to answer for than its immediate and bestial effects.

While I stood on the narrow pavement outside my house (which abutted directly on it, with no front garden), I felt my left leg trembling, and was conscious of a burning sensation over the left side of my cranium, down through my shoulder. I was so unsteady on my feet that I set down the daughter who had insisted on 'seeing grandpa off', by clinging to him and bribing him with a digestive biscuit, which he accepted with quiet dignity.

My father had moved with the times by giving up cycling, in which he had been a pioneer in the eighteen-nineties. He bought his first motor-cycle and basket-work sidecar in 1910, immediately after my mother's taboo had been removed by her death. He was as expert and as much a perfectionist in this new hobby as he had been in the old. I looked, but obstinately aloof in my priggish disapproval, at the machine on which he had driven down from London. It was an 'Ariel', and of forceful appearance, with a smart sidecar like a torpedo. Not a speck of dust or mud contaminated the outfit, and I marvelled again, as I had done all through my life, at this ability by which my father, in all circumstances, contrived to be smart and immaculate, both in his person, and with all things connected: razors, carving-knives, lamps, tools, vehicles. Even his violin and flute, now seldom used, lacking my mother's encouragement, were pronounced by their high polish.

So was the motor-bicycle combination which bore him down Limpsfield High Street, his handsome, aristocratic features concealed by the goggles and latest thing in motoring head-gear. Even so, his figure lent style to the mechanical turn-out, as it had done to the tandem bicycle on which I had pedalled so many torturing miles behind him at the turn of the century.

As he reached the bend of the street by the village inn, The Bull, he waved a hand gaily above his head. All was well. He was on the road again, and therefore in his element, not a care in the world for the time being.

It made him vulnerable, and as he disappeared, I stood momentarily paralysed by a convulsion of strong feeling, for which I could not account, and would not willingly acknowledge. I was rescued by a small hand plucking at my trouser-leg. I turned to go into the house, and to break the news.

[5]

It was inevitable that I should become involved in the family and domestic re-arrangements that followed my father's separation from his second wife. My misgivings about money matters, felt intermittently since the birth of my daughter two years earlier, now grew insistent. After the still-birth of my epic poem *The Deluge*, also in 1920, I had done more reading than writing. All people, not only artists, find themselves from time to time passing through a period of uncreative existence; mere existence it seems to them in that dull-eyed mood. We never fully understand the cause of it. Frustration, impatience, loss of confidence, the frosts of reality, all are contributors to this tide of ineffectuality. When we are young, it nearly drowns us, for we can see no end to it at that time of life. The days, months, years still have not speeded up, and the present, with all its conditions, looms over-large and sempiternal. Achilles, by sulking in his tent after being out-manœuvred by Agamemnon in a love affair, set a morbid example for all mankind.

My temporary defeat left me wondering soberly about the problems of the art of poetry, and I became more reluctant to enter where angels like Spenser and Keats had feared to tread. What had been worth saying in verse a few years ago now was trite. Both in theme and technique I believed myself to be crippled, nor could I see that this state was a process of growth. I could have taken a walk to the home farm at Titsey, to find encouragement and explanation from fields lying fallow under the April sky. Instead, I whipped myself on, anxious to find the cause of this infertility of mind and spirit.

It is a laborious process, making one's own bricks to build the house of knowledge. It was Robinson Crusoe's method, but he was able to practise it in solitude, without the deterrent of comparison with mass-produced scholarship and professional techniques.

However, I had been labouring on, reading my way toward enlightenment, while testing the results against the responsibilities and emotions of fatherhood.

Not many young men have written about the adventure of fatherhood. Now, in the present trend of western society toward a matriarchy, the omission may never be made good. Even the Christian religion is turning from its paternal basis: the Catholics to Mariology, the Protestants to a pseudo-scientific abstraction more in the image of a Life Force than in that of a Father. Indeed, there is almost an element of levity in our references to fatherhood today, and this may be the cause of the loosening of family ties, of the authority of the family, in the structure of human society as it is being remoulded by the Welfare State. We have not yet seen the full consequence of the overthrow of the father figure.

I took that image seriously, however. Experience as a young parent combined with my reading, thus bringing instinct and intelligence together to direct my way of life and my interpretation of it. From my increasing devotion to Wordsworth, I went farther, to the philosopher who had fired Wordsworth's early vision during the creative years, before he sank back into the more comfortable and social acceptances of the Church of England during the nineteenth century. Spinoza was that guide. His divine genius flashed over my dark world at that time, a lighthouse in stormy weather. It has never failed me since. It still stands as the image of unity, of coherence, of mutual, interdependent and sustaining force in all things, the 'rocks, and stones and trees', the organic creatures from mollusc to Man, the superb and indifferent mathematics of the galaxies within the atom, and the cosmic structures, which in their accumulation and rhythm are the Universe, the Substance, the Father.

Years later, in the autumn of 1947, I lay in hospital for a month, between two operations, and in that period of suspension, I read Bertrand Russell's *History of Western Philosophy*. I still burn with disappointment at his dismissal of Spinoza's vision as 'leading to a complete and undiluted pantheism', because 'according to Spinoza, everything is ruled by an absolute logical necessity'.

This is a strange accusation, coming from a mathematician equipped with so lucid a prose style, and so vigorous an emotional temperament. Why has he not explored Spinoza's imagery further, in his quest, which surely must be the quest of all philosophers, even our latterday academic semantists, after the secret of unity, the source of the interacting motion by which the universe sustains itself? Our chemists, physicists and biologists are beginning to reveal more aspects of that secret. But what is now overt to them by experiment and analytical research was revealed in Spinoza's synthesis of Christ's insistent vision of 'the Father', with the more rationalized principles by which the Greek Parmenides expressed his discovery of the One-ness towards whose harmony mankind must contribute if the human family is to survive, and after this voyage over aeons of time, finally to fulfil the craving to reach home, a racial achievement picturesquely and primitively foreshadowed by the Hebrew forerunners of Christ when they prophesied the reception of man 'into Abraham's bosom'.

I saw this vision too, as I studied my first child during those years of early infancy. What gave major authority to my conclusions, and made them permanent, was the commonplace nature of the experience. Indeed, from this point of view, parenthood is disgusting. Rats, viruses, are its most prolific exponents. The seething, anonymous fecundity of organic life is surely a condition out of which the fastidious thinker would wish to lift himself, by celibacy conserving his energy, and his identity. Religious practices and disciplines have been founded on that escapist revolt. The negative aspects of clericalism, in all religious systems, spring from it, breeding epicene and perverse horrors, castes, and tyrannies whose subscription to dualism, that basic evil, has dominated and directed the human drama since the beginning of time.

The real struggle towards serene maturity had begun. The effort to write that long poem, on the regeneration of mankind as symbolized in the story of Noah, was the last agony of the literary amateur, naïvely undertaking a theme beyond his capacity and his technique.

The apprenticeship of an artist, in any medium, is the period during which he is brought down from these heady aspirations, to plant his feet firmly on the earth. An economical way to this is through a university. In the Middle Ages, as in classical times in Greece and Rome, the apprentice artist served a master, to be schooled to a patient anonymity of craftsmanship, so that for the rest of his career the raging fires of that first inspiration would be controlled and given a formality that alone would fully utilize their power.

The arts today are too far removed from the crafts. They are diluted with amateurism, and perhaps with too many external rewards and plaudits. But no doubt there have always been temptations to work for public acknowledgment rather than for the work's sake. The medieval guilds were not wholly free of them, but they and even our contemporary trade unions have worked towards standards of professionalism based upon pride of workmanship.

I have always believed that for the writer, a period in Fleet Street is a good hardening experience. Journalism, practised as an art, produces clarity and economy. It links poetry with bread and butter. I recall the skill of some of the journalists with whom I have worked: H. W. Nevinson, George Russell ('Æ'), H. N. Brailsford, H. M. Tomlinson, Harold Massingham, Rebecca West, Kingsley Martin, Hamilton Fyfe, Frank

Swinnerton, Harold Nicolson, Raymond Mortimer, J. B. Priestley, Edward Crankshaw; these are a few professional writers whose technical mastery has been developed as much in Fleet Street as in the novelist's or the poet's private work-room.

I was now to join that fierce but friendly brotherhood. Necessity drove me. The prospect of advancement in the Civil Service may have been sure, but it was 'exceeding slow'. Nor had I either interest or ambition there. Indeed, so detestable to me was this official life, of routine, standardized work, that as I entered Montague House every morning I felt a sensation of physical nausea, a nervous disturbance that upset my digestion and provoked a mental panic of which I was ashamed.

Even the pleasant and semi-literary work to which Humbert Wolfe had directed me, in the company of delightful colleagues, did not cure me of this pathological revulsion day by day. It may have been caused by distress at having to lose these seven most useful hours that might have been given to creative work. This was no artificial conceit, nor was I conscious of a belief that the world at large was likely to value my poetry. This fury of writing was a condition of the blood, irrational and un-controllable. It has never wholly abated. Even today, in old age, I am restless and guilt-haunted if a day passes without my putting pen to paper. This cannot be explained; nor can a violent love affair, or the afflatus of religious devotion. People who are thus possessed have to follow that possession, and woe be to the people who try to wake them from that somnam-bulation.

My strange variant of morning sickness passed as soon as I settled down to work amongst my highly intelligent and sympathetic colleagues all of them at that time of higher rank than myself. John Hilton and 'C. K. Munro' in particular both guided and stimulated me, though Hilton was obtuse about Wordsworth, and Munro thought that a little too much fuss was made about Shakespeare. This did not, however, prevent Munro from marrying a generous and charming Shakespearian actress, Mary Sumner, from the Old Vic.

Another colleague who made a reputation outside the Ministry was C. E. M. Joad, the popularizer of the study of philosophy. He was an odd figure, Coptic in appearance, untidy and in need of a bath. He had been relegated to an attic room in the mansard towers of Montague House, directly over my room, as mine was directly above the Duke's Library, where Humbert sat in languid splendour. To avoid physical exercise in stair-climbing, to and from the water-closets, Joad used a water carafe which he brought down when he was leaving at the end of his day's work.

He was so often out of his room, that he kept a hat and coat permanently behind the door, to indicate, misleadingly, that he was somewhere in the building. But as this apparel was green with age, and covered in a thick bloom of dust, nobody was deceived.

My feeling was that this trickery was part of the whole man. His manner of speaking with an affected Balliol drawl, and an air of unwarranted condescension, furthered my suspicion that he was a charlatan, bluffing his way through the world of scholarship. That was priggish of me, symptomatic of the isolated self-taught perfectionist. I fear that had I met Dr Johnson, with his bearish gait and manners, his soup-stained coat and rolling eyes, I might have been, at that stage of my life, equally as priggish as I was towards Joad.

Even so, I still think that he was a law unto himself. His subsequent career after resigning from the Civil Service, to become a dogmatic lecturer at Birkbeck College, and a highly popular radio oracle on the original team of the B.B.C. Brains Trust, must have encouraged him in this illusion.

[6]

During those two fallow years after the birth of my daughter, I had nevertheless produced verse, perhaps none the worse for being costively delivered. The *Spectator*, which had been responsible for my meeting with Humbert Wolfe, and thus for the dynamic change in my means of livelihood, had continued to print most of the poems which I submitted.

Why not, I thought in desperation, write to the Editor to explain my need for more income, and bluntly to ask for reviewing work? I did so, and a few days later I had a reply, not from the Editor, St Loe Strachey, but from a woman, the Literary Editor, who signed her letter 'Amabel Williams-Ellis'. She invited me to luncheon at her home in Eaton Place.

At that time, though I was twenty-nine years old and head of a small family, I had met very few contemporary intellectuals and writers, apart from the rather exotic group clustered around the personality of T. S. Eliot and the columns of *The Criterion*. My connection there was a rapidly widening educational process, often agonizing to my mental muscles, but wholly beneficial. It taught me at once to dissociate myself from equality with the immortals, hitherto my exclusive discoveries and possession, from Chaucer to Tennyson and Browning. I was beginning to fall into line, and into step, at a more appropriate place in the procession.

So I presented myself at the house in Eaton Place, somewhat less naïvely than I would have done two years earlier. The boisterous elder-brotherliness of F. S. Flint, the frosty Northern courtesy of Herbert Read, icily impersonal, and the more indefinable but no less tonic kindness of T. S. Eliot had taught me a self-restraint and watchfulness, which now served me well.

I was instantly dazzled by my hostess. She was a superb Titian. I have a recollection of green and gold, of Renaissance jewellery, of gracious approach, and a vitality that swept away my shyness as the sun dispels a morning mist. She was a conflagration, radiating warmth and kindness.

Sitting next to me at the luncheon table was her brother John Strachey, just down from Oxford. I found him, too, receptive and courteous. The gravity of his manner surprised me. I should have expected it in an older man. He had the habit of leaning forward, to listen more intimately to the person with whom he was in conversation, and this deference was most acceptable to an individual frozen by social or intellectual mis-givings. It warmed him out. It gave him confidence. To my astonishment I found myself talking, and being listened to, while a pair of dark, shrewd, somewhat melancholy eyes scrutinized me with increasing interest.

I ought to have been back in the Ministry, to add my stint to the coral-building task on the Dictionary of Occupations; but during that luncheon hour, prolonged to two, I had become enclosed in a new world, hitherto outside my ken, and rec-ognized now only through its resemblances to those created by similar-minded groups in former times: the Johnson Circle, the Coleridge web, the George Eliot secular sanctuary.

Thus, by reflection from my reading, it was sufficiently familiar for me to feel at home in it. I was not aware that Bloomsbury was condescending to an outsider, as it has been said to do by literary historians.

I remember returning to Whitehall on the Underground Railway from Sloane Square Station, still entranced by the courtesy and swift intelligence of John Strachey, still dazzled by the golden splendour of his elder sister. I even forgot to apologize for coming back to the Ministry in the middle of the afternoon, so flushed that I might have been suspected of being drunk. But nothing was said. The discipline of the Ministry was more 'modern', more democratic, than that of the Laboratory in the Custom House, where the staff had been controlled rather like the crew on Captain Bligh's *Bounty*.

Within a week or two of that luncheon, I found myself enrolled as a regular reviewer on the *Spectator*, beginning in a small way with short notices of books of a monumental dull-ness. After a short period of this apprenticeship, I was sum-moned to the office of the *Spectator*, which was then in York Street, Covent Garden, near Drury Lane Theatre, to where it had recently removed from Waterloo Place at the end of the old bridge.

There I was inspected by the proprietor-Editor, St Loe Strachey. I was not aware of the inspection, or of any open inquiry into my credentials and ability. Throughout the interview the famous journalist was buzzing up and down the book-shelves, like a bumble-bee at a baker's shop-window. His monologue never paused, nor did he turn round to look at me. The soliloquy was concerned with the books, as he snatched first one, then another, from the shelves, and the piles heaped on chairs, on the floor, on a table beside the editorial desk. Each book taken in his hand set up a commentary on the subject, the author, predecessors who had handled the theme, how they had handled it, or mishandled it, and what sort of a mess the present author had probably made of it.

Most of the books thus selected and discussed were thrust back into the ranks, but exception was made here and there, while the Editor paused, looked over his spectacles, then thrust out his hand behind him, for me to take the book. 'Two hundred words on it: no more!' The number of words varied, according to his private evaluation of merit, but by the time the so-called interview ended, I had accumulated more than a dozen books, enough reading matter for a month, and enough commissioned verbiage to fill at least three pages of the *Spectator*. Then he dismissed me, with a 'Come in next week, and you can choose some more!'

I carried my harvest into the office of the Literary Editor, but she was just departing. 'Oh, dear,' she said, as she saw the acreage of reading matter in my arms. 'Just choose three of them, but take the rest as well; and do come in regularly. We'll hope to give you more space now that you've been accepted.'

Again I was warmed by that Titian-like splendour, the kindness, the golden glow, the music of the voice; but she was gone, wafting the air out of the tiny office, the draught of her exit causing the door to shut itself. It also shut itself on my amateurism. From that spring day in 1922 I began to earn a supplementary living with my pen. For the next twelve years I reviewed regularly for the *Spectator*, graduating quickly to leading, signed reviews.

CHAPTER SEVEN

The Valley of Dry Bones

[1]

THUS LAUNCHED ON THE MAIN-STREAM of adult life, I began to find my days, and thoughts, more and more occupied with the job in hand. First and last things were still all-important, but now, by being constantly busy, I had an almost plausible excuse for postponing consideration of them.

This is a dangerous condition. It is the cause of those longueurs which overcome most people in middle life. That 'darkness at noon', that *accidie* which halts the traffic between earth and paradise, is the direct result of the loss of creative leisure.

So began the journey away from childhood and youth, about which every individual has a unique story to tell, of fabulous adventures in a dew-glittering world, every detail outlined by a light which gives it an illusory permanence.

People like to hear that story, repeated again and again. Biographers and autobiographers easily satisfy them. But who wants to hear of the gradual slowing-down and subsidence of early raptures, as the individual falls into step with the rest of the breadwinners, worthy but indistinct, for the long remainder of his life?

There is an answer to that gloomy question, but it cannot be given by those who have lost heart, or relapsed into a mild cynicism and sophisticated worldliness, that occupational disease common to all human activities. It attacks us insidiously when we become the prisoners of our own careers: the lawyer, the doctor, the business executive, the housewife. None of us is immune.

The only persons to escape this hardening of the arteries of the spirit are those who remain young, naïve, innocent, while maturing physically and mentally. They are 'the movers and shakers of the world forever, it seems'. They are the only people whose middle and late careers continue to reflect the sunrise, that under-lighting glory of wonder and novelty which alone makes life worth while, and also the story about it.

Both success and failure are irrelevant issues, so long as the story continues to carry those early qualities of hope, of unfolding adventure, of discovery, and the perpetual struggle to understand what the whole experience signifies. Even the recognition of loss, of relapse into mediocrity, can be used to this purpose. We cannot all be master-minds, destined for immortality. Indeed, it is only people who are doped by the drug called fame, either tasted or unduly coveted, who believe that there is such a condition as mediocrity. They should have their living-licences endorsed.

My daily routine was not noticeably changed by the departure from amateur to semi-professional status as a writer. Since I entered the Civil Service thirteen years earlier I had portioned out my day so that the seven hours spent in an office should not prevent me from studying for and practising my art. I got up at five o'clock and read for two hours before beginning the routine of bath, breakfast and train-catching. I read in the train during the journey of fifty minutes. At the other end of the day's work in Billingsgate, and in Whitehall, the time-table was reversed, my two hours of reading or writing being kept until late evening, so that I might have some time for family life. This measured existence was less mechanical in fact than it sounds on record. Nobody, not even a Proust, can reproduce the moment-by-moment awareness, appreciations, and even ecstasies, by which we all live. We take our experience through our pores as well as through our conscious minds, and the impressions are multitudinous. They overflow time and space.

From that first reading done for reviewing, however, I began to suffer from a slight anxiety in the very process of reading. In a mild but prolonged way, it was a form of Examination neurosis. Having to read with an ulterior motive, I began to

H

look for, and note down, *points d'appuis*, on which I might lean
to write the review. Thus pleasure, or the reverse, in the reading
was thrown slightly out of focus. This no doubt was beginner's
apprehension. It can be detected by the reader when it takes the
form of undergraduate learnedness, the airing of book-
knowledge and dogmatic assertiveness and intolerance. Long
experience cures the reviewer of this almost inevitable disease,
though on occasion it hits him, like a migraine, all through his
career, caused, perhaps, by a book of outstanding merit and
authority, or by one of unsurpassable banality. A middle course
of temperate and equable judgment is not easy to maintain,
even after years of practice.

My new work was not wholly detrimental, however. I now
read not only with more determination, but also with pleasure
in mastering the book, in seeking to discover more consciously the author's aim, his skill in pursuing it, and his success
or failure in reaching it. To read thus is a process of living. So
long as a critic can continue to read in this way, he is adding to
the wealth of his personal experience, and is perpetuating the
freshness with which he must have read as a child. Without that
freshness and intensity, he would not have been directed by his
instincts to take up this profession of letters.

[2]

Though the Ministry of Labour in the nineteen-twenties, the
first decade of its existence, was the most modern organization
in the British Civil Service, comparable to a gigantic cartel in
the business world, human nature contrived to creep in,
colourful and various. This was most patent at the Headquarters in Whitehall. Humbert Wolfe was responsible for
much of this picturesque idiosyncrasy in the staff. He believed
that people who showed talent and originality, in any direction,
could apply that ability to the work and development of the
Ministry. He wanted to humanize the relationship between the

Ministry and the public. This was a laudable purpose, because men and women only came into the Labour Exchanges when they were suppliant, looking for work, and therefore they were sensitive to patronage. Sometimes the treatment they received at local Labour Exchanges was even harsher than patronage.

I had no direct experience of this disgusting state of affairs, for my work never once took me into an Exchange; but there was much talk at Headquarters of the problems arising from public resentment of the pseudo-military atmosphere creeping into the Exchanges.

Humbert instinctively hated all this. He derided the stuffiness, the long-winded methods of bureaucracy. I think this made him suspect amongst his more orthodox colleagues. And the majority is always orthodox, submissive to routine and precedent. That, and the fact that Humbert also had outside interests and reputation, may be the reason why he was never made Permanent Secretary in charge of a government department. Yet as an administrator he was a genius. He got things done, and he got them done quickly and simply. He cleaned up those Labour Exchanges, and I believe that the better relations subsequently established there between staff and the public helped towards the general equability that kept the nation sane during the General Strike of 1926.

He fought also for the equality of service between men and women on the staff. When I joined the Ministry in 1920, I found women of first-class credentials and ability working as an administrative team; such people as Beryl Power, sister of Eileen Power the economic historian; Miss Barfield, a solicitor and sister of the philosopher Owen Barfield; Amber Blanco-White, of literary lineage. Beryl Power was a young woman of astonishing physical beauty, but that in no way softened the impact of her incisive and vigorous mind, at least during office hours.

At one time I had on my staff of some half-dozen people a woman named Shakespear. She was a redhead, and inclined to a gaiety of manner that made me suspect a desire to cover up something disastrous. Her name appeared at the bottom of the family tree in Sidney Lee's biography of the poet. It stood beside that of her brother, an officer in the Guards. He had been killed in the war.

She too had an active war service. She served on the nursing staff under Mrs Percy Dearmer, and took part in the great retreat across the Balkans. Night after night she and her fellow nurses slept out in the open, amongst the Serbian troops, and were treated with protective courtesy by them. Her tragedy came later, as the result of an affair with a senior officer in her brother's regiment. That result was long drawn out over the years of her service in the Ministry, and its climax of treachery resulted in her suicide.

Her sense of humour was irrepressible. It cut through the small pomposities of official life like a draught of fresh air through a gaping window-frame. On one occasion she wrote a minute in a file which then was passed to a more senior officer in another department. He minuted it back to her with a comment about her grammar. The next I heard was a telephone call from him to tell me that he was reporting her to the Establishment Department for insurbordination.

In redheaded rage, Miss Shakespear had rushed with the file to his room, and in the presence of other members of the staff, had slammed the file down on his desk, opened it at the minute and its rejoinder, pointed an accusing finger, and shouted, 'How dare you, a creature of *your* name, how dare you criticize the English of a person of *my* name!'

His name was Nussbaum.

I could recall other colleagues whose personalities made them conspicuous among the rank and file of the staff. One, the son of a dean of a northern cathedral, came to the Ministry every day with his official dispatch case (that shoddy-looking, black hand-out) bulging. This was not because he took files home to work at night. The dispatch case contained a lettuce, the daily portion for a pet tortoise which he kept in a lower drawer in his desk.

Another colleague with whom I was friendly wore a *vie-de-Bohème*, floppy bow-ribbon, and a shapeless tweed hat. He was a talented landscape-painter who also had a mystical ambition to write the novel of all novels, more revealing even than *The Brothers Karamazov*, which he was using as a model. I saw some of the pictures from time to time, but never a sign of the novel, whose growth was both interminable and subterranean.

For three years, in a key department called Industrial Relations, I shared a room with a musician, who at the age of sixteen had received the Fellowship of the Royal College of Organists. He was organist in the church of the country town where he lived, and he composed and published much ceremonial music, liturgies, anthems, cantatas and the like. He set several of my lyrical poems, some for solo voice, some for male-voice choirs.

In such a community, I found myself infinitely interested in the play of character and conduct. Had I not been driven by my singular demon, I should have been happy enough in that company, where once again I found myself being petted and spoiled, as I had been in the Custom House, solely because of my faculty of expressiveness, which by now was also beginning to make my name remarked in the outside world.

My contact with Humbert Wolfe was frequent, in spite of the difference in our ranks. This contact was frowned on by non-latitudinarians in the official hierarchy; and they were many, in a Service where seniority was sacred. I sometimes found myself embarrassed, and even apprehensive, to be found by a very senior officer, sitting in the armchair beside Humbert's capacious desk in the Duke's Library, discussing perhaps the poems of Siegfried Sassoon, or the subtle rhythms of Edward Thomas's solitary muse, matters which Humbert declared – loudly and provocatively – were of prior importance to some information for which the Minister was clamouring in order to answer a Question in the House. I detected many a frown of ominous disapproval, as the intruder closed the door, to wait impatiently, and often angrily, on the other side of it in the secretary's room, conscious of the abuse of his rank, and the urgency of his errand.

I was always ready to be aware of my precarious standing in

the Ministry, for I could never believe that I had become an efficient civil servant, in spite of my ability in dictating or writing carefully worded minutes and memoranda. I did this with a gesture, for here I was in my own territory. I ascribe my promotion in 1924 (which nearly doubled my salary) to this, for one day I was sitting at my desk, before a mountain of files, dictating a long memorandum on the state of the catering trade, prior to a public inquiry. The door of my room opened, and a couple of Treasury inspectors entered, ushered by the Head of our Establishment Department.

I was interrogated: my rank; the work I did; the task now in hand. Did I habitually dictate memoranda? To my astonishment, I was promoted a month or two later. At the time, I suspected this was due to the friendliness of the head of my department, a taciturn, capable officer named Godfrey Ince, who subsequently became Permanent Secretary and was Ernest Bevin's devoted right-hand man during the second world war, and with that political chief of genius and gigantic character, was largely responsible for the efficient provision of labour for assuring victory. In spite of his taciturnity and seeming lack of interest in anything outside official affairs, Ince presented me with the World's Classics edition of Johnson's *Lives of the Poets*, to signify, maybe, his approval of my promotion.

[3]

Meanwhile, the colleague from the Custom House, who had filled my garden with beehives, and had taught me his rustic lore about cultivating a vegetable garden, at last found a little house beyond Limpsfield Common, to which he took his wife and her Pleyel pianoforte, there to start a family. The bridal couple came to us in 1919 for a few weeks to look for a cottage. They were an endearing pair, with their music and their honey, their country ways and kindness, and we were sad to lose them, after two years! They could have figured harmoniously in one of Thomas Hardy's novels. Indeed, I often found myself mis-calling them 'Giles Winterbourn' and 'Marty South', though their fate was happier than that of the hapless couple in *The Woodlanders*.

So life's day drew towards noon, and I found myself building up a family environment as static and tangible as that of my childhood in Battersea and Dulwich, with time and eternity almost identical, and nothing to change or come to an end.

Almost – but not quite! Something had intervened, an intruder which claimed my vitality, my hopes, through every working hour. It is not easy to describe this claimant. Its forms are as infinite as the individual humans whose minds it enters, to inhabit there, as a torment and a glory. Its masquerade is most obvious when it takes the form of religious ecstasy. It changes some people into saints, others into cranks or maniacs. It some-times carries the rare and dubious gift of genius. It has no generic name, and may assume the disguise of any kind of obsession, taking charge of mind and body, leading the possessed individual to courses of action and achievement out-side the influence of logic and the persuasions of environment.

Such was my *doppelgänger*, who first tapped me on the shoulder when I was a boy of fifteen, standing at the foot of my brother's bed and opening his copy of the poems of John Keats. From that moment, the world around me had been set back, beyond the range of my full, unthinking acquiescence.

There is a wonderful moment in Shakespeare's *Henry IV* when Falstaff staggers to the front of the stage, holds up a leathern flask of canary sack, as though it were the Holy Grail, and cries, 'It is an Inflammation!'

All my life, hitherto, I had been subject to an inflammation, first in the stomach, whence the disease kindled illusions of levitation. But these proved to be a blessing, for they tided me over the humilations of childhood and youth. At the moment while I stood before my brother's bed, the fiery condition took another form, the fen-fire of art. This curtain of flame has flickered ever since, between me and the immediate actualities of life. I suspect that all people who are controlled by an

overpowering interest, enthusiasm, faith, are similarly removed
in some degree from reality or those aspects of reality which
make up our concrete world, of events, conflicts, palpable
things.

The artist's need is to raise that curtain of fire, while retaining
its warmth and light. There is no other way to unite himself
with the life around him, and to give purpose to his illumination.

I may have been groping towards that achievement but it was
still a blind and desperate effort. The excitement of living in an
exquisite country setting, with a family of my own in a house
now free from guests, could not satisfy my craving, nor banish
the unease, the misgivings, which began to possess me after the
death of my mother, and increased after the experience of
marriage and fatherhood.

I went after more literary journalism, hoping that a larger
income would reassure me. During the next few years I worked
regularly for the weekly magazines: *The Nation*, the *New
Statesman*, the *Westminster Gazette*. I joined the staff of the
weekly literary page of *The Daily Herald*, whose Editor was
Hamilton Fyfe, an amiable martinet. I still worked for the
Spectator and *The Criterion*.

Later, when Middleton Murry founded and edited *The
Adelphi*, I wrote for that too, but not happily, because I could
neither trust nor like him. He was a dark, slippery character,
who looked over my shoulder (probably into an invisible
mirror) when talking to me, and referred to himself always in
the third person. Narcissism is not a social virtue. I was not
peculiar in this lack of confidence. Both D. H. Lawrence and
Aldous Huxley have portrayed him cruelly. S. S. Koteliansky,
a leonine Russian liberal self-exiled in England early in the
century, was a colleague of Middleton Murry and Murry's wife
Katherine Mansfield when they edited *The Athenaeum* for two
years immediately after the first world war. Koteliansky was a
seeker after truth, and he divided mankind into two camps, the
seekers and the obscurantists. He put Katherine Mansfield
amongst the seekers, and thus parted husband and wife in
theory, long before Katherine's death parted them in actuality.

In spite of these characteristics which made Murry so equivocal socially, and in his relationships with individuals, he was possessed by a strong literary sensibility. It was this which lifted him out of the lower middle-class environment of his childhood in Peckham, a period of his life to which he never referred. This reticence may have been an unattractive by-product of that sensibility. In the world of books he functioned with more candour, and developed a critical faculty most fully deployed in his book on John Keats. Even there, however, he tends to spin an elaborate web of commentary on which his victim is finally caught, to be devoured at leisure. Where he was also personally concerned in the life of the poet under analysis, as in his writings about Katherine Mansfield, his criticism became ghoulish.

He so over-inflated the delicate but somewhat self-conscious work of his wife, that he harmed rather than confirmed its reputation. In consequence, not only Katherine Mansfield's creative talent, but also Murry's unique gift as a critic, continued to be under-rated, nearly half a century after they flourished so romantically in literary London. At least two stories by Katherine Mansfield, 'The Doll's House' and 'The Life of Ma Parker', are masterpieces worthy to stand with the stories of Chekhov, H. E. Bates and V. S. Pritchett, in both kind and quality.

[4]

This launching into semi-professional work on so many journals and magazines brought me into contact with more and more writers. I began to live two lives at once: that of the Civil Servant in the midst of officialdom in Whitehall, and that of the literary journalist hovering between Fleet Street and Bloomsbury. Added to these two mildly remunerative activities, were the demands of this craving, this 'inflammation' which has dominated my life and conduct since boyhood.

The stimulation of my work as a reviewer must have become an intoxicant, for I wrote and studied poetry more fervently than ever. The passing of youth did not allay this passion. Nor was I daunted by the fact that the trend of poetic fashion, which followed the example and teaching of Eliot and Ezra Pound, was uncongenial to me. I remember being indignant when Ford Madox Ford once proclaimed, in his tendentious and wholly inaccurate way, that I was a *dévoté* of Pound. This bit of perversity was Ford's *riposte* to my indiscreet outburst against the influence at that time of the American-Montparnasse expatriates on our native English literature.

I spoke thus at Ford's dinner table, in a flat where he was lodged temporarily in London immediately after he set up a ménage with the Australian portrait painter Stella Bowen, a woman of selfless courage. They left soon after for Paris, where they lived for many years, while Ford wrote the war-novels that made him widely known in America. Stella meanwhile made a reputation as a portrait painter, and exhibited at the Salon.

Ford, whose real name was Hueffer (he was the son of *The Times* music critic of that name), was an extraordinary man. He could not differentiate between fact and fiction. This made him an amusing companion but a mischievous friend.

He lived within a cocoon of illusions, that confined both himself and all his acquaintances to a drama of events that never took place, caused by characteristics that were non-existent. But such was his bright and gusty personality that nobody objected to the subsequent inconvenience and misrepresentation. I have always been amused by the contrast between him and his grandfather, Ford Madox Brown, whose biography he wrote early in a curiously disjointed literary career, and whose paintings offer evidence of a meticulous devotion to facts.

Ford prided himself not only on his prose style (and on having formed that of Joseph Conrad), but also on being a cook of *Cordon Bleu* calibre. Unsuspecting hostesses, at least once, were inveigled into allowing him the freedom of their kitchens and pantries, where he created chaos. All was part of the great illusion.

We all have our oddities, and I find that no sooner do I begin to capitulate those of my friends, and even people more remote, than I find myself in a hall of mirrors which throw a thousand reflections of an all too familiar figure, most of them open to ridicule. All of us are prone to these saline moments of self-conscious reflection. As we shrink like snails into our shells, we may perhaps console ourselves with the hope that it is these oddities and vanities which endear us to our friends, and shall keep us remembered long after our grandeurs are 'interrèd with our bones'.

From time to time during those middle years of the nineteen-twenties, grim years of post-war confusion, betrayal, and inadequate international machinery for the recovery of world peace, I put out books of verse.

Fortune favoured me in this matter by bringing me once again into contact with the Gollancz family. More than ten years earlier, Professor Israel Gollancz had encouraged me in my literary ambition. Now I was to meet his nephew Victor, who was running the editorial office in the firm of Benn Brothers, which flourished mainly on trade journals.

Victor Gollancz proposed to carry the imprint into general publishing, and one of his first ventures was the bold under-taking of the definitive Julian Edition of Shelley's poetry, prose and correspondence, in ten expensive volumes, edited by my friend and former publisher Roger Ingpen, with notes as copious and learned as those of Birkbeck Hill to the edition of Boswell's *Life of Johnson*.

Gollancz was not content with reprinting the classics. He took a more precarious and revolutionary step. He introduced paper-covered brochures of new poetry, at a shilling a time, and he started this series in 1926 with a long narrative poem of mine called *The Portrait of the Abbot*. This won commendation from John Masefield, when it subsequently appeared in my *Collected Poems*, a volume undertaken at his suggestion. It also brought me a letter from Sir Edward Grey, the statesman and ornithologist, praising my description of herons in flight. I dared not confess to him that my blank-verse picture was not founded upon knowledge. At that time I had never seen a heron in flight. I had written, at fever heat, as my imagination directed. This creative activity is quite unaccountable, and can only be vouched by examples, such as this one, and others already offered in the course of my fugal story of the journey of one individual towards the ever-elusive home for which we all crave.

In the course of the next few years Victor Gollancz added two more collections of my verse to his shilling brochures. In the days before broadcasting provided a new instrument for popularizing poetry, Gollancz's venture was the only practical means of introducing a young poet to the general public.

A man of such daring and energy could not long be constrained as a lieutenant. Gollancz set up as a publisher, under his own name, introducing new, streamlined methods in book-production, and in advertising. His Left Book Club became the platform for radical political and economic discussion, and his general list carried the names of new novelists whose success brought grist to the mill, and a worthy reputation to the authors, among them, Ivy Compton-Burnett, Phyllis Bentley, A. J. Cronin, Louis Golding.

His method, in all the facets of the business of publishing, was dynamic, *farouche*. He *proclaimed* every author whose book was on the production line, and this galvanic technique succeeded as often as not.

Behind this professional bravura, however, the man himself has survived unchanged: a passionate enthusiast for the things and principles he loves. Outstanding among these are two, music and friendship. He has a large capacity for both. For some years in the nineteen-thirties I was his neighbour in Holland Park, and could observe him at close quarters. An occasion arose, during that period, when a distinguished poet-scholar fell on hard times, owing to a chronic sickness and the needs of a large family. The poet Robert Trevelyan and I went round the literary community cap in hand, and collected enough money to tide him over the difficulties for a while. The most instant and generous contributor was Victor Gollancz. It is wholesome to record such gestures long after the event, even though the giver may be embarrassed. 'Let us now praise famous men' is a healthy as well as an authoritative injunction.

[5]

All through those early years of professional writing, my connection with the *Spectator* was close and constant. I saw changes in its staff and its contributors, some of my acquaintance there developing into friendships, amongst them those with Celia Simpson, the Literary Editor's secretary, who later married John Strachey; V. S. Pritchett, incorrigibly urban in his muse, with a strain of lethal Welsh derision in his prose; Alan Porter, the Literary Editor; and Evelyn Wrench, the founder of the English-Speaking Union; Basil Maine, the Music Critic, and Peter Fleming, the Assistant Editor and distinguished journalist, accurate and lucid.

Alan Porter was an unforgettable character. He was the second of three sons of a craftsman in Manchester. All three boys won scholarships to Manchester Grammar School and to Oxford. Alan was at Queen's College with Edmund Blunden, and while still up at Oxford, collaborated with him in unearthing and re-editing the poetry of the almost forgotten John Clare. This was the most impressive act of literary exhumation since Sydney Dobell rehabilitated the metaphysical poetry and prose of the seventeenth century Thomas Traherne.

I met Alan Porter when he was appointed to the Literary Editorship of the *Spectator*. He was then twenty-five, thin, feline in figure and movement, pale of face with black hair, and large, prominent brown eyes, strained as though by exophthalmic pressure. He was a chain-smoker, and his long-fingered hands trembled as they mechanically extracted the next cigarette from the packet, an action of which the rest of the person was unaware.

Alan Porter was also unaware of so much other of the mechanics of daily life, because he was concentrated throughout his waking hours, with aquiline equilibrium, hovering over the theme which happened to be occupying his field of spiritual and mental vision.

I have never known a man so intense. He was like a falcon about to be unhooded. He lived with his wife, Iris Barry the film critic, in a flat in Guilford Street, a few doors from Jacob Epstein, near Coram's Orphanage. It became my habit to go there at least once a week to luncheon, hurrying to and from Whitehall like a creature possessed, in order to listen to his oracular monologue, or to meet the other poets, novelists and journalists who gravitated there on a similar mission. My first meetings with Richard Hughes and Peter Quennell were in that flat; memorable because of my pleasure in their work, scanty but of rare quality.

Porter was a latterday Coleridge, squandering his energy in semi-mystical monologue. He published only one book of verse, *The Signature of Pain* (Cobden-Sanderson, 1930). I have put two poems from it in my anthology *Poems of our Time*, in Everyman's Library. They represent his austere personality, which delighted with masochistic relish in renouncing possessions and all the burdens and ties of the world, and finally even of the world of the intellect. The poem beginning

> Hard above all things mortal is
> To sacrifice our love's return:
> We shudder and are bare of bliss,
> And our hearts mourn, . . .

sums up his disposition.

His friendships hovered precariously on the brink of this desire for renunciation, and finally his marriage succumbed to it. His nervous mind went seeking restlessly for solutions to the mystery of mere living. He even followed the ancient Gnostics right through the centuries to their latest dogma in Rosicrucianism, and he spent many of those luncheon hours drawing geometrical graphs to demonstrate to me the structure of the Cosmos and the hierarchies of its inhabitants, from God rank by rank down to Man.

I listened spellbound, but sceptical, as I had listened, and indeed still continued to listen, to the religious and aesthetic theories of the *Criterion* group, at our weekly luncheons, held in another upper room, over a public house in Beauchamp Place near the Victoria and Albert Museum, to accommodate Herbert Read who had got himself transferred from the Treasury to this less arduous department.

I was spellbound by Alan Porter's personality, not by his theories. I saw that these reflected the strange and somewhat sinister influence of a man named Mitrinovic, a liberal Serbian exile, another pedagogic philosopher who tried to capture my adherence, and failed. He was the *éminence grise* behind Orage, the editor of the weekly review *The New Age*, to which I was contributing at that time under the pen-name of 'Eccles', an abbreviation which I believed would sufficiently disguise my patronymic, then too lavishly displayed in the press.

Mitrinovic and Porter, in their zeal for saving souls from the grasp of the Moloch of the Machine Age, founded the Adler Society, to expound the doctrine of Individual Psychology taught by Alfred Adler after he broke away from the tutelage of Sigmund Freud. This organization became known to the master, and finally he visited England to investigate its principles and its members. Mitrinovic persuaded me to attend a weekend 'school' in the house of Miss Slade, a saintly lady who subsequently translated herself, and her metaphysical luggage, to India, to become vestal to Gandhi. She is thus likely to become as immortal as the women who were in attendance on Calvary and at the entrance to the Tomb.

Adler was unimpressed by the Adler Society, but he singled out Alan Porter and laid an episcopal hand on him, with the injunction to go to America to preach the gospel of Individual Psychology. Thus Porter disappeared from his native land and his friends. I saw him once again many years later, when we met during a conference at Oxford. He looked even more ascetic than in his earlier years. Time had not thickened either flesh or mind. He was Professor of English at Vassar, the women's university. But he had little to say during this belated return to England. Maybe he had expended himself as the apostle of Individual Psychology, and in awakening the literary sensibility of young American women. It was not his silence that disturbed me, nor even the expression of bewilderment and a vague fear in those still prominent brown eyes. I saw, and pretended that I could not see, a large growth emerging out of the hair at one side of his head.

He appeared to be able to make little contact with his former friends in England, and I wondered, with sadness, if he had dogmatized himself too ruthlessly in the effort 'to sacrifice our love's return', a form of renunciation which, in his poem, he had declared to be 'hard above all things', and therefore desirable to his proud spirit.

I wondered also if his experience of life in America had overwhelmed his laboriously built cosmology, and made those elaborate graphs of the structure of the universe lose their meaning and authority, as maps of the journey home. He had been so sure of the way when he spoke and demonstrated during those inspiring luncheon hours in Guilford Street.

We said good-bye to each other in the Broad, outside Basil Blackwell's bookshop, an appropriate background to this last portrait of a friend whose scholarship and fervid eloquence had so enriched my life. He went back to America and within a few months was killed by a tumour on the brain. He was forty-four years old. The last stanza of his poem 'Love in Constancy' is an appropriate epitaph.

> After much argument and pain
> He finds at last the enigma plain.
> Love's honour is no whim,
> Love lies with him.
> He makes himself, by prayer and fasting,
> Constant: and love is everlasting.

A number of his friends wrote 'commendatory verses' to that one book of poems which Alan Porter was persuaded to publish so reluctantly. That by his Oxford contemporary, J. Isaacs (later to become Professor of English Literature, first at Jerusalem University and later at King's College, London), contained a line which I endorse, thirty-three years later. I believe it will still be valid when the centenary of Porter's death spins past, in times and manners beyond our conjecture today, at the threshold of the atomic age. Here is the line:

'Alan, in mood and music Coleridge's peer'.

[6]

So, in the second half of the nineteen-twenties, I moved into environments ever more crowded with acquaintance in two professions, that of the Civil Service and that of literary and journalistic London. The vista of childhood and youth, its solitude and close horizons, receded and shrank. The figures in it ceased to move. Sound died out of it, and its light diminished into a twilight that made it mysterious, primitive, heroic, like the drama in the Iliad, or the stilled gestures of the figures in the frieze on the Greek vase saluted by John Keats, the poet who had loomed so large in my boyhood. He was now almost lost in the crowd, as the procession debouched over the open country of my middle years.

The open country! Here too I felt the intrusion of new, ever-increasing interests. My first years, during the 1914–18 war, when a recurrence of bad health drove me to Limpsfield out of London, had been rapturous with discovery of wild flower and bird life, of woodland and downland, of the seemingly insignificant things of rustic life in the village, on the farm, in the isolated lanes and copses. The colours, the sounds and absence of sounds, the perfumes and pungent stenches, the night skies with moon and stars for the first time fully revealed, the

Wordsworthian mystery of it all, in leaf, bloom, decay, and near and distant focussings: these populated my imagination and played upon my nerves so that I could hardly contain myself. Here was a more sensuous rival to my world of books, and a localization of my religious cravings.

The phase was reflected in the verse by which I was forced to express it, a profusion that fell short because it was so indiscriminate and so artless. But a poet's most tonic challenge is to have too much to say, rather than too little. So I persevered, urged on by a kind of ecstatic despair.

To be unaware of fatigue is like walking towards an ambush. The days, the months, the years passed, seemingly timeless, and I took no heed because I believed my way of life to be quite normal. I got up at five o'clock, in that primitive little house in Limpsfield High Street, stirred myself out of sleepiness by a cold sponge-down at the kitchen sink, brewed a pot of tea, then settled down to work for an hour or more before the family awoke. On winter mornings before daybreak, this was an easier routine than in the summer, when the whole magic gamut of out-of-doors began whispering through door and window, like lover to lover. Sometimes, when the dawn was irresistible with level sunlight, and riotous birdsong, I succumbed, and instead of reading or writing, I crept out, and clicking the carriage-gate into the private road through Hookwood park to the dowager's house, I disappeared into fairyland.

That fairyland was the large garden insecurely fenced off from the park where the wild honey-bees colonized in the ancient oaks. The home to which it belonged stood immediately opposite to my cottage, frowning through small windows on the High Street. Its occupant was an elderly spinster named Miss Sidney, somewhat removed and austere. Her father had been a Lord Mayor of London, an historical fact mentioned with awe in the village. I shared the awe, and my too easily instigated imagination so apparelled her with glamour that I found myself addressing her one day as Miss Whittington!

I say one day, but it was one dawn, for she was up betimes on a summer morning to survey her garden, probably to think out the daily duties for her gardener. She saw the young man from the small house next door to the grocer's shop, and may have been alarmed at the possibility of a trespasser coming to steal a cabbage, or a punnet of her raspberries. There he stood, skeleton-thin, wearing a disreputable old green velvet coat. He was more like a scarecrow than a living creature, silhouetted against the newly risen sun, and shuddering in parallel with the shuddering of the uncertain beams of dusty gold.

I was about to slip shyly back into the shadows of the oak-trees along Hookwood drive, for though I had been her neighbour for nearly ten years, we had never met. She was a church-goer, and I was not. No doubt, as a good Victorian surviving into an age of chaos, she had fixed ideas about social status. It was a marked characteristic of the rich mercantile class at the turn of the century. Its members were either more 'county' than the aristocrats, or more 'aesthetic' than the professional artists.

'Come here, young man!' she cried, as though about to admonish a naughty young gypsy for prospective pilfering. Mischief entered into my soul, and I obeyed Miss Sidney.

'What are you doing in my garden?' she demanded, with a voice like that of Florence Nightingale at Scutari.

'I am worshipping the sun, Miss Whittington,' I replied demurely, resisting the temptation to touch my forelock.

That rather startled her. She hesitated, but only for a moment. Training and tradition came to her support.

'Where do you come from?'

I told her, and I said that I had been her nearest neighbour since 1918 when I moved into the boxlike house which I had christened 'Redfern' in preference to its previous name of 'Wandsworth Lodge'. I added that if she knew Wandsworth she would appreciate the incongruity and irrelevance of the name 'Wandsworth Lodge' for a pretty little Regency dwelling in the High Street of the most enchanting village in the south of England.

This was a long explanation, especially as I embellished it with innuendos that implied my recognition of a discrepancy between her practice and precept, over the most vital axiom of her Christian faith 'Love thy neighbour as thyself'.

Suddenly her manner changed. She stole my mischief. We both found ourselves laughing and the disturbance alarmed a blackbird, which had been scouting around the wire enclosure of her raspberry beds. He flew off, squawking with indignation.

Miss Sidney then confessed to having heard that a young writer lived 'in the village' and she claimed to be interested in the arts. I knew instantly what that interest would be. She would have dull prints of Giotto's illustrations to Dante's *Divine Comedy*, as prescribed by the popular lecturer and commentator, Philip H. Wicksteed, at whose feet no doubt she had sat with other daughters of Birmingham, Manchester and the West Riding, carried on the tide of wealth to Kensington and the Home Counties, there to disguise their shrewd, grimly realistic origins under the 'greenery-yallery' garments of the aesthetic 'Nineties, in spacious homes prescribed by William Morris, and furnished by Mr Liberty.

Miss Sidney and I resumed politeness, and after some five or ten minutes of mutual and almost ceremonious congratulation, she implored me to walk in her garden whenever the fancy took me. I assured her that this privilege was unlikely to be abused. With that, she retreated and I did the same, moving with quiet dignity while she was in sight, then scurrying like a rabbit back to Redfern, for fear of being late for breakfast and the train that was to take me to my other world, in Whitehall.

[7]

Promotion in that other world brought more official work and responsibility, and this coincided with an increase in the family, and the consequent anxiety that drove me to more literary journalism. This last was not solely bread-and-butter work. The more I wrote, the more I learned. The mere practice of writing, the penmanship and the manipulation of words through the pen onto the paper, was an activity so real, so absorbing, that by comparison the rest of my daily comings and goings seemed mere dream gestures, interruptions of the true purpose of life.

Such a concentration of energy, hope and talent may be insane, but I believe that this is the way in which the big things, the perfect things, are conceived and carried through to a triumphant finish. It is symbolized for me by examples here and there. I think of Trelawney's story of the day he went off fishing while staying with the poet Shelley in that forlorn villa by the waterside near Lerici. He left at daybreak, and saw Shelley standing up, reading from a volume of Plato, which was propped on a shelf. Trelawney returned at dusk, to find Shelley still standing, but pale and exhausted, intent upon the book.

Musicians frequently offer examples of this singleness and concentration of purpose. I have watched Julian Bream, the guitarist, Nathan Milstein and Menuhin, the violinists, and recognized in their performance a complete and unself-conscious identification of self with the instrument and its technical demands. That is the mark of an artist, an almost maniacal devotion to craftsmanship and all its concomitants, the instrument itself, and the deft, inspired handling of it.

My brother had this monomania, and I suspect that it was too much for his body to sustain. The change of school from St Peter's, Vauxhall, to the healthier one on the hill near his house, did not arrest the deterioration in his health. His vitality flagged, and he settled into a quietness, hardly to be called melancholy, almost serene in its gentle resignation.

I recognized it with foreboding, for precisely in this mood our mother had begun to compose herself during the last two years of her life, releasing one by one the ties of love, interest, hope that bound her to husband, sons and to the world in which she had played so eager and joyous a part. It was as though she were moving house, and in spirit had already departed to the new home.

I watched my brother Jack quietly making the same dispositions, and I saw too that his wife was also alert, for she had known my mother during those two preparatory years for departure. But neither of us dared to confide in the other.

It was better to be practical. The couple bought a piece of downland in Kent, above the Pilgrims' Way at Otford. It was aerated chalk land, on a spur of the Downs looking westward along the Westerham valley, and out to the south across the wide arena of the Weald. There they put up a bungalow where they could spend weekends and holidays, five hundred feet up, breathing the untainted air purified by height, and drawn over the dwarfed medicinal flowerets that carpeted the chalk. This retreat was only twenty miles from their London home, but thus disposed by height, view, and silence except for the flattened sounds half-rising from the plain, it might have been two hundred miles away from any metropolis, a dreamworld of assured convalescence. For four years my brother spent longer and longer periods there, coming and going with increasing ghostliness, ever more inscrutable, except during the small influxes of health, when he turned to his music with a kind of autumnal exultation, too colourful, too fervid.

I moved under the shadow during those years, not daring to recognize it. I drove myself faster and faster, as though in a sleigh beset with wolves. I kept away from the old house in Peckham and the bungalow at Otford, in the hope of assuaging this sense of repeated doom. I told myself that I must be more mature, more philosophic; that my intensity of feeling was an embarrassment to the loved couple and was certainly not reciprocated. I even manufactured grievances, to serve as spiritual torniquets, as that my brother had no right to disapprove of my marriage, or that his former monitorial interest in my work as a writer had fallen into indifference. It was a torturing self-deceit, and served no purpose except to add emotional confusion to misery and foreboding.

During those four years, indeed, I was advancing into the valley of dry bones. The absurd devices of pique to assuage anxiety over my brother not only failed, they turned inward and poisoned other activities, interests, and relationships.

It is a bleak experience, to stand helplessly watching the fire of youthful enthusiasm dying down into ashes. I began to live mechanically, or like a sleep-walker, going through the gestures required by daily life, but aware that no impulse, no belief, lay behind them. To write about such a state of mind ensures boredom for the reader. It is too like self-pity, that condition of malaise which causes its victim to be treated like *The Man who ate the Popomack* and thus began to stink so obnoxiously that all mankind fled at his approach. That was a play written by W. J. Turner, the poet and music critic whose work has remained, since his death in 1946, in the mortuary trough, the literary Purgatory, through which even that of the greatest of the immortals has to pass after its creator's death.

[8]

Everyone must recognize the scenery of this mental and spiritual condition, for none can escape it, at some time or other on the journey from the cradle to the grave. Even if circumstances are serene, there seems to be a biological reason for men and women, when they reach the middle thirties, to find themselves beset with misgivings, unanswerable, agonizing inquiries, and a loss of zest. Is it that state which the medieval schoolmen called *accidie*, the cardinal sin of spiritual sloth? I believe it is; and I believe it is as ancient as the human race, and that it can attack not only individuals but whole communities, dragging nations and empires down into the trough, just as cosmic inertia gradually exhausts galaxies.

All this may be the rhythm of a systole and diastole that neither physicist nor metaphysician can yet comprehend. We know only that it is an irresistible force, moving in and out with a tidal indifference to the structures of morals, religion and science which mankind builds and tries to maintain, in defiance of it. Sometimes, during a springtide not so much of disaster as of sheer inanition, it sweeps all such erections away, leaving us naked under the dark night of the soul.

Such was my condition in 1927, though I went about my daily life with as much resolution as I could summon, in the effort to break out of this enveloping despair. The desperate loneliness that accompanied it was almost welcome. Everything material belied my malaise. Colleagues at the Ministry were increasingly considerate and friendly, and amongst them I made friendships, such as those with Harold Emmerson and C. K. Munro, which have deepened and endured, as did those with Humbert Wolfe and John Hilton until death put them into a more remote perpetuity.

Further, a change of house ought to have made me believe that I was living in paradise. The little Regency box in Limpsfield High Street had become restrictive. Traffic in the village began to increase as Morris and Austin got into their stride, threatening the roads in town and country with the inundation that by the end of the twentieth century will have swept away the last vestiges of historical Britain.

Through the efforts of Lewis Fry, I was offered by the squire, Mr Leveson-Gower (brother of the cricketer), the lease of a fourteenth-century house on a clearing in Staffhurst Wood, beyond the southern side of Limpsfield Common and overlooking the Weald towards the county border at Kent Hatch, where Edward and Constance Garnett lived in their house called The Cearne, vividly described by their son David in his book *Beany-Eye*.

My lease was an ancient one, that gave me all kinds of rights, in obsolete legal terms, for grazing cattle and pigs, for felling trees of a certain girth, and other activities as futile as the gestures of dog or cat when they scrabble at cushions or carpets before curling up for sleep in the sitting-room.

The cottage had low ceilings and a vast open fireplace. It was draughty but picturesque, and it was blessedly quiet. We had grown so used, after nine years in the High Street, to a background of man-made sound, that our first days and nights at Comfort's Cottage (a name attached to it when it housed a Huguenot refugee named Comfret) were almost intimidating. I found myself sitting by that cavernous hearth, listening to the nothingness that came down the chimney-stack, along with daylight or star-shine, a kind of ghostly infiltration that permeated the whole of the wood-scented interior, reducing light and temperature by a fraction of a degree, and creating the suggestion of a presence in the cottage, and indeed in the woods outside it, of intangible form, but emphatic power.

The exterior of the cottage was rose-red and mossy, 'half as old as time'. Its eaves came down to first-floor level on one side to the north, and contorted, crusted apple trees scratched at the windows on the south. We had main water, but no electricity and only cesspool drainage. Life there was almost a return to the Elizabethan Age, and I should not have been surprised to see a loom set up in the shelter of the open hearth, or to see myself clad in homespun, plucking at a spinet, to accompany my own madrigals, a latterday Dowland or Campion.

My neighbours, a mile away on another lane through the wood, were a musical family named Harrison. The three daughters were professional instrumentalists, and the 'cellist, named Beatrice, was already well known. The B.B.C. came to her home and gave the first broadcast of the song of the nightingale, induced from the surrounding woods by the sound of Beatrice's violoncello as she played the hackneyed but irresistible Indian maiden's song from Rimsky-Korsakov's opera *Sadko*. When I hear that tune today, sprayed over the tables in a Palm Court tea-house, these nightingales of Staffhurst Wood come back to me, and I press my breast against the thorns of memory, under the dewy night of nostalgia, while Comfort's Cottage glimmers on the clearing, drenched in moonlight.

That, however, is not why I turn in dismay. I see too the paradox that had by then begun to work, changing light to dark, sweet to sour, true to false, and love to hate.

The translation from the noisy village to this utmost solitude and peace failed to cure me. Indeed, as I became accommodated to the remote setting, and to the increased expenses connected with it, I found myself working harder than ever, under the dread of falling into debt.

Freedom for creative work was more elusive than ever. I was

reviewing for some half-dozen magazines, and this increase of
literary hackwork coincided with a new post in the Ministry
that carried work both urgent and onerous. Fortunately my
new chief, a highly intelligent but explosive character named
Kingham, was also sympathetic to the literary temperament.
He was a friend of the poet and star reviewer at that time,
Gerald Gould, of *The Observer*. Kingham and I set up one of
those workmate friendships, restricted but peaceable, which
can endure indefinitely. Ours lasted some thirty-odd years until
his death. It never penetrated to intimacies; it was rich in undertones, and put no stress upon obligations. During the sickness
and horrors that were shortly to overcome me, Kingham stood
by me in silence, and never afterwards referred to the crisis. A
relationship of that kind grows only between people who work
together. It is partly a team-bond, but it also serves as a protection against the chafing and other irritations (some of them
otherwise deadly) which occur in every team.

The pressure of work in both my occupations not only
increased, but it felt as though it were increasing. I grew
conscious, more and more as those late springtime and summer
days at Comfort's Cottage crowded upon me, of a loss of
opportunity, and then of regret for that loss. This numbness,
indifference, towards the values and quests which had been my
world since the great awakening in my boyhood, worked more
evilly than the more concrete problems of time and physical
fatigue.

I began to dread things and functions normally taken for
granted. The problem was how to combat this dread, to prevent
my will and my mind from paralysis, that *rigor* of cowardice
which Herbert Read had described to me only a year or two
before this crisis. His words came back to me during my
misery. They might have been uttered by the Accusing Angel,
and I tortured myself by discovering, belatedly, that Read had
spoken prophetically, foretelling my moral collapse.

I believe that he had no such personal accusation in mind, for
he, like T. S. Eliot and the other members of the *Criterion*
group, were as friendly at that time as they had been from 1921

when we first met, and as they have since remained. By keeping my intangible troubles to myself, I was able to keep a sane contact with my friends, and to draw, unknown to them, a degree of hope and self-respect from the healthy ordinariness of my relationship with them.

So too I held on to sanity by my contacts with people outside the *Criterion* contributors. I found them freely: Harold Massingham, Desmond MacCarthy, Viola Garvin, Hamilton Fyfe, C. Henry Warren, Max Plowman, the American poets John Gould Fletcher and Conrad Aiken. These are but forerunners of the literary colleagues whose personalities and talents have enriched my life. Those I have named, with the exception of John Gould Fletcher and Henry Warren, knew nothing of my morbid condition during that fateful year, which was to reorientate my loyalties and to turn me to a more resolute habit of mind and conduct. Deeper troubles were to follow, involving more than my own mental and emotional state, and those two friends broke through my reserve, determined to help me.

[9]

The deeper and more active troubles began from the day when I sublet the little house in Limpsfield High Street. A neighbour who knew that my household was moving sent another family to inspect the house. Hindthought brings back that picture to me, and loads it with a significance hardly to be appreciated at the time.

The family consisted of two sisters and two brothers. Three of them were passive. The negotiator was the eldest, the sister who obviously mothered the rest of the family. She was small, neatly proportioned, her face shadowed by a broad-brimmed black felt hat. Her speech was beautifully modulated, and it was made more noticeable by a roughness of tone that came surprisingly out of so petite a figure.

I listened, then I listened again and more attentively,

committed despite my guardedness and the self-concern due to my neurotic condition. A strange curiosity fastened my attention on the young woman whose features I could not see because they were hidden by the broad-brimmed hat, and she was bowing nervously over the back of a dining-room chair, up and down, up and down, while she croaked, with that enchanting pronunciation, to inform me that she would take the house, but that the landlord must be persuaded to convert the lobby at the back of the house into a bathroom.

I was listening to the magic of the voice, and not to the content of the words. I nodded, my head moving in rhythm with the figure bowing over the chair. All that I noticed was that the rest of her family stood huddled together by the door, eager to escape but penned there like sheep cornered by the watchdog.

I saw the visitors out, and watched them clamber into a bull-nosed Morris car, to be driven away by the small person whose resolution at the wheel was still almost hidden under that stiff-brimmed black hat.

I watched them disappear, as I had watched my father go, after his visit to tell me that he and his wife were separating. That was some years earlier, and in the meantime I had been poised uneasily between the divided parties, though my sympathies, my instincts, inclined heavily towards the father whom I so priggishly censured, with filial mercilessness, first for having so prematurely superseded my mother, and second for having chosen so dreary a widow to take her place. My brother Jack solved the problem by evading all contact with her. I had manœuvred myself into a position that permitted no such easy way out.

It all came back to me at that moment while the family of strangers disappeared, as I thought finally, after this momentary contact, as twigs float down a fast-flowing stream. I do not know why my sub-conscious mind associated my father's marriage, and therefore my own, with this quite irrelevant interruption from the outside world.

I stood pondering these matters, half bemused by my own

misery and by the sound of that hoarse, lovely voice, and the face hidden beneath the brim. This time, no daughter came out to touch my arm, and to recall me to my duty and the domestic undertaking that had gradually overlaid the glory of language, and my youthful resolution to grasp it and make it mine. Perhaps it had flickered up again at the sound of that voice issuing from a hidden throat, to challenge me, to put me to shame because of my surrender to despair.

[10]

People who lead a settled life, centred in one place, un-intentionally fill and overfill their homes with worthless stuff which they are reluctant to discard. A writer specializes in superfluous books and papers. The late Augustine Birrell said that a man of letters should not be content with a library of less than four thousand books, and that he should sit amid them, day by day at his work, to let their wisdom penetrate, by a kind of osmotic pressure through his skin, to improve his literary style and inform it with knowledge.

That fanciful counsel is acceptable until one comes to move house. I started to collect books at the age of fifteen, just before I left Dulwich Hamlet School in 1908. The process was slow until 1922, when I began to review books, and thus opened a second source of supply, other than by buying. During the five years of that double intake between 1922 and 1927 I had filled the shelves put up by my brother Jack in the little house in Limpsfield. Books stood about on chairs, tables and floors, blocking the domestic traffic and causing much complaint. Manuscripts also accumulated. I am not sure which created the greater grievance, the books or the papers. Unless a writer is professionally organized, with an office to work in, where he can file his papers methodically, he cannot avoid a confusion of cast-off writings. I was still only semi-professional, though prolific, and the family had to wade ankle-deep through the fallen leaves of my literary forest, as they piled up year after year.

Here then was another task to add to my binary activities as author and civil servant. For weeks before moving house I sat up late at night, after the books for review were read, or the reviews written, sorting out the sheep from the goats, reluctantly setting aside books to be sold secondhand, and wading through odd sheets of manuscript, exercise books filled with verse, yellowing typescript, to be sure that no nuggets or dust of gold be thrown away.

There were none. Ruthlessness suited my mood. I had an unaccountable premonition that something was about to happen; that this moving from one home to another would mark an even greater shift in the direction of my life and the lives of those connected with me. I must, in future, travel light.

I must be ready for desperate ventures, and prepare to be blown before the storm. The tension had been gathering for several years, to fill my days with misgivings and my nights with fear. By suppressing these negative forces I only increased their threat.

This childish action of destroying old writings and selling half my books was intended, so far as I was aware of my state of mind, to propitiate whatever it was that threatened me. I was offering danegeld to the invader.

It was a futile gesture, but it served to ease the job of moving house. There could be no help now from Jack. Early that year he became too weak to take the short walk to and from the school near his home. During that spring and summer he led a desultory existence, between his home in London and the hillside bungalow at Otford. His pianoforte was heard less frequently, and finally it was silent. He continued to read, to draw and paint, though even those sedentary occupations were diluted, thinned away by the dreadful quietness and resignation that settled over him: a twilight of the soul.

Before the moving day, when we left village life and took to the woods, the future tenants of Redfern came down again. My first impression of the elder sister was confirmed, and it began to work upon my imagination, adding to the several impressions of foreboding that had been gathering round me, year by recent year. I had not believed an individual personality could so impress me, at least since the death of my mother, and the quiet, inevitable surrender by my brother of his authority over my boyhood and youth.

The acquaintance, and the half-dreaded attraction, deepened after the family was installed in a modernized Redfern. The landlord, who was also the village postmaster, had evidently been spellbound too: the bathroom was installed, and the house decorated throughout; the nine years of my occupancy distempered away forever.

I almost resented the change when I visited the house; the exquisitely harmonized colour schemes, the sense of greater spaciousness. I stepped into another world that appeared vaguely familiar. It absorbed me, and I only half-recognised myself there, talking more freely, eager to escape, eager to remain, touched once more by precognitions of hope and renewed confidence in myself as a person, and in my capability as a writer.

I dared not allow such recognizances, and I resolved to keep away from this attraction. My new home was unique, in its beauty, its isolation in the woods where the nightingale haunted, its antiquity that called to my historical imagination, which is the half of poetry.

I tried to write again, and felt the fever in my veins, the familiar sense of a fire consuming my stomach, an intoxication spontaneously induced. But the effort failed, because in the meantime I had lost the naïvety necessary for assured creative work. I had read too much, and too variously, as a reviewer. The fret outweighed the fever. All that I produced was the symptom of a greater fear. Delusions touched me, and even during the day when I was at work in the Ministry, behind the mask of official anonymity, I failed to combat this sensation of being drawn away, lured away, to some new, strange field of existence, which nevertheless I recognized, and rejoiced in, though I dared not approach it.

The daily journey to and from Oxted Station was now much longer. Lewis Fry, who was responsible for our translation to Comfort's Cottage, now insisted that he should advance the money to buy a small motor-car. I accepted uneasily, for this general change in our way of life meant larger outgoings, and the old, puritanical dread of debt revived. It is an obsolete fear now, in mid-twentieth century; the morals of the Old Testament have been replaced by those of the Hire Purchase System. Thrift is almost a social crime, for it impedes the processes of mass-production, and consumption.

I had gone so far, that I had to go farther. Lewis Fry, curmudgeonly, asthmatic, was an artist, and he had the values of an artist. His gestures of friendship were never condescending. He told me, frequently, that he valued my verse and wanted me to have more opportunity to produce it. So I accepted the help, as I accepted his friendship, on the assurance that both would be fully repaid. But I could not quite dispel that sense of guilt.

This was a minor shadow, for darker clouds were gathering. Work at the Ministry increased in range and responsibility with every new Act of Parliament and Order in Council, as the machinery of the Welfare State gathered momentum and scope.

I began to lose my methodical control of my two lives. I found myself one day staring out of my window at the Cenotaph in Whitehall, suddenly to see it obliterated by a flurry of snow. But the flakes were black, for this strange occurrence took place on a warm day in June. Before me on my desk was a bowl of early roses, brought to the office by a temporary clerk, a quiet, middle-aged man who had spent three months of his soldiering during the first world war, disguised as an Arab, in the company of his officer, buying up camels for army use. The officer was T. E. Lawrence, described by his assistant as 'a funny little fellow, until he lost his temper. Then he was uncanny, a proper fiend, who frightened even the Arabs.'

This optical aberration, accompanied by a slight headache and sense of depression, startled me at my work, or what I had thought was my work. I looked up again, but the Cenotaph was now clear, though the daylight was dimmed around it. A semi-iridescence in the air made the monument flicker, and the colours of the spectrum washed over its white surfaces, to disappear and reappear, then vanish.

I looked down hurriedly, refusing to believe the evidence of my eyes. But I found no reassurance in the file on which I had been working. There, on the minute sheet on the left-hand side of the dossier, opposite the correspondence, was a poem! I had, unconsciously, while studying the letters and previous minutes in the file, written a poem in *vers libres*, as follows:

> How heavy the foliage.
> Tree trunks are stocky,
> Like Atlas bearing the world.
> Hills are brought low,
> And valleys are lake-deep
> Under the clotted green.
>
> It has triumphed over the hope of Spring,
> The many colours;
> All that rebellion of flowers
> Is beaten down
> Under this passion of green,
> This burden,
> This marriage.

I looked round guiltily, and I felt the blood flushing to my cheeks. It was the guilt one feels after losing one's temper, that momentary trespass into hell, where there is nothing civil, or responsible, nothing but blind hate, and repudiation. Fear succeeded guilt; fear not only of the irrational act, but also of the contents of the verse. What was at the back of my mind? I dared not allow myself to examine that question, to explore the bitterness, the satiety, the stalemate.

The poem was written on a clean sheet of paper, which I had put into the file preparatory to writing a minute. I began to remove the sheet, but suddenly stopped. I could not face this experience alone. I had been carrying the burden of depression

K

too long, and always alone, confessing to nobody except that eccentric old American poet John Gould Fletcher, who had attached himself to me with the desperate gesture of an exile. Perhaps I had turned to him with fellow-feeling.

Without further self-struggle, I picked up the file, carried it into my chief's room, and laid it open on his desk.

Kingham was a man of Churchillian presence, stout and irascible, given to glaring furiously over his glasses, and firing annihilatory remarks at anybody regardless of rank whom he believed to be pretentious or stupid. Life had treated him badly, and he was an unhappy, angry man. People steered round him.

'Look!' I said, pointing hysterically at the minute sheet.

'Look at what?' he growled, scowling at my violent intrusion.

'See what I've done!'

I tried to explain, hopeless of being understood. I said that this verse had got itself written without my being conscious of it. I had prepared to write a normal, official minute, had looked up to see black snow pouring down on the Cenotaph outside my window, then looked down to find this verse on the file.

The frown on Kingham's face became almost a grimace. He would not look at me. Murmuring and muttering, he leaned over the file and read the poem. There he stayed, frozen for a terrible quarter of a minute. Then he spoke, still without looking up, and his voice was gentle, awe-stricken, like that of a person whispering in church.

'Marriage! My God, marriage!'

I realized that he was frightened too; frightened of his own despair.

He removed the sheet from the file, folded it in half, and handed it to me.

'You'd better keep that. It will enhance your next book, and find a larger audience there.'

There followed one of those conversations rare in everyday human relationships. We both talked, but impersonally and from the perimeter, about ourselves, creating instantly a confidence from which it is impossible wholly to withdraw. Kingham told me that I had been planted in his Department,

rather against his will, by Humbert Wolfe, because he was
likely to understand 'that sort of chap'. He confessed that he
was not anxious to have 'that sort of chap' on his staff. 'The
Civil Service is a necessary evil,' he said, 'and it has to be run
without regard for individual temperament.' He suggested that
I should see my doctor and supply a medical certificate pre-
scribing a couple of weeks' rest. 'It's no use my saying that you
should give up burning the candle at both ends.'

'I can't risk giving up the Service,' I replied.

'That wasn't quite what I meant,' he said, and a smile of
delightful mischief flickered over that thundery countenance.
'But I don't presume to advocate anything. So far your work
here hasn't suffered. But if it does . . .'

He waved me out, using the file as a fan to raise the necessary
draught. I took the file and fled, curiously light of heart.
Returned to my chair, I accused myself of being a flipper-
tigibbet, too easily moved, to pleasure or distress, by the way
people handled me. But I knew that below this superficial self-
estimate, lay the recognition of a most obstinate purpose, to
which circumstances, the ups and downs of chance, were
subordinate. The poem inadvertently appearing in an official
file was a demonstration of that purpose, and no doubt Kingham, who from that time became an ungrudging supporter of
my writings, had that in mind when he removed the poem from
the file and returned it to where it belonged. It found its place in
the experimental volume, *Mood Without Measure*, which T. S.
Eliot published under Faber's imprint. At that time I was
experiencing mood without measure indeed, not in a technical
connection.

[11]

That minor aberration in Whitehall was the first open sign o
the breakdown towards which I had been heading during the
past five years. For some days I went up to the Ministry as

usual, and persuaded myself that the lapse was due to a bout of indigestion. I told myself that I must take more exercise, and decided to walk home from Oxted Station every evening. This would take at least an hour from the time devoted to literary work, but I lacked the persistence to face that problem.

During the walk on the third evening, I had reached the top of Limpsfield Village, where the road divides into three, to penetrate through the middle and extremes of the Common, when utter bewilderment seized me. I could not decide which road to take. All were tracks into a desert.

I halted, and found myself breathing heavily, gasping like an asthmatic. Sweat ran into my eyes, and this may have been the cause of the second optical illusion. The black snow began to fall again. I stood watching it blot out the June landscape, the long, rambling house nestling under the flowered bank behind me; the inn farther down at the lower crossroads; the hill dropping to the village street, and the distant heights of Titsey Woods and the lime-pits cut out of the Downs. They all wavered, thinned, as the solid flakes of darkness settled.

I found myself making little murmuring noises of protest. Someone, it might have been a man or a woman coming towards me down the hill, stopped, looked nervously, walked on a pace or two, then returned to ask, 'Are you all right? Nothing wrong, eh?'

I apologized, turned, and walked away down the High Street, hurrying faster and faster as I approached Redfern, my former home. I could think of no other home, and of no other person than the new tenant there.

She answered my knock at the door, looked at me, and showed neither surprise nor alarm. 'Come in,' she said, quietly, and took me into the familiar but strange little sitting-room. I found myself sitting in an armchair, looking out of the window at Miss Sidney's house opposite. Passersby almost touched the window, their bodies throwing momentary shadows into the tiny room. This was what I had known for nine years. It was something to grasp at. I put out my hand and found it holding a cup of tea from which I must have been drinking. I heard that curiously hoarse voice, with its precise articulation; it was telling me something, quite objectively. It was asking me something unconnected with myself, my ghostly, incoherent self. It was asking me if I had noticed the spoon in the saucer, since it was handmade: made by the hand which had drawn me into the house, led me to the chair, poured the tea and passed it to me.

The irrelevance was my salvation. I looked at the small teaspoon, and saw the interwoven decoration of the handle.

'It's like an initial letter from the Book of Kells,' I said. The black snow had ceased to fall. Only a headache remained, like a drumbeat inside my skull.

'It *is* the Book of Kells,' she said, 'which is a wealth of design for a silversmith.'

'You are a silversmith?' I asked, studying the small figure, the small hands, and the steady, blue eyes.

'*And* a jeweller,' she said. 'Would you like to see some, while you rest? Then I'll drive you home.'

I stared at her, hungry and craving. 'But I *am* home.'

She looked frightened for a moment, then laughed gently, sympathetically, and took my cup to refill it. I sat, sipping the hot tea while she disappeared, to return with a cigarbox, which she opened, to take out rings, necklaces, brooches, displaying them on her lap, turning them one by one to the light: silverwork on semi-precious stones; her own designs worked out in the metal and the gems. In taking one brooch to examine it more closely, I touched her hand, and was instantly overcome by that sense of premonition, of doom, which gripped me when I watched her leaning over the back of a chair, the day she came to view the house. That was only three or four months ago; but I had moved into another world meanwhile, a world of doubts, fears, the shadow of death, and of a far distant landscape of sunlit glory, impossible to reach.

Her hand was cool against the fever of mine. We looked at each other, and she stepped back.

'I think you should get home now,' she said, gently. 'I've got the car outside.'

I was passive. My will-power had deserted me. I could not even be positive enough to thank her, or to apologize for intruding so absurdly.

She drove over Limpsfield Common and down through Staffhurst Wood. Neither of us spoke. I could see that she was distressed, but I could do nothing to reassure her. I believed I had no right to try; I might say more than I intended. But I *did* intend it; and I knew, with a sickening of the heart, what it was. I told myself I was sick, irresponsible, likely to rouse incalculable mischief if I spoke.

[12]

The weeks that followed lengthened into two months, and still I was not allowed to return to my duties in Whitehall. The summer passed into early autumn, while I wandered about in the woods, looking for nothing with a kind of eager absent-mindedness; or sat in the neglected garden, trying to read but halted by loss of attention. The little things of nature became all-important: the blindworm gliding over the gravel path; the butterflies flickering over the cabbage bed; the sparrows and finches perpetually busy; the robins inquisitively approaching me and staring at the immobile figure in the deckchair and at the pile of books on the stool; beady-eyed robins with a knock-kneed stance, miniature Lloyd Georges, impudent and provocative.

The weeks passed, and I struggled against the inanition into which I had lapsed, body and mind. Maybe the village doctor, who had taken a strong line about the daily journey to London, was using his bottles of tonic to disguise a sedative. But I needed no sedative. Despair and fear were sufficient warders.

Then it was decided that I must have a change of scene. Some neighbours suggested a quiet hotel in Paris, called the Hôtel Jacob in the street of that name, where once Laurence Sterne stayed while writing *The Sentimental Journey* some two hundred years before I made mine.

For my first visit abroad was more sentimental than it should have been, if it was to cure me of this strange, uncharacteristic malaise which had struck me down in the noonday of life.

My brother Jack, also on sick-leave all that summer, came down to stay for a week before my wife and I went to Paris. He had never before stayed with me during my married life, and I was apprehensive of what might result. But he was too weary to show any preferences or prejudices. He sat in the garden with me, coughing drily from time to time. This so distressed me that I persuaded him to be examined by my doctor, who said that he could find nothing wrong. He seemed more concerned about me; but I could find nothing wrong either, except this black despair, with its minor demons of shame, humiliation, self-consciousness.

I tried to amuse Jack with the new-fangled radio, as a substitute for his music; but after several attempts he had to give up. The weight and pressure of the earphones were too much for him. The two children approached him, shy and curious, attracted by this undefinable quality that had made him a beloved teacher. They brought him gifts, wild flowers, or tit-bits from the larder, and he accepted with a gentleness that, for me who watched, was more cruel than anger.

He was able to go home alone, and a few days later I was in Paris. Paris in September, when the myriad little shop-keepers and restaurateurs come back refreshed from the annual vacation in the provinces, is a haven for the most sophisticated of travellers. I saw it as a novice, reduced to a state of *tabula rasa* by nervous illness, and the photographic impression has never since been erased.

I see the gravid chestnut trees in the Luxembourg Gardens, dropping their fruits into the grass, their foliage already flushing. But nobody wants another person's pictures of Paris, unless they be those painted by Sisley, or Utrillo, or Degas.

Almost against my will, I found myself haunting the Cluny Museum, to study the antique jewellery there, and the silverware.

I would not admit to myself why I furthered this new interest. It took me into another world, not unaccompanied. The companion was not wholly welcome. She was no more than a conjuration, like the Helen of Troy seen by Faust, under the evocation by Christopher Marlowe, to provoke the immortal question, 'Was this the face that launched a thousand ships, And burned the topless towers of Ilium?'

I was no less provoked, and tried to exorcise the devil at my elbow. But returning physical and nervous health only fed the provocation. The conflict between duty and longing raged on, so unintermittently that I grew accustomed to the din of it, and could almost stand aside as a disinterested spectator of my own temptation and defeat.

My torment of mind found no expression at the time, but a year later, when the silversmith and I were examining Anglo-Saxon jewellery in the British Museum, the following poem began to take shape, catching not only the reactions of my imagination to the exquisite little works of art, but also certain aspects of the sacrifice I had since made, and asked of others, while following the demands of a destiny from which I had been unable and unwilling to escape.

MUSEUM PIECE

That afternoon in the Museum
I felt my spirit die from the present,
Slip from the clasp of loved hand
And touch the dust of a lost land.
There I met a Saxon child,
Upon her fingerbones a ring
Whose gold was faded as in Spring
Rainwashed primroses shine.
A little garnet blind with time
Was set within it, shared the sleep
Of milkwhite skin and August hair,
That hair of Autumn wheat, with deep
Sunflecks, and the windy shadows

Kissing the gold, and settling there
Like happy thoughts on innocence.
But now the garnet glowed, the gold
Clung to the living flesh that gleamed
And pulsed as the blood flowed beneath.
From the awakened eyes there streamed
The light of mind: and I heard breath
Make music in her mouth, not old
Harsh rustling from the grave of thought,
But tenderness, sweet enquiry,
Quick with suspense, rapid with running
After life, after colour, tasting these
With timid, child-bold ecstasies.

It was a voice I knew, calling
'Father! Father!' in the Saxon speech;
Falling on my heart, falling
From a century where I could not reach,
Shouting over her shoulder as she ran,
'I have left a message! Make haste!
Follow me, Father! Follow! Follow!'

Striving after her, to come to her side,
And clasp my darling, my spirit died.
Echoed in my ears 'Make haste! Make haste!'
And the faith of that eager, 'Follow! Follow!'
Then the dust of the Museum settled low,
The dust of time and human waste,
And I said, my voice drawn thin and hollow,
Said to my loved one, 'Shall we go?'

[13]

The convalescence in Paris, which might have been interminable, was cut short by a telegram. My brother Jack was ill,

and we were summoned home. We got back to an England that stood motionless under a mantle of October glory.

We drove through Staffhurst Wood, and it seemed as though every tree were individualized by its own choice of colour. The air was so still, half visible with fine mist, that nothing moved. Comfort's Cottage nestled in the midst of the silent wood, its rose-red, lichened tiles toning with the foliage, so that it might have lain unseen by a passing stranger.

But I was no stranger. This was known to be my home, the centre of my world. The children had put up a toy flag at the gate, to greet us. I should have had a sense of certainty, to give me courage to face what was coming. Instead, my heart was leaden. Fear gripped me again as I entered the old house and stood before the great open fireplace, the bread-oven door, the recess for the salt-jar, the iron dogs and the spit.

I was an intruder there. What meaning, what claim it may have had when I left for Paris were now quite relinquished, as though the house itself had given up an association that had never come to life. I felt the children round me. I greeted the dog who was performing his canine ballet of ecstasy; but everything took place at a distance, like the gestures of musicians seen by a man stone-deaf.

That drab person, combined stepmother and mother-in-law, greeted me too, and I stared at her without recognition. Her sister, the aunt who was now a factotum of the household, too simple-minded to go out into the world to earn her living, also greeted me, simpering and nodding her head under the impulse of vague, universal kindness. But I had no responding smile for her, either. I could hardly recollect who they were, these two elderly women, perpetually bereaved, perpetually grateful for nothing in particular. Blessed are the meek; but I could not bless them, or acknowledge that they had been in charge of the house and family during our absence.

They were not rebuffed. They attributed my strangeness to anxiety for my brother. So did I, and I was partly right. The anxiety drove me out again within an hour, after a hasty meal. The autumn afternoon was sinking into twilight, and darkness had almost muffled the splendours of the countryside by the time I reached Otford, and the recess by a heap of stones on the Pilgrims' Way where I left my car.

I opened the gate to the footpath over the Downs, and walked up the hillside to the acres and the bungalow where Jack now lay. The blind was not drawn in the end room, and an oil-lamp shone like a golden sovereign in the window, tiny and gentle under the gloomy weight of the hill rising beyond, and the sky over all.

The emotion of anti-excitement, that dread negative, made me conscious of myself approaching the bungalow, where the two people most bound to me, my past, my hopes, my intellectual aims, were waiting. I should be there before they expected me, for the journey home from Paris, like most return journeys, had seemed to take only half the time taken by the journey out.

I went round to the door, which was at the back, against the slope of the hill, and knocked quietly, for he might be asleep.

I was greeted by the sister-in-law who for nineteen years since I first met her had been growing to more intimacy in my life, my life once secret but now beginning to emerge with professional confidence. We had little to say, and spoke in the undertones of anxiety, the reluctance to face facts when they are too harsh to be believed. I learned how, a week earlier, Jack had been on a bus, travelling down from Town for a weekend at Otford, she to follow later when school was out. At Farningham, while the bus stopped at the inn, Jack had coughed and brought on a haemorrhage that left him badly shaken and confused. But he managed, by an effort of will, to reach the bungalow and to put himself to bed, where she found him when she followed some hours later. He had not left the bed since, and meanwhile a sickroom routine was established, with visits from the unhopeful local doctor twice daily. He too was a sick man, who grumbled about the climb up from the Pilgrims' Way.

All this information was given to me, standing just inside the threshold of the little bungalow. Darkness closed down for the night, and my sister lit a candle so that we might continue to recognise each other, rather as ships greet in mid-ocean.

I touched the panel of the sick-room door, making just enough sound to announce myself if Jack was awake. I heard a slight movement. He must have raised his hand, or stirred in the bed. So I went in.

He lay propped on pillows, his head turning to greet me as I entered. I pretended to be casual, though what I saw in that first instant killed all hope. He was strange because he had grown a beard. Above it, the familiar ascetic face was puffed and swollen. The prominent brown eyes were shrouded by drugs, and lay half shuttered by the lids, now more sombre than ever.

In that instant I had a sudden recollection of the model steam-engine which he made from castings, under directions from *The Boy's Own Paper*, and of its trial in the garden of our home in Battersea. That was a quarter of a century earlier, but here was the same Jack, stern but patient, even benevolent in a monitorial way. When the little locomotive blew up, Jack's face bore the expression which I saw on it now, through the mask of disease: reproachful surprise, a perplexity because something had gone wrong which, after his careful calculations and performance, ought not to have gone wrong.

But now the creative energy was lacking. He lay there resigned. He had surrendered. I had never known that before, and it brought tears to my eyes. I turned my head away, to hide them, and this made him more alert. He moved his hand and put it over mine, on the quilt. His was hot, and dry. I looked at the filbert nails, the long fingers, the bones within the almost transparent flesh. It was Jack's hand surely enough, but sublimated already.

He whispered to me, and as he framed the few words, one by one, tears of weakness troubled him, making him move his head from side to side angrily.

'I thought you would not get here in time.'

For nearly two weeks I drove to and from Otford from Staffhurst Wood every day. On one occasion my bee-keeping friend, now living at Hurst Green, came with me and rigged up a crystal set and arranged the earphones so that Jack might help himself to music from Savoy Hill. He made one effort that night; but it was useless. Nor was he disappointed. He lay there inert, relinquishing all interests in preparation for the departure which we knew had to be made very soon.

Our father came frequently, and stayed during the vigil of the last night, while we waited for the end. It came at six in the morning, as another October daybreak flushed over the hillside and along the Westerham valley. So Jack died to a riot of colour, as he was buried in Otford churchyard three days later, when after the ceremony we walked back to the bungalow, numbed into silence under a sunset that blazed and triumphed, a colossal refusal to recognize grief.

I went down afterwards to the road, to see my father off. His motor-cycle and sidecar stood behind my little car by the heap of stones. He took my arm as we walked down the footpath. Something he had said or done must have upset the two women whom we had left indoors, and they had responded with some resentment. I looked at him when he touched me, and to my distress I found him crying. Only once before had I seen this happen: at the graveside of my mother, seventeen years before. That had marked a closure in my life, and the opening of a new chapter, cold, clean and almost hostile, because of its break with the past.

So now my father's tears affected me with premonition of something finished. I thought at the moment that it was solely due to Jack's death, and the many finalities involved, in life, in art, in brotherly love. But I was soon to learn that the severance was not complete. There was more to come, with a new kind of suffering, compounded with remorse, and almost overwhelming responsibilities that were to fetter my life for another fourteen years.

CHAPTER EIGHT

Vita Nuova

[1]

SEVEN MONTHS LATER I was living again in London, my hometown, after twelve years in Limpsfield as an amateur countryman. What happened in the meantime after my brother's death is hidden in darkness, and horror enacted and re-enacted in that darkness. I, and the others concerned, finally emerged to an equitable and stable relationship. But all large wounds leave an area of cauterized organism from which sensation has been burned away. It is a process of nature, and probably a merciful one, the anaesthesia of pain, both physical and spiritual.

The death of people we love affects us in that way, cutting away from our estate of consciousness a whole area of feeling, of responsibility. Often we are dismayed by what we suspect is callousness in ourselves as we recall the memories of the dead, even the recently dead. We know that really we are heart-broken, desolate: but we cannot feel those finalities. We are merely numb, spiritually paralysed. Half the misery of grief consists of remorse because we cannot feel more acutely. We have passed the pain-barrier, into an over-speed of the emotions. Even memory is crippled, and permanently. We live, so far as that event, or loss, is concerned, in a condition of supreme cowardice, unable to face the circumstances and the de-privation. It is the dreadful state which Herbert Read spoke of to me, as he had observed it in the trenches of Flanders. Dante refers to it in the opening lines of Canto 9 of the *Inferno*:

> Quel color che viltà di fuor mi pinse
> veggendo il duca mio tornare in volta,
> più tosto dentro il suo nuovo ristrinse.

That 'cowardice that blanched my outward hue' made me go about my daily life for those seven months more than ever wraithlike and cut off from all health-giving communion with my fellow-creatures at home and in Whitehall.

At home! There was no home. I had gone out into the wilderness, maddened to a cold anger and faithlessness by the death of my brother, a loss too closely repetitive of the death of my mother, that now almost mythical being so like the son who had joined her; his sensibility hers, his musical talent hers, his intolerances hers.

The Christmas of 1927 was a white one. The snow cut off Comfort's Cottage during the twelve days of the Festival. I recall it only vaguely: the pain of making an effort, within the family for whom my love was so tortured and shattered.

I went out alone, to wander about in Staffhurst Wood, and over the Common. Twice I found myself back in the village, staring hungrily, hopelessly at the little house where I had lived for nine years. The consequences of those pilgrimages of despair were to be immediately catastrophic, but they led to the changes that started a new life, new hope and expectation, and a rebirth of the creative energy and intellectual activity which have since commanded my life, and made it an active gesture of worship and wonder.

[2]

The immediate consequences were, of course, a need for strict economy. Two households are dearer than one, and I had to expand my literary work accordingly. But now there was a purpose and a challenge. The nervous prostration disappeared, and in the care of the silversmith my health was not only restored, it was transformed. For five more years I worked on at the Ministry of Labour, almost enjoying the various assignments, and wholly enjoying the acquaintance made among my colleagues. So many of them are still living that it is difficult for me to describe them without embarrassment. That is one of the major difficulties of the autobiographer, especially if his mature career takes him, and so many of his contemporaries, out into public life and the distorting glare of the limelight, in politics, or the professions that command wide attention.

Civil Servants have hitherto made a discipline of anonymity, almost of facelessness. In private, and in the course of their work, they are no less idiosyncratic and interesting than the rest of humanity. In the past, before the Welfare State made life economically secure for everybody, the Civil Service was the only profession, at least in its lower ranges, that offered this security. In consequence, many creatures, like myself, moved to it because they had no inclination, ability or courage to dare the open jungle. It is not fanciful to say that there was less intrigue, less redness in tooth and claw in the Civil Service than in the business world or the professions, where individuals had mostly to fight for themselves, against the rivalry of other hungry men. The orthodox means of promotion in the Service, by seniority, put a certain restraint on the power-lust with which nature endows us all, as a weapon towards survival. That official tradition is despised nowadays, and rightly, for it encourages sloth, and the ascendency of the mediocre. That danger has been largely removed from the post-war Civil Service, and passed to the community as a whole.

In the course of my essays in autobiography, first two static presentations, forming a diptych with childhood hinged to youth, and now the present one in a more fugal form to suit the flux of mature life under the increasing compulsion of time, I have drawn several examples of the eccentricity and vagary of individual Civil Servants, whose sheltered professional life enabled them to cultivate a second activity, in the arts and sciences. I worked with musicians and mathematicians, painters and boxers, clockmakers and champion swordsmen, religious cranks and mystics, *bons viveurs* and prigs, collectors and gardeners. There is no end to the variety attracted by short office hours and the sense of security.

With all this dispersion of vitality, the British Civil Service has been, and remains today under much altered circumstances and conditions, the most efficient and uncorrupt Government executive machine of any country in the world. It lacks the power of the French executive, and the pedantry of the German, its only rivals. It has never had to administer a diseased legislation, a function of the otherwise efficient South African Civil Service.

I have watched, with admiration, several colleagues move through the hierarchy of our Service, and I know of no characters more impressive, both in administrative ability and in cultural range. People such as Edward Marsh, Harold Nicolson, Edward Bridges (son of a Poet Laureate), Eric Leadbitter the novelist, Alec Randall, Herbert Read, James Laver, C. K. Munro, Rostrevor Hamilton, Bernard Newman, Humbert Wolfe, Alan Barlow, Harold Emmerson, David Milne, Godfrey Ince; these are a short rosary of names to tell of true patricians in the control and manipulation of public affairs, responsible to Parliament and upholding it.

It would be delightful to paint intimate word-portraits of these, and other, representative figures to be seen, or formerly seen, coming and going between the Government Departments in London and the provinces. Some of them would be coloured by friendship, others by a touch of malice. But there would be less malice than I should introduce were I painting a gallery of literary contemporaries.

For here is a profession uncertain in its status, both economically and socially; dealing also in uncertainties of aesthetic standards, and having no assurance of an increasing and constand good will, or supply of raw material and technical equipment. Like the publishers who handle them, writers are doomed, by the very nature and authority of their work, to an almost morbid individualism. Though writers have a commonalty in their art, exacting and tyrannical, and publishers have the Publishers' Association to protect themselves against the rapacity of paper manufacturers and the printers' unions, there is in the literary world none of the *esprit de corps* that binds the Civil Service into a sodality comparable to those

L

of the fighting services, and of the religious communities. This is no sentimental estimate, nor is it blind to the friction, rivalries and often mean intrigue that goes on in all organizations, religious or lay, military or civil. A picture could be made of life in Whitehall that would alarm the ratepayer and the simple-minded citizen. It would be true; but it would be inadequate.

I recall my twenty-four years in the Civil Service with pleasure. Beginning in 1909 when I was a boy of sixteen, straight from the Elementary School in Dulwich Village, I was shaped by a discipline, (much against my pliant young inclination, which was towards Byronic grandeur) that must have conditioned habits of work for the rest of my life. For a long time it was too protective, and kept me in a kind of nursery, softly cushioned against the elbows of the outer world.

The world of letters corrected that, especially when I entered fully into it, in 1933.

[3]

During the five years prior to my emancipation from Whitehall, I turned novelist. I did so with misgiving, for I recalled a remark made by T. S. Eliot many years earlier, that when a poet took to writing novels, it was likely to be the end of him as a poet. I was unnecessarily frightened, for I believe the magister spoke light-heartedly (he is prone to poking fun).

It might be argued that the novelist is a lyric poet turned epic poet, driven to change his medium from verse to prose by the demands of a sophisticated society no longer credulous of myth, or an agreed standard of literary values.

Efforts are made from time to time to rehabilitate verse as a vehicle for popular stories, histories, philosophies, and some impressive work has been done to this purpose in the English-speaking world and in Europe. Browning's *The Ring and the Book*, and Hardy's *The Dynasts* are masterpieces in this anachronistic kind. Maurice Hewlett, with *Song of the Plough*, and Francis

Brett Young, with *The Island*, are novelists who have interrupted their work in prose fiction to revert and to ascend to long poems.

There are many examples of such survivals of the epic and narrative poem, crashing through the jungle of modern life, huge as the mastodon, fierce as the sabre-toothed tiger. But they make short headway against the sawn-off prose of contemporary journalese, the weapon with which the popular novelist rounds up the public, and warns off any writer who tries to revert to a medium that employs the devices of rhetoric and prosody. Nor will the public accept such experiments, for it condemns them, perhaps rightly, as self-conscious posings, comparable to walking along Piccadilly in a suit of armour, or wearing Elizabethan doublet and ruff to travel on the Underground.

Poets who have not dared, or deigned, to attempt the novel have persisted in writing long poems, but they have found small audiences. Robert Bridges's *The Testament of Beauty* was an exception, for it sold many thousands of copies. Critics who disapproved of its quantitative verse form (always foreign to the rhythmic English tongue), and its episodic structure, frivolously attributed its success to its title, which had deceived the majority of its female purchasers, who expected the book to be a guide to cosmetics and their application. I wonder how many of those purchasers looked farther into the poem, to discover that it is really a gallery of rare English water-colours, hung on a wall of orthodox Episcopalian-Stoic philosophy. Both ingredients are out-of-date in the latter half of the twentieth century.

John Masefield is the most conspicuous poet in our time who has combined the two activities, of verse and prose as vehicles for narrative, and has commanded vast audiences. Passionate, simple and prolific, he is a master story-teller, his work not two-dimensional like that of William Morris, but solid, earthy, and human with sudden outbreaks of flowers, in the manner of Chaucer.

For a while, it has been thought that verse would succeed in rehabilitating itself in the theatre, a return due to the diametrically opposed talents of T. S. Eliot and Christopher Fry. But neither of them is frequent enough in composition to consolidate the victory, or to command reinforcements. Death has removed Louis MacNeice, who carried the battle into the field of Sound Radio, followed by a host of younger poets capable of no more than short, lyrical gestures.

It was not only these technical problems, however, that drove me to experiment in prose fiction, turning from one medium to another as a carpenter selects oak in place of mahogany to suit the job in hand. Whatever his choice, he remains a worker in wood. So too the poet, whether he use verse or prose, remains a worker in verbal imagination, tooling it into the desired shape.

The other incentive was a more personal one. I needed to increase my income; a dreary necessity too obvious to discuss. Further, I was still being tossed about in the aftermath of the storm which had almost wrecked my faith in life and driven me to despair.

The horror had gone; but no artist is serene until he has utilized past experience in some form of creative effort. So, by way of catharsis, I began to write my first novel, setting it in the Limpsfield scene which I had left only a few months before. I saw Limpsfield through the eyes of a self-exile, with an intensity that was obsessional, under the compulsion of a remorse that had to be exorcized if I was to find the energy and confidence to be able to carry the new responsibility which I had so eagerly, so passionately undertaken.

The pull both ways was expressed by two poems, written at the time. Here is the lyric which looks back to what I had left:

The Return to the Orchard

> Overblown with seeding grass
> The old orchard was:
> The brickpath and ashpath
> Laid but a year,

Now hidden. Creeping near,
I saw no feet had trodden
There. They were rain-sodden.
Great hemlocks, and sorrel
With fingers of coral
Moved with the breeze
Under the bearded trees.
No birds were singing,
No children swinging.
I wondered, calling,
'Hallo! Hallo! I've come!'
No little ones ran out
With welcome and boisterous shout.
Only the ancient trees
Stood secretive, dumb.

Here is the poem which looks forward to the new way of life,
yet to be proved. At that time it was undertaken ruthlessly, and
on trust founded in an intuition that began to ferment in my
consciousness from the moment I watched that small figure
bobbing nervously over the back of a chair in the tiny house in
Limpsfield High Street:

Your simplicity of heart;
The open candour of your mind;
Though I search in every part
Of the worlds of thought and sense,
Where shall I such freedom find
Though lifelong I wander hence
Through the jungle of my being
Where the sensual tigers tread
Tirelessly behind the fleeing
Deer of gentleness, until
Outworn, they tumble dead,
And the tigers take their fill:
Though I cross the desert then
Of my unknown fellowmen,

> Finding sphinx and pyramid
> Where their cryptic thoughts are hid
> Arid and unanswerable
> Till the mind's divisions fall,
> And united knowledge leaps
> Impersonal to apocalypse?
>
> Though these void adventures take me
> In the treachery of unrest
> From the home that you would make me
> In the shelter of your breast,
> I shall come again and find
> Your simplicity of heart
> And the deep wisdom of your mind,
> Nor a second time depart.

Such was the personal situation which I had, first, to support and, second, to incorporate within the imaginative world of my writing. If I failed in the one, it would be the end of myself, of two households, and of the persons concerned. If I failed in the second, I believed (such was my self-confidence) it would ruin a now firmly based lifework, on which the superstructure was just beginning to appear above the scrub and wilderness of indiscriminate emotion and appetite, the blinding jungle of the senses.

Out of it all must emerge a coherent life-structure recognizably like that which I had glimpsed, far off, when I began as a boy to write, and to realize that this activity was a form of worship likely to sustain me in my vision, as the mystic is sustained in his.

> Ah! Let me close my eyes on this.
> What I beheld shall thus remain
> Recorded lifelong on my brain;
> A scene of mingled hurt and bliss,
> A sculptured and arrested strife,
> A still epitome of life.

This shall become, as time wears on,
A legendary thing, that bears
An immortality of tears;
A joy mankind shall feed upon
When we, our matrix-moment past,
Have crumbled from this perfect cast.

Time has worn on over four decades since then, nearly toppling our whole human civilization in its flood. Perhaps history will name it as the period of genocide, during which the vices of the human race flared up into one worldwide insanity, whose ravings drowned the 'still small voice' of the reasonable mind, which is the godhead, symbolized in the figure of Christ, and the other gods of gentleness, truth-seeking, and neighbourly love, erected and revered by this mysterious genius of conscience that makes man somewhat different, in a small but significant degree, from the animals.

A vast requiem, in all the arts, has been raised for the myriads who have perished: the Holy Anonymous on the battlefields, the home-fronts, in the concentration camps. It will be added to, for the last word of compassion and remorse will never be said. And still there remains a necessary tribute to the survivors who are maimed, in body, mind, even in soul, generations of them still unborn, but destined to a share in the consequences of scientific warfare and the over-armed politics of the major part of the twentieth century.

The desperate individual, especially if he be a survivor from the comparatively paradisal nineteenth century, is tempted to shriek 'A plague on *all* your houses!' forgetting the actualities of those years of his infancy before Armageddon began: the filth, poverty, privilege; the clumsiness and messiness of the early machinery of the Industrial Age, as it functioned even through the first world war.

But we have now, surely, gone beyond the stage of recrimination, and we can observe the opening of the phase of exhaustion, and the resultant quiet, above which the 'still small voice' will again be heard. That indeed will be a Second Coming, to be welcomed in such a way as will prove that mankind in the mass is, after all recent history's evidence to the contrary, capable of evolution, in the Darwinian sense, and thus of fitness to survive.

But generalizations are boring; anathema to the artist, and meaningless to the simple citizen who rightly sheers away from them, even at election time when politicians offer them free, or at the cost of one vote per person.

During those years of my private holocaust, I went through a microscopic version of the world-change which has overtaken us all. I came out on the other side, to sunshine, serenity, renewed hope and rapture. This condition may lack drama; it may be impossible to be conveyed to an onlooker; it may appear to be callously self-concerned in a society whose disturbance I have just referred to. But it is real. It is fecund. It holds the future protected by its warmth and gesture. It houses that third authority of the Origin of all things, the Holy Ghost. That was my own discovery. There is no other way of discovering it than by individual experience, with its shaping tools of suffering, fear, enlargement, and humiliation. Every religious initiate refers to that experience, and tries to pass on the dictionary of its terms, so that all may express it. But the extremes by which it announces itself to the man, the woman, the child, at all times in their lives, have no fulfilment along the nerves (as the poet Keats said) until it is of their own doing, their own receiving, and consequent degradation, total sacrifice, and gradual conquest.

How gradual, indeed, is that conquest: a slow getting up, lifetime long, after the knockout blow, the moment of accosting such as that met by the rather unlikable person Saul, on the road to Damascus. I have the feeling now, in my old age, that I have at least risen to my knees. But I dare not look down!

So it was that I turned to the art of prose fiction at a time of spiritual and economic need. I wrote the first novel to brand upon my memory the period of my life spent in Limpsfield, during and after the first world war, fighting against the threat of renewed tuberculosis, which had dominated my childhood and poisoned my young mind with delusions of grandeur and godlike privilege superior to the laws of gravity.

Living in close quarters on the seamy side of Holland Park, I appreciated the talents of my companion, who had the gift of making a home wherever she might be. If she were stranded for an hour or two in the waiting room of a railway station, she would convert it, by a few deft touches and disposition of her luggage and available furniture, to make the place homelike, a centre to be left with reluctance when the train arrived.

Such was my appreciation, and the wonder which increased day by day as my new life developed and took deeper root, that I did not miss the woodlands, the silence of the countryside, the habits of the familiar past. I was translated, and encouraged in this adventurous freedom by the character of the person with whom I had grasped at it, at the moment of drowning.

From the beginning of this new life, we punctuated the long sessions of work with explorations abroad, travelling third class, tramping with ruck-sacks. The first of these journeys was to the Black Forest, searching the small river valleys and walking along the northern shore of the Bodensee.

A year later we were lent a farmhouse in the canal country in mid-France, near Grez-sur-Loing, the village where the composer Delius lived. Those were the first periods of escape into a world larger than I had ever known, and I stored up the experiences, to use them later in novels and poems, enriched by authentic and first-hand material. That process, of seeking and using, has gone on ever since, ever farther afield as our circumstances gradually improved, and latterly as our responsibilities have lightened.

[4]

During the months immediately following my brother's death, I dared not listen to music. I lived in a kind of twilight of sound, adding thus another aspect to the torpor within which I had been cocooned during the last stages of my life in Limpsfield. So acute was this condition that often I found myself crouching in my chair, with my arms folded across my chest, my legs drawn up and my head sunk forward, the posture being taken unconsciously while I brooded, open-eyed but sightless, on nothing in particular, since brain was as rigid as limbs. I might have been an amoeba in the womb, waiting to be born.

I *was* waiting to be born; and I have tried to describe how that new birth took place, and at what cost of conscience and torn loyalties. Like all major experiences in an individual's life, it gave a lasting change of direction over the rest of the journey home.

Many years later, the charmingly idiosyncratic critic Cyril Connolly, reviewing one of my books, suggested that I was a 'schizophrenic'. This set me thinking, for it was a frightening accusation, especially when directed towards a person who has followed, lifelong, the practice of an art. For the main purpose of the arts, in all mediums, is to reduce the chaos of life to a pattern and a unity. He would be a poor practitioner who could not carry this purpose into the clarification of his own life, no matter what the odds against it, and the caprice of chance. There can be no homecoming for a schizophrenic, for he wanders in no-man's-land, like Vanderdecken, the Flying Dutchman. And homecoming is also the arrival at that point of truth which the inspired John Keats said 'is all ye know on earth, and all ye need to know'.

What troubled me, in Cyril Connolly's accusation, was that he too, as a sensitive and acute critic, so obviously travelling toward home, would not recognize another pilgrim on the same road. A writer has to learn, however, to take the knocks indifferently with the bouquets; no easy matter, especially in his early years, when his professional skin is of a maidenly thinness.

Temporarily deprived of music, I turned with all the more fervour to writing, and have never touched a pianoforte again. Grief was not the only surgeon. Sophistication made me impatient of my own lack of skill. Now that I lived again in

London, and could go to recitals and concerts, I could nourish the taste and needs in music which Jack had awakened in me when I was a child.

I had read regularly in the literature of music, biographies, letters, treatises, following up the excitement caused by the correspondence of Hector Berlioz in a book bought for twopence when I was still a schoolboy. He became a hero, and my French as well as my musicology profited accordingly. He gave a direction to my taste, and I have never lost a special delight in the work of Gluck, Vivaldi, Fauré, Dvořák, and all composers whose music is marked by a resolute melodic gesture, as though pointing homeward to the sun. Mozart above all is of this kind, and so, I find, is Benjamin Britten: makers of an imagery instantly recognizable, like the voice of someone loved, a member of my own family, in the circle of home.

It is a mystery, this sense of contact, or of repulsion, where instinct works with lightning speed beyond the range of reason, to pick out what is one's own kind, in the arts, and to reject what is detestable. Certain single works can be thus miraculously singled out: such as Beethoven's Triple Concerto in C, Op. 56, Berlioz's *Nuits d'été* song-cycle, and for me, its companion cycle, Britten's *Sonnets of Michelangelo*; Mozart's *Requiem* and Britten's *Requiem*; absurd juxtapositions, a professional musicologist might say; but I could offer many such couplings, as examples of work that have a privacy of appeal for me, to set moving the unaccountable and almost uncontrollable machinery of creative activity which I can only serve with humility and awe, and no little incredulity, through the medium of my own art, which functions, in common with all the others, architecture, painting, sculpture, cooking, sports, on the ground base of rhythm, and command over timing and spacing.

This hunger for music has never been assuaged. Even street music puts a spell upon my senses, if not upon my mind. I can recall sitting in my office during a period at the Ministry of Labour when our department was housed in a squalid and dirty block of buildings opposite Dartmouth Street, near St James's Park Underground Station. To Broadway, below my window, street musicians frequently made their way, with fiddle, trumpet, and three-stringed double-bass. As soon as their music began to float up, dustladen from the street, my attention to the Dictionary of Occupations wilted, like cut flowers in the sun, and I sat there, hypnotized, a lump in my throat, and often tears in my eyes, much to the consternation and bewilderment of any colleague who might enter the room to find me in that nostalgic condition; nostalgic for I knew not what.

[5]

I showed my first novel to Edward Garnett, that legendary figure in the world of books. He was the publisher's reader *par excellence*, responsible for the prestige of two publishing houses, first of Grant Richards and later of Jonathan Cape. He fostered the careers of John Galsworthy, Joseph Conrad, Stephen Crane, W. H. Hudson, W. H. Davies, Edward Thomas, and many other writers since established in fame. The last of his discoveries was H. E. Bates, whom I met through his recommendation. My friendship with Bates has become more than a professional affinity. There is something 'old-fashioned' about it: genial, inexpressible, tough enough to make it survive differences of appreciation, and occasionally severe criticism of each other's work.

Bates has a fertility which has flourished since he began to publish at the age of eighteen, in 1923, when Garnett first recognized the promise in his short stories. For years, after Garnett had attached him to Jonathan Cape's distinguished list, Bates wrote for a small public, winning a *succès d'estime* that tempted connoisseurs, here and in America, to buy his manuscripts. During that period before the second world war he wrote some of the most sensuous short stories in the English language, based on no dramatic mechanism, but exciting enough in their poetic tangibility and handling of the basic emotions and human relationships, presented against a

background of nature observed and re-created with a closeness
that makes the reader suspect the author of possessing not five
but six senses. Perfume, colour, temperature, light and dark,
impregnate his paragraphs, with a Hardyesque poignancy.

By the time his creative work was suspended during war-
service, Bates had published several novels in addition to his
volumes of short stories. At least one of them, *A House of
Women*, has a substantiality, in all aspects, that I look for before
I call a book a masterpiece. It possesses the close poetic detail of
the short stories, and adds the element of constructive destiny
ordained by character. We see that destiny working through
the narrative, using events naturally and plausibly, and never
against the grain of the temperaments of the people whose
actions make the plot.

During the war Bates, under the pseudonym of 'Flying
Officer X', wrote sketches for the R.A.F., which sold by the
million, building up a publicity for the Air Force where
perhaps none was needed. Thus, after the war, Bates found his
public multiplied so much that it almost damaged his reputation amongst the exclusive critics who tend to write off an
author after he has become acceptable to the world at large. But
Bates continues to embarrass those critics by producing, from
time to time, work that maintains and enhances the standard of
that on which his reputation was founded before the war, under
Edward Garnett's blessing.

Garnett invited me to visit him to discuss my first novel, and
I presented myself in Bedford Square, very shy because I had
never met him before, though we had lived with only Limpsfield Common between us, from 1916 to 1928, long enough,
had he been interested in my work, for him to summon me
earlier into the presence.

I was therefore somewhat guarded when I confronted this
strange figure: strange, because his physical appearance was
more that of a Chinese brush-drawing of a Mandarin, than of a
living Westerner. His figure was portly and shapeless, and sunk
into it was a formidable head, slightly tilted forward over a layer
of chins. A pair of eyes, enormously magnified and distorted by

thick, pebble lenses, flashed at me like headlamps. I conquered the inclination to leap aside for fear of being over-ridden.

It took me some moments to realize that I was being addressed by a voice of remarkable kindliness. It was detached, impersonal. Garnett made no personal inquiry about my conditions of work, how, when and where it was produced. He said that the book was a faithful study of rural life, that the heroine, daughter of a village grocer, was a real woman, of flesh and blood, and that her temperament was convincingly feminine. He commended the disciplined writing, and concluded these encouraging remarks by saying that I should send the book to the house of Dent, whose list it would suit admirably.

This expertise astounded me. To be able to place a book precisely with one amongst the hundreds of British publishing houses suggested to me a professionalism so cool that it froze my blood. I shivered with an apprehension that I could not define. I thanked him for the advice, and almost retreated backwards, bearing the refrigerated typescript in my arms.

But I took his advice, gratitude having overcome intimidation. I sent the books to Dents, a house which hitherto I had known mainly as the publishers of Everyman's Library, that godsend to the impoverished scholar, that friend who had indeed, as the flyleaf of every volume proclaimed, 'gone with me, to be my guide, in my most need to sit by my side'. My first literary prize, won at Dulwich Hamlet School in 1908, for an essay, was the three-volume Shakespeare, bound in sultan-red leather faintly tooled in gold, at eighteenpence a volume. My mother's last gift to me, two weeks before her death in 1910, had been the works of Macaulay in seven Everyman volumes.

Everyman's Library therefore had an emotional as well as a literary appeal to me. I regarded it as almost a private possession, as no doubt did many thousands more like-minded readers avid for knowledge and vicarious living.

These associations of our childhood and youth never lose their magic. They remain our secret possessions, and when in later life we happen upon them, the coldness and complexity of our adult condition are put aside. The hopes, the grandeurs and extravagances of the young spirit revive as we touch these tangible relics, to conjure again the certainties of home, the confident mystery of family life, and the first intimations of love for individuals, for vague ideas, for the very concept of home, a wider and more comforting assurance than home itself, the four walls, the mother, the father, and all that surrounded them.

These emotions revived, therefore, when I posted my typescript to Dents, though by 1929 I was sufficiently hardened by experience to be able to live behind a façade of professional equanimity. I had met death for the second time. Its cauterizing touch had perhaps healed the nervous sickness that put me out of action during the months of my brother's last illness. I was working just as hard again now, in my double capacity as Civil Servant and author-critic. Indeed, I was working harder, for in both careers accumulative good will brought ever-increasing responsibilities and commissions. I was about to reach the state in which I should no longer be able to serve two masters.

[6]

I was already aware of that dilemma, but dared not allow myself to face it, because my domestic commitments were so heavy. Even so, I was no longer distraught by the ever-multiplying work. The whole rhythm of my life was more free. I felt no break in it, no resistance to it. Happiness, that welcome by-product of a harmonious relationship between personality and environment, shone like the sun, invigorating mind and body.

About this time I realized that something had dropped away. It was the childhood habit of imagined levitation. That mechanism of escape had served me well, balancing the handicap of tubercular sickness and its dormant consequences, through youth and early manhood. Now that I needed no such compensation, the conjuring facility had gone. I realized it suddenly, lying in bed one day, touched by bronchitis. I was re-reading Edwin Arlington Robinson's long poem *Tristram*, which I had reviewed two years earlier for the *Spectator*, and was subdued almost into physical comfort by this undertoned verse.

I needed to be up and active, for the backlog of work was accumulating, at the Ministry and at home. Formerly, this set-back by sickness would have started up the machinery of worry, my breathing would have deepened, as though I were inhaling an anaesthetic gas, my arms would have stretched out at an angle of forty degrees from the shoulders, with hands palm downwards consciously pressing horizontally upon air, and I would have felt myself rising, free, unimpeded by the obtuse force of gravity.

That was the means by which I used to escape from Billings-gate, when I left the Custom House each afternoon, madly eager to get home to my rooms on Denmark Hill, to the intoxication of my books. It was a puerile device, abnormally prolonged in an individual whose conscious effort was to command himself and his work reasonably, and who selected his reading to that end, in philosophy and those poets who made philosophy tangible and concrete.

All this was over now. I looked back upon it that morning, turning from Arlington Robinson's two-dimensional poem in the tone of a wall-piece in tempera by Puvis de Chavannes, and I felt a deep distaste for my former device. It was a form of jumping the queue, and unfair to my fellow-creatures. Just as, in Bible morality, a man who looks upon a woman with lusty eye has committed adultery, so I by my invalid trick of mind had cheated in the struggle of life, the 'daily round and common task' by which people have to earn their living, in circumstances and labours no more congenial to them, than I found the Battersea Board School and Billingsgate congenial to me, young, naïve and self-crowned laureate.

Thus, in being advised by Edward Garnett to send my novel to Dents, I felt that something had come full circle: a small circle, hardly mid-stage in my life, but at that time it seemed adequate, since my cup of happiness was so full.

Two months later, just as we were about to set off for our long walk in the Black Forest and round Lake Constance, the novel was returned from Dents. Even this disappointment did not cloud that first holiday abroad. The visit to Paris two years before had been in different company, at a time when I was nervously sick and oppressed by foreboding caused by my brother's fatal illness.

The railway banks and the valley beds in the Schwarzwald were kneedeep in wild valerian, columbine and iris, whose purple and carmine gave a royal gravity to the character of the Forest. The footpaths through the Forest was still signed with splashes of coloured paint, on the tree trunks or posts, for at the end of the nineteen-twenties the *Wandervogel* were still active. The motor-car had not yet made human legs obsolete. We penetrated up lonely valleys, so quiet, so overhung by steep slopes of pine that we expected them to be inhabited by creatures out of Grimms' fairytales, sinister but enchanting. We visited the museum of clocks at Furtwangen, at the head of the Elz Valley, and reached Donaueschingen, the source of the Danube. We collected a tiny parcel of semi-precious gems from the stone-polishing factory established in the Middle Ages near Waldkirch, and still powered by the musical stream that ran through the building. These were to be worked on by the silversmith at the bench in her bedroom when we got home, embellishing rings, necklaces, brooches, expressive of a personality ever various, ever creative.

Nobody wants to read accounts of other people's holidays, and I am not sure that I want deliberately to recall my own, for adventures abroad are no more rich in wonder than my life at home, under the hazards of work, and the teeming excitement of the so-called monotony of the habitual daily round.

One scene in that German holiday stands out, however, and my memory often returns to it, as to a phrase in a symphony. We reached the extreme western tip of Lake Constance one evening when darkness was settling prematurely and threateningly over the countryside as an alpine thunderstorm gathered. The dark forest lay behind us, thinning out to smallholdings

M

and picturesque wooden farmhouses as we approached the little town of Radolfzell, which stands on the north-western arm of the Unter-See. It is here that the great lake, eight hundred feet in depth, appears to gather up its waters for the titanic task of feeding the mature stream of the Rhine, for its flight northward.

We stood, travel-stained, weary, apprehensive, at the water's edge. The level lay higher than the land, and we could not understand what contained the water within its banks. It had the appearance of a convex surface, as though it were straining in muscular contortion, as layers of mercury do under the oppression of their morbid specific gravity.

But we could not study the water for long because the storm broke, with lurid flashes across the lake that increased the illusion of quicksilver. Under a cannonade of thunder we fled for shelter to a small inn near by. It was a peasants' haunt, but clean and welcoming.

Nor were we the only refugees from the storm, which raged all that evening and through the night. A band of Hungarian gypsies came in. They were on their way to north Germany, to play for the summer season in a sophisticated restaurant in one of the great towns. But here they were *au naturel*, and they played for their supper and night's lodging. Cembalo, fiddles and deeper strings, the music challenged the storm, wrestled with it into the early hours, extemporizing on themes some of which I recognized as folk tunes rescued and civilized by Korbáy, Bartók and Kodály, under the impulse of Franz Liszt.

We lay in the room above, the bed and the crude furniture vibrating in the conflict. Sleep was impossible, though we were physically exhausted after walking all day, bowed under rucksacks. We cursed the storm and the musicians, but listened nevertheless, spellbound by the wildness of sound and setting, under the threat of the brimming lake.

That night evoked the emotional impulse which led me to plan a second novel, whose purpose would be to bring this elemental contest between man and nature down into focus, within the character of a young woman seeking to escape from the ready-made shelter of parental home and then of marriage, so that she could begin her own homemaking. The theme hovered over me like an eagle for the rest of the tour, as we walked on day after day round the Lake to Lindau. I began to write the book, called *High Summer*, soon after we got home.

[7]

I had some encouragement to do so, because a letter from Dents awaited me. It said that a mistake had been made, and asked me to return the typescript of my first novel, *Oliver's Daughter*, as they proposed to publish it.

This began an association that lasted for twenty-one years. During that time Dents' imprint appeared on over twenty of my books. The relationship was congenial, and the firm made no objection when, from time to time, I was asked to write a book, on some special theme, for another publishing house.

This happy relationship between publisher and author was maintained for over two years, coincident with my work at the Ministry, and during that time I delivered the second novel and occasionally advised the firm when they wanted a further opinion on a manuscript.

A novelist's second book always causes anxiety, especially if the first has been well received by the critics and has sold reasonably well. The critics, usually kind to a beginner, withhold their fire. They are waiting to see if the tyro has the staying power and creative objectivity necessary for a professional artist. Too many first novels are the one book which every amateur can wring out of a limited but self-concerned personal experience.

If the beginner lacks that creative energy, he may be tempted to brush up an earlier and frequently rejected manuscript. Or he may not even have the humility to brush it up. His temporary confidence may persuade the publisher, who is inclined to be indulgent after the success of that first venture, to accept this second offering, this little bit of bubble-and-squeak. It is then that the critics pounce.

If, however, the second novel is more mature than the first, the kindly praise from the critics becomes respectful, and much more attentive. If the public's interest is also won, a new novelist joins the ranks of the professional writers, and his publisher's catalogue is thereby enriched. Sometimes, of course the author whose books are now a sound business proposition is lured away by another publisher, and considerable ill will is engendered in the profession of letters.

This trick, common, and said to be legitimate in the business world, will continue so long as human nature follows the law of the jungle, based on fear of starvation. The blame for indulging in it can seldom be placed accurately. The publisher who took the risk in that gamble with the author's first book may be hard-fisted over further contracts. The author, resenting this and hot-headed with vanity over his premature success, will be an easy prey for the poacher. The infidelity may double his income: and incomes are precarious for a writer proposing to make a living from books alone.

Even so, he is ill-advised to break a good-will relationship. It is the beginning of a habit of suspicion, restlessness, and finally of cynicism. Professionally, he will be a homeless man. That is a fate more dreadful the more one contemplates its effects. It means no continuity, no coherence, in the handling of his work; no sympathetic, personal relations between him and the editorial members of the publishing houses with whom he traffics. And personal relationships are important to all artists because of the intangible nature of their work. Good will is a basic need; and good will is homeliness; an ease, a freedom and an unquestioning trust. When an author feels that he is at home within his publisher's imprint, he is able to add confidence to his effort, the unaccountable and always elusive activities by which he lives as an artist.

Further, the practical results are valuable, as are all stable conditions. The lasting association between an author and his publisher is noticed in the profession and by the more intelligent reading public. It is felt, instinctively, that there must be something good in the continuous union. Again, a sense of *home* is created: something recognizable, part of the enduring assets of the community, trustworthy and positive. Like marriage, it is an ingredient in homemaking, and nobody likes to see such a relationship broken.

My association with Dents prospered in this way. After publishing my second novel, *High Summer* (still fragrant with those wild flowers of the Black Forest), Hugh Dent the Chairman of the firm took me out to luncheon one autumn day in 1932. He was obviously uncomfortable, and this made me nervous also. He was a small man, quick, irritable, given to 'good works' and patronage of the arts so long as they were in the Ruskinian mode popular at the time of his boyhood, when his father launched Everyman's Library in covers reminiscent of William Morris's designs for the Kelmscott Press.

But Hugh Dent was also truly benevolent and single-minded. He was somewhat guiltily aware of the parsimony with which his father, a man of genius, had been forced to establish and consolidate the business which now made the son a rich man. The son's loyalty was not to be questioned, as his biography of his father reveals. He was not conscious of a sense of guilt; but it gleamed – a vein of gold – whenever he referred to the history of the firm, and the character of its founder, whom he called 'the Chief'.

His discomfort at that luncheon was due to some personal matter that he wanted to discuss. Usually he fought shy of personalities, especially with authors, a breed that he was not quite prepared to understand. For instance, he thought Joseph Conrad and W. H. Hudson, two masters finally published by Dents, to be 'very queer, very difficult', as no doubt they were. But, with him, their personalities ended there. Not that he blamed them, or penalized their heirs. On the contrary, his generosity to the relics and children of authors proved how sorry he was that they should have had to be dependent on men of so unreliable a profession. He had much more trust in real estate; something concrete, substantial; no nonsense.

His discomfort was thrown off with a violent gesture; very characteristic.

'Look here, my dear fellow,' he burst out, as we stirred our tiny cups of coffee. 'The way you're going on will kill you in a couple of years! How many hours a day are you working? What are your plans? Do you expect to keep it up and maintain the quality? I've only to look at you to know you can't do it! Why, you're a walking skeleton. What d'you weigh?'

'About eight stone,' I said meekly.

'Pah! I'm not surprised!'

His spectacles flashed angrily, and he sat back like a robin defying a songthrush.

'I've a suggestion to make. I don't know much about the Civil Service, or what your prospects are there. It's obvious you have done well, but can you go on at this rate, putting in a full day in Whitehall and doing your writing morning and night? It's not possible. I'll tell you this—'

He leaned over the table and glared at me fiercely, motioning away the waiter who was hovering with the coffee pot.

'—I'll tell you this, my boy. You've got to choose one or the other career.'

'I don't regard the Civil Service as a career,' I said quietly. 'It has never interested me in the least. But I had to earn a living, and I have a family to maintain.'

'Yes, and there's more than that, isn't there?'

This was hardly an accusation; neither was it an approval. I looked into his eyes, whose pupils were enlarged by the lenses of his spectacles, so that they gave the impression of being perpetually dilated by a touch of belladonna. I saw genuine perplexity there, and anxiety on my behalf. I was grateful.

'Quite right,' I said. 'And that adds to my responsibilities.'

There was a pause. I thought my last remark had closed the conversation, and I stood up, preparing to leave. But Dent, who had jumped up (he was always spasmodic in movement, in parallel with his irritability), put a hand on my arm.

'Look here, my dear sir. I'm making a suggestion, and I make it in the light of all we know about you. My colleagues agree.

We propose that if you are willing to take the risk, we will guarantee a long contract as Advisory Editor to us.'

We walked out of the restaurant together and I left him at the dark oaken door of Aldine House. We had not spoken.

'Let me think it over for a day or two,' I said. Our handshake was warm and friendly. He was a wholly trustworthy man.

I walked back down Whitehall to the Ministry, thinking not so much about the offer, as of its coincidence with a conversation held only a week or two previously with Beryl Power. She too had been admonitory about my physical fragility, much to my surprise. Those early years of my new home life had released such confidence and creative energy that I was contemptuous of all obstacles.

Beryl Power was as shrewdly generous as she was beautiful. Her interest in my work was therefore appreciated, and now that she extended it to a concern over my personal affairs I was not affronted. She quite openly urged me to resign from the Service, on the assurance that wider recognition of my writings must certainly follow.

It was a flattering idea, and I was tempted. But to walk out into the wilderness as a freelance literary journalist and occasional novelist unequipped with easy inventiveness was something I dared not face. Not only was I held back by the ever-present realization of my domestic commitments, an absolute responsibility; I was also, by temperament and heredity, wholly remote from the competitive outside world. My parents and grandparents had been salaried workers, in safe occupations. This was so deep-seated an acceptance in my instincts, that the City, all business life, anything to do with money as a primary consideration, connoted dishonesty, as well as the utmost peril. On the other hand, I detested bohemianism, its squalor, incoherence, discomfort and humbug.

Dent's offer, following Beryl Power's disturbing suggestions, moved me successfully out of this nursery-minded fixation. The coincidence of the two approaches took on a super-human authority. I put the matter to the silversmith, as the person instantly concerned. Her answer was equally instant. I must take the risk. I must accept Dent's offer.

[8]

After twenty-four years' service I sent in my resignation. To my astonishment, not only my colleagues, but the higher officials at the Ministry of Labour and the Treasury congratulated me on my decision. I began to suspect that they wanted to get rid of an incompetent incubus! Humbert Wolfe, always generous to me and my work, told me not to worry: the step was inevitable, and that, in addition, certain matters were afoot. I was to learn later what he meant by that last remark, but at the moment I thought it merely one of his picturesque gestures.

I went across Whitehall to the Colonial Office to tell Edward Marsh that I had flung myself over the precipice. He and I had been friendly since we first met some years earlier, but as he never mentioned my work, either prose or verse, I presumed it was repugnant to him. I was not depressed by this, for I thought him to be rather spinsterish, timid, and therefore deprived of a healthy literary appetite. How wrong I was. He had a mind like a gimlet. It showed its steel in his official work. He would not otherwise have spent so many years as private secretary to Winston Churchill, the last man to suffer fools gladly.

I had occasion one day to go over to the Colonial Office to discuss a matter that concerned his Minister as well as the Minister of Labour. I sat in the Private Office with Eddie (as he was known in Whitehall) and, after we had disposed of the official problem in a couple of minutes, we talked of more congenial matters. Any reference to the arts quickly brought Eddie Marsh to the contemporary English painters, whose pictures he bought out of a small civil list pension paid to his family as descendants of Spencer Perceval, the prime minister murdered at the door of the House of Commons by a madman, early in the nineteenth century. Eddie's chambers in Raymond Buildings, Gray's Inn, were cluttered up with masterpieces. They filled the walls of his rooms. They hung on the doors and swung perilously when the doors were opened. They occupied most of the chairs.

I found another overflow on the walls of his room adjoining the Minister's, and of course I had to inspect them and hear their merits pointed out by Eddie with ecstasy, and dramatic gesture. He was a remarkable figure, the last of the Edwardian dandies, bandboxed, Savile Rowed, monocled, the sartorial confection crowned by an almost Mephistophelian head marked by jutting eyebrows with which he semaphored shrewd judgments and murderous unspoken comments on works of art distasteful to him or beyond his comprehension.

With this Augustan wit and social artifice, however, he combined an extreme emotionalism. It showed itself whenever he approached one of his collection of Christopher Wood's paintings. This temperamental artist had committed suicide at an early age, a fact recalled to Eddie when he approached the paintings. The reminder caused him to produce his handkerchief and dab his eyes, from one of which the monocle was simultaneously dropped.

A similar display of grief marked even a casual reference to Rupert Brooke, to whom Eddie had been devoted in those halcyon days, for the privileged few, during the years on the eve of the first world war.

While Eddie was angling for my appreciation of his collection of pictures, after the inspection, we were interrupted by the telephone. I sat in his guest-chair and watched the expressions fleeting across that histrionic face while he listened to the interrupter, who was obviously keyed up. I could hear the excitable voice from where I sat some three yards away. Eddie sighed from time to time, and the famous eyebrows expostulated. An important, but importunate, person from one of the Dominions was demanding to see Winston Churchill. No doubt it would have been difficult to keep him at bay by orthodox procedure. Eddie solved the problem in an instant.

'Impossible,' he whimpered down the telephone, almost in tears again. 'Impossible! The poor dear has *such* a headache!'

And he calmly replaced the receiver and turned to me as though there had been no interruption of our art-talk from the tedious world of officialdom. As Eddie opened the door to see me out, however, he whispered, 'He would have slain me, my dear, he would have killed me, if I had let that dreadful man get near him.' I crossed Whitehall, and as I raised my hat to the Cenotaph, I realized that I had been taught a lesson in the technique of conducting the game of high politics.

I was to find that this technique was not so unusual, and that with infinite variations it was practised outside Governmental circles. It is not principles but personalities that lead, in the arts, the sciences, the Church, in business; wherever men have to contend with each other for place, power and *estime*. Publishing houses are no exception.

[9]

Eddie Marsh taught me more than that. Our acquaintance deepened into friendship when we became near neighbours. In 1935 my wife and I were offered a set of chambers by the Under-Treasurer of Lincoln's Inn. In those uncrowded years, when England was less obscenely populated than it is in the second half of the twentieth century, the Benchers of the Inns of Court liked to have representatives of the arts in residence among their own members. Harold Nicolson lived in King's Bench Walk in the Temple, Edward Marsh in Gray's Inn, Tyrone Guthrie in New Square, Horace Horsnall (of *The Observer*) and C. W. Brodribb (of *The Times*) in Stone Buildings, Lincoln's Inn. I was offered chambers on the top floor of 13 Old Square. Possibly no other writer could be found who was willing to associate himself with that unlucky number. Writers are superstitious creatures, because they work viscerally rather than with their brains, and thereby over-exercise the organs of consultation.

My next-door neighbour was Pethick-Lawrence, the rich, benevolent Labour politician, who with his wife had been a pioneer in the struggle for women's suffrage. He was old and physically shrivelled when I knew him, but his ever-diminishing figure gave off energy like a crumb of radium. It continued to do so as late as 1959, when he was with me at a literary congress in Frankfurt, during a heatwave that prostrated the younger delegates and those from the tropical countries. Such conditions merely increased Lord Pethick-Lawrence's atomic energy.

The chambers below mine in 13 Old Square were still occupied professionally by Sir Frederick Pollock, an international lawyer in his nineties. He had been a famous swordsman, and was still an authority on Spinoza, on whose philosophy he had written a book. This drew me, a devotee of that divine master, like a moth to the flame. Pollock was also distinguished, within a small circle, for having conducted over many years a correspondence with the American judge, Oliver Wendell Holmes, son of the author of *The Autocrat of the Breakfast Table*, that literary breakaway from a Calvinist ancestry.

Until we were driven out by fire during 1940 (a latterday Adam and Eve expelled from Eden), this was our home, principal to a country cottage for family retreat during school holidays. It was a congenial setting, within walking distance of every civil amenity that London could offer. My workroom overlooked the solitary plane-tree in the small square beside Inigo Jones's chapel, and was thus comparatively quiet even during the day. I sat at my table, soothed by the shuffle-shuffle of lawyers' leather as the members of this close fraternity walked between chambers and the Courts, sometimes robed and bewigged. Outside the western gate of the Inn, opening on to the Fields, stood the Land Registry where I began wage earning, at fifteen shillings a week, when I was a boy of sixteen years, starry-eyed, weak in the stomach, and already bewitched by words.

At six o'clock in the evening, and throughout the weekends, a strange, haunted silence fell over the City. The footsteps died away in New Square and Old Square, except for those occasional to a resident, or perhaps a reverent sightseer. The loud roar of traffic up and down Chancery Lane, below the east window of our long sitting-room, died to a trickle, finally to stop with the last bus late at night. The only sounds from midday on Saturday until Monday morning were the whirring of pigeons' wings and the gargling murmur from their throats.

Every quarter of an hour, a sprinkle of chimes fanned out from the clocks of the innumerable City churches, headed by that of St Paul's or Big Ben (as though Wren and Barry could never agree on the matter of procedure, and so submitted to vagary). The sound fell like flower-petals over the dusty streets, to be lost in their emptiness, but not ineffectually, for it left, four times an hour, a faint perfume of history, a conjuration of memories, peopling the deserted city with ghosts.

Our acquaintance was not solely within my own profession. We met many lawyers, and found in common with them a necessary search for precision of language. With one, in particular, we made a family friendship. Edward Holroyd Pearce lived in Stone Buildings with his wife and baby. When not engaged with briefs, he was busy with brushes, as a gifted painter of Alpine landscapes. This secondary passion did not prevent him from rising to the top of his profession.

[10]

The only person who disapproved of my retreat from Whitehall was my father. He was living alone in rooms in Eastbourne, following some disagreement with the 'landlady', who had looked after him since the failure of his second marriage. During this long period of autumnal homelessness, he graduated from motor bicycle to motor-car, to which he remained faithful, through a third matrimonial term that lasted happily until his death in 1955, at the age of eighty-nine.

His passion for the open road mastered him until the end. Fortunately, his last wife, a gentlewoman of small private means, who in spite of having been a sedentary spinster until she married him was tolerant of his gypsylike habits, willingly accompanied him on what he called 'jaunts' at all times of the year, exploring the by-lanes of Great Britain.

Only once did she rebel, when he proposed, in his eighty-fifth year, to buy a trailer caravan, so that they could explore the Western Highlands of Scotland without being restricted to hotels every night. I was called in to dissuade him from this venture, and I was successful only by pretending to be very grave over my brief.

I was saddened by my success, because I knew it must be the prologue to his final surrender. After he agreed to my veto, he looked at me reproachfully out of those clear grey eyes. They were the eyes of a boy eager at the threshold of adventure.

This aspect of his temperament was in contradiction to his play for safety in the matter of earning a living, but I think that both sprang from an innocence, an immaturity, often found in old soldiers.

It was this that dictated his reaction to the news of my resignation from the Civil Service. My letter brought him posthaste from Eastbourne to our flat in Holland Park. It was a Saturday afternoon in March, a week before I was to gain what I believed to be my freedom. I was feeling rather low, because that morning at the Ministry had been spent ceremonially in official farewells, with halting speeches, formal understatements, handshaking all round, the presentation of a gold-banded fountain pen (with wisecracks about 'putting it to good use'), and many private gifts of books and good will, demonstrations that almost reduced me to tears.

I showed these gifts to my father as soon as he arrived. My object was to barricade myself against his reproach, for I knew that must come. After studying him all my life, I had a good working knowledge of what would be his next move.

He looked at the gold pen sorrowfully. 'A good lot of chaps,' he said. 'You'll never find better.'

The old soldier, and the glory of the Regiment, were uppermost. My wife, who could never accept this dominant aspect, fled to the kitchen, leaving me to face the battle alone. I heard the distant and angry sound of crockery, and I recalled, as a drowning man recalls the past, similar occasions of hostility toward my father, shown by someone of a personality entirely different from hers.

'Had you been neglecting your work at the office?' he inquired, after ignoring the other gifts.

I crushed my reply to this, and he attacked from another flank.

'If you'd stayed on, you'd have had a good pension at sixty.'

Again I held my fire. Now he advanced all along the front.

'This writing business! It's all right as a hobby, but you can't expect to live on it.'

This was the strain of Woburn blood showing itself, in a contempt for scribblers. I could sympathize with him there, or at least appreciate his prejudice. But I could no longer restrain myself. Now was my moment, in a contest that had smouldered since my boyhood, beginning with his sarcastic remarks one mealtime about my premature claim to be a poet. That had been dreadful, because I had lost my temper and grasped the bread-knife. My brother Jack, telepathic in his understanding, had saved that situation. He was not here now, but his influence survived. I remained calm.

'It's not as bad as all that,' I said, smiling at my father priggishly, knowing that I was taking advantage of his un-teachability, as my mother had never done. 'You see, though I resigned, steps were taken up above, and I have been given a reduced pension.' He stared at me incredulously. His conception of the Civil Service was almost military, based on his own experience in the Post Office, which in his time was run on a severe discipline.

'Not only that,' I pursued, and I told him about the offer from Hugh Dent, my publisher.

This altogether confounded him. The whole idea of anything outside the Civil Service being stable was beyond his belief. Further, that 'this writing business' could be a respectable remunerative activity, on which a man might support a family without the hazard of starvation and throwing his children on the parish, was outside his range of consciousness.

I knew that I should never convince him otherwise; and I never did. Every time we met during the subsequent twenty-two years, he would shake his head sadly, with the remark, 'Pity you ever left the Service, my boy,' and follow it up with the unhopeful inquiry, 'Are you making a living with this writing business?'

He refused the evidence of his eyes, as he watched, year by year, our homemaking, in Lincoln's Inn, and then in our Kentish home, where on a hilltop, and a corner of a remote cherry-orchard, the silversmith put her skill to work on larger and more various materials, expressing always in concrete form a personality which continued to overflow into mine, with energy and enterprise.

My father always acted as though suspecting all this to vanish overnight, a figment of my wilful fancy, the daydream for which he had always reproached me. The distrust made its last appearance on his deathbed.

One cold February weekend in 1955, I was at Cambridge, taking part in a debate in the Union. The morning that we were leaving the house of our host, the Master of Pembroke College, I had a message to say my father was failing.

My wife drove us home to Kent, and there I got more details of the illness. An hour later I set out alone, through the Wealden country white with moonlit frost. The road along the mid-Weald ridge, through Kipling's Burwash, was empty, except for one badger which I saw at the entrance to a wood beyond Heathfield. He stared up at my headlights, which threw up his white markings, so that he looked like Grimaldi the clown crouching there.

The moment registered indelibly on my mind, as though to ensure that the larger occasion should not be distorted and destroyed by the conflagration of anxiety and grief. For I was indeed full of grief, though I had had no close association or dealings with my father since I left his widowed home in 1911, forty-four years earlier. We had lived in affectionate conflict, foreign in our attachments, our fervours. He had refused to acknowledge my career in the world of letters, and had been hostile to my ménages both as young bachelor and as married man. I had been angered by his irresponsibility and obtuseness, and alarmed by his absurd matrimonial ventures, to say nothing of one extra-matrimonial.

As I drove at speed that night through a world purified by frost, I reviewed this troubled relationship between father and son, and saw it clear itself, simplify itself into the old, Biblical bond on which most religions are founded, and all biological evolution. I once even found myself shaping the word aloud, 'Father! Father!' so powerful was my emotional concentration on something troubling me by its profundity, its vast significance far beyond the scope of reason, or the prejudices and personal conflicts within the confinement of any two individuals bound by this tie, father and son.

I reached his house just before midnight. It stood exposed below the racecourse, on the heights above Lewes prison. I looked up after I had left the car in front of the garage. The red curtain was drawn across the lighted window of my father's bedroom. I stood for a moment, wondering how I was to get into the house; for his wife was stone-deaf. The red glow from the window answered me; the signal of someone waiting.

The front door was on the latch, and I went in, shutting the door after me, for I knew the old lady was terrified of burglars, and indeed of all strangers.

She met me in the hall, and whispered in the loud, off-stage voice of the deaf, to tell me that father had been sent home from the hospital because he was so troublesome. He had insisted on coming home, and had even struggled with nurses and male attendants, in efforts to get out of bed, dress himself and make for home.

I pacified the old lady and persuaded her to go back to bed.

Then I went into my father's room and sat down beside him. He lay on his back, drowsily murmuring. I could distinguish only a word here and there.

The frosty wind sighed over the house, and the gasfire flickered under the down-draught. The glow from it was sufficient to light the room, and I switched off the light; not, however, before I found myself, shamefacedly, looking at the reading matter which had been pushed aside to make room for the usual paraphernalia of the deathbed.

He had been re-reading *Highways and Byways in Wiltshire* and *Awheel in the Welsh Marches*. The latest issue of *The Motor* smelled fresh from the press. It had not been opened.

I wrapped myself in a blanket and sat waiting. I even dozed off, weary after a long day on the road, a day that would have delighted the old warrior. I watched him closely when his restlessness woke me. The firelight gleamed on his nose and cheekbones, now more prominent. Age and decay had not robbed him of his good looks.

In the small hours I was wakened by the cold. I rewrapped myself in the blanket and was about to doze off again, when Father stirred. The uncertain rhythm of his breathing changed, becoming less stertorous. He turned his head, and I saw that his eyes were open. He was looking at me.

'Well, my boy,' he said. The words were somewhat slurred. 'Left the car inside? Don't waste the battery. Hope you've given it a wash-down.'

I assured him that all was well, and that I had not betrayed his training. His mind wandered a little, then he returned to ask about the drive, state of the roads.

'That's a nasty corner, coming into Burwash. Took it carefully, didn't you?'

Something was still worrying him. He muttered and fretted, and I tried to make him more comfortable in bed, but he waved me away.

'No good now; doesn't matter. Tried to keep me away from home. I wouldn't have it. Want to be at home for the end.'

This peevishness died away into vague murmurings. Then

N

he rallied, the grey eyes refocussed on me, clear and suspicious.

'Are you all right, my boy? Making a living, I mean; writing business?'

It was useless to reply, so I tried to reassure him by putting my hand on the bedclothes, above his arm. A moment passed, and then he spoke again, but less distinctly.

'Pity – pity you left the Service, my boy.'

That was the last coherent sign he ever made. Toward daybreak he slipped either into sleep or unconsciousness, lingering in that purgatory for another day and night, before he finally reached home.

After the funeral, during the drive back to our oasthouse, we talked about him dispassionately, there being no cause for sorrow. But I had a sense of nakedness. The last opposition to my choice of work and career had been removed. I wondered if I could do without it, in a life which seemed perpetually new.

CHAPTER NINE

On the Threshold

[1]

THE CAREER AND WORK which my father had so anxiously deplored took instant command as soon as I was released from Whitehall. I had no misgivings. I realized that a man can have no greater happiness than to earn his living at work which is also a vocation, work that is rounded and whole, to contain the worker's substantial personality, both subconscious and philosophic.

How wise were the Christian mythologists to represent Jesus as a carpenter. In his day the work was a handicraft, carried through from start to finish by a marriage between the wood and the worker, the medium and the man. It is a wholly expressive union. I find today, even in this machine age, that wood has a unique significance for me, and whenever I hear that a man is a carpenter, my imagination clothes him with simplicity, benevolence and holiness.

I remember that my first sensation, on leaving the Civil Service and taking up my editorial post at Dents, was of serenity, as though I were a carpenter. At last I felt at one with my tools. The morning that I left Montague House for the last time, I hurried away, but halted when I reached Trafalgar Square. A curious association of ideas, or emotions, arrested me.

Though I was eager to rush home, drunk on liberty, I went first and stood outside Charing Cross Hospital, to stare at its façade, from outside the shop-window of Bains, the bookseller. I knew, or rather my bones knew, that inside the hospital was the surgeon who had begun his working life with me in 1911 when we were boys, in the Government Laboratory in the

Custom House. He had been more courageous than I; sensible enough not to trammel himself at the beginning of his career with a young family. So now I wanted to ask him about his sensations on stepping into the freedom of a chosen vocation, out of the bondage of an uncongenial wage-earning job. This indeed must have been a step homeward. I knew what a resolute, incisive character he was. Could it be that I was now putting on a similar garment of self-confidence?

A surgeon, a carpenter, a poet, maybe even a soldier: all men of vocations, and only secondarily careerists; something mystical about them.

I stood there for some ten minutes, thinking of my friend at work on that top floor, in the operating-theatre. Then the fantasy faded, and common sense took command, to drive me home to Holland Park, though I still walked on air when I emerged from the Underground station and followed the crescent of Holland Park, beside the woods which contained the bottom of the grounds of Holland House, sheltering owls that hooted at night, waking us to illusions of remote country.

Remote country! How absurd, to foster this fantasy. Nobody quite loses it. Even when it shrinks to some petty desire which reason repudiates, it is of the same origin as this dream of spacious adventure. Most great human achievements spring from it, and they in their sum make a civilization.

I had not much to show, as I walked from the Underground suburban station that Saturday midday, a middle-aged Government clerk released from what he believed to be servitude, touched with something of the apprehension felt by Charles Lamb's Superannuated Man. But I snuffed the odour of the April sap rising in the trees of Holland Park wood, and once again the exultation seized me, the sensation of complete translation of my restricted self, body, mind and soul, into the world around me.

Now I was experienced enough to recognize this condition. I stopped outside the house next door to that where we had our flat. It was the home of the London Music Club. Someone was practising the piano, deft-fingered at the scales. The delicious stream of sound, in its pulses of eight, made me catch my breath as though I had stooped and put my lips to a cold fountain.

The pianist stopped playing, and I returned to earth. I was about to move on, when the music began to flow afresh; but now it was a gay movement from one of the Vivaldi concertos transcribed by Bach for the keyboard. I recognized it at once, and I saw my brother Jack sitting at the instrument, in our rooms, on Denmark Hill twenty years earlier. He turned his head as he was playing, and nodded to me, approving, assenting.

The perfume from the budding trees beyond the railings opposite the house, the music that shared its speed and in-sinuation, the reappearance of my brother from beyond the grave, all these tangibilities united to celebrate my home-coming, enlarging a minor, private event into an oratorio, universal and loud with praise.

[2]

Hugh Dent insisted that I should go away for a complete rest before taking up my editorial duties. So my wife and I went off without delay to the south-west corner of France, where the Pyrenees come down to the Mediterranean at the Spanish frontier. Before the Spanish civil war and the second world war, Collioure and its neighbouring villages round that curve of the Côte Vermeille were untouched by tourism. The sculptor Maillol still lived unmolested in his native town of Banyuls.

The night before we left, however, our friend and neighbour Lascelles Abercrombie called, bringing two strangers, a young newly married couple. Abercrombie was a saintly person, of wide literary scholarship, a quick, vivacious temperament, a happy family man whose benevolence showed in his children's characters and later achievement. He was at that time Professor of English at Bedford College, and was the only poet, besides Robert Bridges, to have his collected verse published during his lifetime by the Oxford University Press in the Standard English Poets series. This distinction, however, failed to impress him. He was so busy living, and encouraging other people to expand their capacity for living.

It was characteristic of him, therefore, to undertake to find a home, though only temporary, for this young couple who had been enthusiastic enough to get married without ensuring that they should have a roof over their heads. The bridegroom was a lecturer in history at London University. He had just been snatched from his job by Lord Rutherford (whose genius was a law unto itself), to take on the secretaryship of the Academic Assistance Council, an organization set up to receive and find posts for refugee professors and lecturers turned out of German universities by the Nazis, who had come into power in April 1933.

The bride was a White Russian girl of noble birth. Her family had escaped via the Balkans during the Revolution, and had existed, homeless, in one European spa after another, Dostoevsky fashion, its male members dropping off the family tree, sometimes self-assisted, as time gradually withered the exposed roots. She was, inevitably, a stoic who drifted on the tides of fate with complete equanimity and good humour.

Abercrombie peered at me through his little steel-rimmed spectacles, like a High Court Judge. In facial appearance, he reminded me of another friend, Alfred Bucknill, who *was* a High Court Judge, and also *was* a saint. I was condemned by the Court to receive this young couple into our spacious flat for a few weeks during our absence, until they could find a place of their own.

They were still there when we returned six weeks later, and there they remained for two years until we gave up the flat and removed to the chambers in Lincoln's Inn. For the second time in my life a newly married couple had come to stay for a few weeks, and had remained for two years. I still am not sure which sojourn I enjoyed the more; that of the beekeeper who filled my little house in Limpsfield with honey from his hives in the garden, or the brilliant academic administrator who filled my flat in Holland Park with an unbroken stream of refugees from Germany, most of them Jewish.

I remember that we housed one for some weeks while he was waiting for arrangements to be concluded that should establish him in a post in America. He was a civil servant named Jaffe. He was sitting with me, during the evening before his departure, and the name of D. H. Lawrence was mentioned. 'Yes,' he said in faultless English; 'He was a wonderful man, and I owe much to him.'

This was said with so personal an inference that I probed further. It appeared that his mother was a sister of Frieda Lawrence and that when he was a boy of fourteen he fell ill, and was sent out to Mexico to stay with his aunt and the irascible poet. He told me that Lawrence had befriended him, talked to him of books, shown him how to light fires in the open, to build a wall, to handle animals; to discover himself. This confirmed what Richard Aldington had told me about Lawrence, and what Aldous Huxley revealed in his preface to the edition of Lawrence's letters.

It is a remarkable thing that most men of genius radiate this magnetic virtue, attracting people by their candour and simplicity. It is known that John Keats possessed or was possessed by this divine quality of childlike directness, this innocence, this naïvety. Such a person is the opposite of the political man, who is needed to be the administrator, a leader in the ordering of social life. If this genius should appear in the character of a politician, it carried him up from the hurly-burly of politics into statesmanship. Abraham Lincoln was a prime example. So have been Herbert Asquith, Ben Gurion and Ernest Bevin: marked by simplicity, a homing sense, massive and unbreakable.

I have already shown how it contained, within a miniature compass, the nature of the poet W. H. Davies. I found it too in other poets, Edmund Blunden, Walter de la Mare, Edwin Muir, Laurie Lee, Edith Sitwell, Dylan Thomas. As their work reveals, these are creatures of genius as well as talent. The talent has given them industry and method. The genius has added a wilful, elusive quality to their work, to make it immortal.

Edmund Blunden was our first visitor when we set up home in London in 1928. I had heard his name, and read his poem 'Almswomen', ten years earlier. I showed the poem in *The Nation* to W. H. Davies, when visiting him at 14 Great Russell Street. We both admired it, and he read it aloud, rubbing his hands together before taking the copy of *The Nation* from me. He had just stoked up the basket-stove, placing the coal piece by piece with his fingers. As he finished reading, he looked up in alarm, an expression frequent in a man prone to persecution mania.

'But *mon*!' he said, 'I've read this poem in Squire's magazine, *The London Mercury*! What has the boy done? He'll ruin himself!'

Everything was liable to *ruin*, in Davies's world. The word was dominant in his conversation. But Blunden survived. Both J. C. Squire of *The London Mercury*, and Harold Massingham of *The Nation*, were ardent advocates of his work, and I never heard further reference to the simultaneous appearance in two magazines of the now immortal 'Almswomen'.

Blunden had returned to England in 1928 after three years as Professor of English at Tokyo, where he made himself so endeared that later in life he was sent there again as a cultural plenipotentiary.

Though he is a shy, distrait person, he has a gift for inspiring students. After his terms at Tokyo, he was given a Fellowship of Merton College, Oxford, and there the magic of his personality worked as it had done in Japan.

At our first meeting, I watched him while he sat, back to the wall, at the dining-table in Holland Park, and I had the impression that he was a bird of passage, blown in by the storms of life, exhausted but wary. The beaky face, the keen, staring eyes, the sensitive body that seemed to be quivering with nervous apprehension, confirmed my impression that here was a being, half bird, half man, like one of those figures drawn by Stone Age artists in the caves of the Dordogne.

In face-to-face conversation he was hesitant, self-interrupting, a habit possibly emphasized that night by shyness at a first meeting. I could not have helped him, for I am likewise conditioned at first contacts, and am liable to lapse into silence, or to offer mechanical remarks that must make me appear to be half imbecile.

Blunden went off late that night, to catch the last train to Oxford. He had made a lasting impression on me, to confirm my belief that the truly fecund, creative person is invariably candid, simple, and direct. No matter how subtle, complex or volatile he may be, in mind and character, all is fused into unity by the fire of genius, the unaccountable, indefinable addition that differentiates him not only from other people, but also from his social self.

A few lines from one of Blunden's poems sum up this dichotomy, and express not only the secret of Blunden's own nature, but that of other individuals, such as his friend Alan Porter, and Walter de la Mare, whose attributes and achievements are drawn together by a single purpose.

> So rise, enchanting haunting faithful,
> Music of life recalled and now revealing
> Unity; now discerned beyond
> Fear, obscureness, casualty,
> Exhaustion, shame and wreck,
> As what is best,
> As what was deeply well designed.

[2]

As a result of my work on various journals and magazines while I was still a Civil Servant, I had already met a large number of writers, especially journalists, before I became a whole-time professional. There is a quality common to journalists. It is generosity, the mark of soldiers of fortune. They live dangerously, and this gives them that tough kindness always to be found on the battlefield. I made many friendships among such men and women, and profited both in person and in literary technique, and this in spite of the fact that most of these people were concerned mainly with politics, of which I knew little; and what little I knew I abhorred and distrusted, after so many years of washing dirty Parliamentary linen in the privacy of Whitehall.

Harold Laski I had met in 1922, at one of *The Criterion* luncheons. He had just returned from America, primed with up-to-date theory on international affairs. The austere atmosphere of that luncheon table froze his young exuberance, and I watched the constriction gathering in cloud over his eloquent brown eyes and neat features.

He was a small, almost tiny figure, hardly strong enough to carry that domed head, with its burden of knowledge, gathered and stored in a prodigious memory. Behind the display which was so obviously disapproved, I suspected a strong emotional directive that would carry this load of academic theory into practice.

I walked along Knightsbridge with him after the luncheon, and he unburdened himself of the resentment stored up during the meal. He never changed his opinion of that group, and I think he was wrongly prejudiced, suspecting political opposition, whereas the snubs had been those administered to a precocious, effervescent junior.

Our liking for each other, like most friendships, was due to no particular bent. I was mildly indifferent to his Labour leanings, and I loathed the arid Fabianism whose documentary, card-index techniques had begun to transform the Civil Service from what it had been in the days of Trollope and Edmund Gosse, to what it had become under the influence of Beveridge and Passmore. I got out just in time to save myself from desiccation.

Laski was a bookman, however. He was a browser in the twopenny bins. He loved first editions, and gloated over rarities. But he also loved the contents, in verse or prose, and had the ability for remembering page after page, verbatim. It was awe-inspiring to listen to his talk, either in private or from the public platform, as the periods rolled out upon that slightly metallic voice, the arguments illustrated by quotations, paged and numbered, or from speeches which he had heard from authoritative lips years earlier. Computers had not been invented in those days of the nineteen-twenties; but Harold Laski was endowed with such a mechanism in addition to the human sensibilities, and a great and generous heart that compelled my love and respect.

H. W. Nevinson and H. N. Brailsford were both great editors under whom I served. They had often worked together, their most notable duet being their exposure of the Belgian atrocities, at the turn of the century, when the rapacious King Leopold of the Belgians exploited the Congo, as a private estate, enslaving its natives in the process.

I met both journalists on *The Nation*, before it was merged into the *New Statesman*, and I continued, in their company, to write for the amalgamated weekly while Desmond MacCarthy was in charge of the literary pages. Brailsford became Editor of the Labour weekly *The New Leader*, and I worked for him there, learning to appreciate what journalism can be at its best. He was a noble character, Cromwellian in principle and doggedness: small in figure, with iron-grey hair *en brosse*, and unsmiling eyes behind large-lensed spectacles.

Our acquaintance moved, without comment from either of us, into a quiet friendship. His wife, the engraver Clare Leighton, had craftsmanship in common with my wife, the silversmith and jeweller. He and I, meanwhile, would stroll about in the beech woods of Buckingham surrounding his home at Whiteleaf. We discussed the demerits of William Godwin, the mental fervours of Shelley, the fiscal pioneering of Robert Owen, and the aesthetics of William Morris. Brailsford's grimness tended to bring socialism out of the picturesque medievalism of its Kelmscott manifestations, as expressed in Robert Blatchford's weekly paper *The Clarion*. But he was too spiritual, in a passionately secular way, to lead it into the statistical corridors of the Fabian Society. He was a deeply emotional man, and a revolutionary worthy to keep company with the Old Testament prophets, Amos and Jeremiah.

His friend Henry W. Nevinson, tall and handsome, with the grand manner, was a belated Elizabethan, expansive in his scholarship, and a reckless privateer in his attack on all that he believed to be evil. Goethe was one of his idols, and in the eighteen-eighties he went to Weimar University to learn the language, enriched by this master.

In 1931 Nevinson published an essay on the life and work of the poet-scientist-statesman, as a tribute for the coming centenary of his death.

At the time when this book appeared, we were on holiday with him and his wife Evelyn Sharp (a pioneer among women journalists), in the Black Forest. To be in his company was to be tempted to exuberance, and as a result of this influence I said, after introducing him to the friends with whom we were to stay in Waldkirch, 'He is a splendid fellow!'

Throughout the visit he was addressed as 'Herr Splendid', by the doctor, his wife, daughter and the two peasant women who served in the professional household. There could be no more apt description of him. It covered his regal appearance, his grandeur combined with modesty, his gestures of spontaneous heroism.

Our holiday was cut short by the news that the British pound sterling had crashed. Nevinson, who at heart was an old-fashioned English patriot, behaved as though universal chaos was at hand. He insisted on going home, and I feared that as soon as we landed he would rush to support Dover Cliff with his gallant shoulder.

So the party of four, headed by Herr Splendid, were seen off at the railway station by an almost tearful family, and I was deprived of the opportunity to take the Nevinsons to see the museum of clocks farther up the Elz valley at Furtwangen, an enterprise which I thought to be of much more importance than salvaging the wreckage of international currencies.

Nevinson's peer in the possession of a magnetic personality was Robert Lynd, Literary Editor of the *News Chronicle* and weekly essayist on the *New Statesman* under the initials 'Y.Y'. He combined an obstinate individualism with tolerance toward all folk: bigots, criminals, even Civil Servants. He had an Irishman's disregard for time. Whenever I called for him, at lunchtime or early evening, at his office, I had to dig him out of the dusty room set solid with books and papers. They rose in barricade from the floor to waist height, and over them could be seen a shambling figure lying back on a chair draped under a bit of carpet, his feet occupying the only clear space on the desk before him, his two hands clasping an open book held up to conceal head and face. From behind the book a blue spiral of cigarette smoke rose leisurely. The composition was Robert Lynd, reading.

Thus enthroned, he administered the literary columns of the paper, in a pool of quietude amid the distant thunder of the presses, and the time-neuroses of his fellow-journalists. He had a gift for gathering talented young men round him, who subsequently went out to wider and less tranquil fields. Norman Collins and Lionel Hale are notable examples of that novitiate.

My entering would cause him to lower the book, look at me over his spectacles, without raising his bent head, and make a statement, standard as an opening of conversation:

'Ach! I've given up looking at books nowadays. The giants have all gone!'

We might be late for a luncheon appointment with other Fleet Street worthies, but Lynd must always stop to buy a midday or evening paper from the man at the corner of Shoe Lane. And having bought it, shaken it out, and scanned the stop-press, he then discussed the odds with the vendor, passing from that theme to life in general. After I had taken him by the arm and persuaded him farther toward the rendezvous, he would explain, 'An old friend of mine, Joe. Keeps his blind mother; has done, for the past thirty years.'

It was not easy to follow his broguish conversation, especially amid the uproar of Fleet Street and its taverns. He never turned his head toward the person addressed. Thus his speech had the quality of soliloquy. Further, it was delivered in a ventriloquial manner, from lips compressed over a permanent cigarette-end, which semaphored up and down with the semi-articulations.

Walking or sitting, he stooped, a stance that caused him always to be looking upward from eloquent brown eyes, full of pathos. But what devastating shrewdness they concealed. It was too powerful an ingredient in his nature to be suppressed, and it escaped through snide remarks dropped as parentheses to his general good humour and kindliness. In profile, the bent figure had the quality of a Fra Angelico painting: saintly, and sustained almost entirely on double whiskies, for he merely toyed with solid foods.

He lived in a charming country villa in Keats Grove, Hampstead, near the Wentworth Place where the poet sat under the mulberry tree and wrote the 'Ode to a Nightingale'; and where the wrongly maligned Fanny Brawne and her mother nursed him during the middle period of his fatal illness. Keats's noble character, an emanation of good will, haunts the grove still, and I believe that Robert Lynd must have been attracted there as a bird of the same feather.

His home was a nest of literary hospitality, for his wife Sylvia, the poetess, was an active hostess. The rooms had the quality of depth, of the absorption of sound, to be found in country houses where the family has been established for centuries, amid an accumulation of intimate treasures, possibly worthless or worn but creative of a general impression of endearing privacy, each item adding its history to the unique personality of the interior, and to the illusion of permanence.

[3]

How inadequate are a catalogue of names, and a gallery of thumbnail word-portraits, as a means of evoking the riches and the mystery of friendship. Merely to discuss it, thereby giving it publicity, seems like a betrayal or, what is no more pardonable, a boast. But nobody can portray his own life without introducing his friends. Without them he is likely to appear as a monster, lacking sane measurement, incapable of establishing, and finally ascending to, that home which is the last continent of all living creatures, and especially of man. Without this sense of home, and its sanctity, there can be no religions, and no civilization.

Friendship is the life-blood of that reality, the home. Without it, the confinement becomes a prison, a religion becomes a dogma, a civilization hardens into a slavery. I think of how it began with me, with the Biblical circumscription of Mother, Father and Brother: capital figures in my infant universe, remaining as cornerstones of it even today, surviving death and the attrition of time as it rubs away at my emotional vitality and dulls imagination, that sole instrument for measuring ordinary things and proving them to be infinite.

There was no need, in those infant days, to try to identify home. There was no other environment. Beyond the house-door lay nothing but vagueness, twilight and shadows, dark-ness and fears. Gradually consciousness ventured farther, made new emotional and even rational attachments. The seedling of friendship, the tree of life, was taking root, and spreading.

But as soon as we begin to discuss this awe-inspiring growth, we fall into generalities, with words that mean little because they have served too long: upon altars, in marriage-beds, in times of danger, and of conviviality. The nature and power of friendship meanwhile elude definition. We are reduced to recollecting examples of it in action, in embodiment, in records of sacrifice; and indeed of every virtue of which the living creature is capable, either consciously as with man, or by instinct as with animals. Friendship is ever active, where there is warmth, blood-pulse, the magnetism of desire, the discipline of thought, the recognition of duty. Those are also old-fashioned words, but their validity remains constant.

I remember talking about verbal fashion, and the ebb and flow of moral standards, with Harold Laski and Felix Frank-furter, one summer day in Essex, between the wars. For six years after I left Whitehall in 1933, my wife and I had a fifteenth-century cottage on the plateau between Saffron Walden and Thaxted. It had been the dower house to the nearby moated Tiptofts, the manor of the notorious Earl of Worcester, known as 'The Butcher' because of his Renaissance cruelties during the Wars of the Roses. He was more than that, however, for he had studied in Padua, was an elegant scholar, and brought some cultural refinement even to those cold East Anglian acres. Caxton said of him that he 'flowered in virtue and cunning, to whom I know none like among the lords of the temporality in science and moral virtue'. That was great praise from England's first printer-publisher.

Something of the earl's personality, an emanation both sinister and stylish, still lingered about that old manor, and our eight-roomed, thatched cottage two meadows distant. We had three vast open fireplaces, one of them containing a bread-oven which projected outside the brick chimney-stack like a rounded pottery kiln. The River Pant, later to become the Blackwater, rose in a spring-pond in our garden, and was our only water-supply. None of the children caught dysentery or typhoid.

Harold Laski and his wife Freda had a cottage in Great Bardfield, to which they retreated whenever Freda decided that her husband needed a few hours of rest. He would not have survived without her passive but resolute care. His frail body would have sublimated into radioactivity, wave-lengths of eloquent talk and cerebration. But at home in the book-lined house on Addison Bridge, near Olympia, or in rustic Bardfield, Laski remained irrepressible. In town and country, he wore his black coat and striped trousers, with a black hat slipping back over that great domed head.

No more incongruous setting could be found for the summer afternoon's conversation held that day, between myself as host, Laski, and the already famous American judge whom he had brought over from Bardfield. Frankfurter was big, rough, leonine. His voice boomed across the plateau and reverberated from the Gog Magog Hills. The great elm trees round our garden shivered, and the grove of poplars clashed their hair-sprung leaves in applause. For once Laski had to listen, instead of leading the talk. I sat spellbound before this giant's vitality, and my old Aberdeen terrier lay at my feet, his nozzle on one shoe, blinking at the bombardment of words. I have never known such a dynamic. Not even Kingsley Martin, then Editor of the *New Statesman*, also a frequenter of our cottage, from the old beerhouse which he had put back into privacy near Dunmow, could have remained in action against such a verbal onslaught of wisdom, in politics, philosophy, philology, the arts, and comparative religions. In all these branches of human knowledge both Harold and Kingsley were at home, and authoritative; but Judge Frankfurter, later to become President Roosevelt's remembrancer, was the whale who could swallow, and retain, both these Jonahs in one gulp.

It is a curious characteristic of editors. All those I have known, and worked for, are what I call bearers-down: great and overwhelming talkers, perpetually ebullient. Brailsford was the only exception. He exerted his conductorship by remaining in one position, quiet but dogged and unshakable. The rest, J. L. Garvin, of *The Observer*, St Loe Strachey of the *Spectator*, H. W. Massingham of *The Nation*, Kingsley Martin, Desmond MacCarthy and John Freeman of the *New Statesman*, Hamilton Fyfe of the *Daily Herald*, Wilson Midgley of *John O' London's*, these are a few examples to prove that the vocation of editor of any periodical, if it is to be successful, demands a person who is expressive, and seen and heard to be expressive: one who not only is loquacious in the editorial chair, but is able to draw his contributors, whatever their gifts and idiosyncrasies, to a willing unity as a team.

Perhaps I am writing too mysteriously about the hackneyed quality called leadership. But one word cannot contain it, for it is ubiquitous, and it emerges in all walks of life: orchestral conductors, financiers, industrialists, great doctors, soldiers, lawyers and clerics. Invariably, all are expressive. They pronounce themselves with emphasis, at least in their work. Sometimes they do it with grace and charm, sometimes with brutality and ruthless egoism. They are not necessarily creative, but they

o

are always leaders. We should not have a cohesive human society without them. But they need the contemplative, the mystic and the artist, to remind them of the deeper and more lasting authority of home, with its attributes of tenderness, intimacy, and the final discipline of solitude.

[4]

My editorial work at Dents at once brought me into contact with a younger generation of writers, and part of my function was to encourage them, seek them out, in the search for new literary talent. Having publication to offer, and payment for it, I was overwhelmed. So long as a man is in office, he need not fear a lack of suppliants, with their attendant flattery.

I was warned of this, among other dangers, by Frank Swinnerton, whose literary life has been somewhat similar to mine, though he had a harder struggle at the beginning, as he has revealed in his memoirs: for instead of sheltering during the sapling years in the Civil Service, he started his career as an office-boy in Dents, when the firm was building up under its formidable founder, J. M. Dent.

Nobody in the profession of letters, therefore, has had a more comprehensive knowledge of it, from the extreme points of view of publisher and author. As an author, his work needs no bush. He is a master craftsman in the art of the novel: subtle, tense, dramatic in characterization; comparable to George Gissing in his evocation of atmosphere; unique in a personal overtone of shrewd wisdom. Like J. B. Priestley, he has been too successful to be idolized by the literary fashion-mongers. Both these men are valuable critics, not only at large as reviewers, but privately as friends. Their silences, where they disapprove, can be salutary. They have a large literary perspective, and have indulged a healthy appetite for reading in English letters over the centuries. Thus they do not ignore the giants of the past, nor accept without discrimination the giants of the present. They are believers in the selective judgment of Time, that most dispassionate of all critics. They both write pure, virile and nervous English.

I first met Priestley at a housewarming given by the poet Frank Kendon, then newly married. Worldwide fame and prosperity had suddenly floated Priestley out of the semi-privacy of the restricted field of the weekly reviews, the occasional essay, and the scholarly literary biography. His novel *The Good Companions* had done for him what *The Pickwick Papers* did for Dickens a century earlier.

None of this, however, appeared to interest Priestley that night. He had just returned from a holiday in Italy, and was enthusiastically concerned with the wonders of the famous marine aquarium in Naples. He could hardly contain himself, and had to impersonate the character and goggle-eyed appearance of each of the deep-sea monsters in turn.

This endeared him to me instantly, and I have never since lost that attraction. He too has the virtue of simplicity, to be found in most people who have mastered a craft, or any means of self-expression. Priestley may present a mask of Yorkshire truculence to the world at large, but behind it is an artist, sensitive to quiet values, shrewd in judgment.

As we parted that night, he smiled wickedly at me and said, 'We like each other more than we like each other's work.' This was too complicated for me, and I could not retort. It would have been premature, perhaps unctuous, to say that I enjoyed his work, especially his essays, a form in which he is a master. His later development as a dramatist was still to come. *I Have Been Here Before* and *Johnson over Jordan* brought not only new ideas but new courage to the theatre. His constructive critical survey *Literature and Western Man* puts him with George Saintsbury, Quiller-Couch, and Van Wyck Brooks. They are all enjoyers of literature, and have imparted that enjoyment to millions of their fellow creatures, most of whom have had no opportunity to savour so much, and have small confidence in academic pundits of limited and often invalid appetite.

Swinnerton and Priestley are professional men to a degree

that few reach in the world of letters. They are successful novelists, columnists, reviewers. They know the art of publishing and have both been publishers' advisers, a difficult and often thankless occupation. When a book fails, the publisher believes he has been badly advised by his reader. When a book succeeds, he attributes that to the prestige of his imprint and excellent sales organization.

In fact, literary success and failure are largely unaccountable. Publishing is a mystery, and a gamble. On that assumption, a man may venture, with capital, hard work, experience and a personal flair, and is likely to become an established publisher, provided he aims at building up a catalogue of substantial titles that need no advertising. This cannot be done to a prescription. Luck plays a part. A general election, or public catastrophe, may suddenly occur, and ruin a publisher's seasonal list. For books are the diet of tranquillity, and if the retort is made 'What about wartime reading?' I would suggest that war is not one long crisis, but rather one long boredom which has at all costs to be relieved by mental and aesthetic exercise.

Frank Kendon also had a professional knowledge and experience. After being a literary editor in Fleet Street, he went to the Cambridge University Press as Second Secretary. This post was but sparsely involved in commercial problems, and it admirably suited this strange, otherworldly poet. He had been up at Cambridge after the first world war, with Priestley, Gerald Bullett, and other ex-combatants. He came from a remote hamlet in the hinterland of Kent, an upland valley in the ridge that runs through the centre of the Weald from Folkestone to Lewes. Kipling's Pook's Hill is to be found along that ridge, and there is a Pook's Wood adjoining the hamlet where Kendon was born in 1893. Such recurrence of the name is proof that this countryside has been the resort of the Little People. Their benevolent if mischievous influence survives.

Into this scene Kendon's grandfather, a sick missionary, retired in 1866, and set up a school. It is now a flourishing boarding-school for boys. There Kendon was born, the eldest son in a large family. While he was in Fleet Street, he wrote a

little book about his infancy in that school. It is a masterpiece
because of its insighted recollection of a child's view of life. It is
written in a prose that matches the theme. I would compare that
prose to a glass of water drawn up from a deep cold well. The
mist collects on the outside of the glass. That is the poetry in
Kendon's prose. The book, *The Small Years*, was published,
with an introduction by Walter de la Mare, by the Cambridge
University Press in 1930, and I reviewed it in the *Spectator*.
Shortly after, no doubt consequently, I was introduced to him
by C. Henry Warren, who served with him in the campaign in
Palestine, though they did not meet until they were on a home-
ward-bound troopship.

Kendon's experience in the Holy Land resulted in a long
narrative poem called *The Life and Death of Judas Iscariot*, which
was published by the distinguished Bodley Head press, who
also put out several collections of his lyrical poems. All his
verse is marked by simplicity, a controlled passion and tenderness sometimes almost too intense to be borne, although always
held back by the discipline of traditional verse forms. Here is an
example of that combination of passion and restraint, a lyric
called 'The Immigrant':

> When Ruth was old
> She'd take her children's children on her knee.
> They never wearied to be told
> Tales of her girlhood in a far country.
>
> For though her eyes grew dim,
> Men said of her, 'Her heart is always young',
> And Boaz, while she spoke to him,
> Loved the faint accent of a foreign tongue.

The tenderness, deep and penetrating, in that last line is
wholly characteristic not only of Kendon's poetry but of the
man himself. He was a countryman as well as a scholar, and this
was apparent in his woodcuts as well as in his writing. He had
no dramatic sense, and his one attempt at a novel was therefore

a failure: as I knew to my cost, because I commissioned it for Dents. His life at the Cambridge Press enabled him to withdraw more and more from the modern world of violence, advertisement, and sensation. He became a quietist, and joined the Society of Friends. A certain rigidity of character rooted in his puritan inheritance and upbringing became more obsessive as his health deteriorated. He was made a Fellow of St John's College, but he took no part in University life, preferring to confine himself to his work at the Press, and his garden in the Cambridge suburb, where he loved to sit in unfathomable contemplation under a gigantic copper beech tree.

He was revered at the Press, as he was by his few friends, Priestley among them. Four years after his death in 1959, the Cambridge Press put out a handsome memorial volume. It consists of new versions, made in free verse by Kendon, of thirty-six of the Psalms. He had been commissioned to set the Book of Psalms for the *New English Bible*, but his death prevented the fulfilment of the task. The whole job had to be started afresh, because it would have been false to finish with a pastiche of Kendon's style.

I have lived for a quarter of a century in a block of oast-houses converted by my craftswoman wife into a home. It stands at the end of a large cherry orchard, on the same hilltop as the school where Kendon was born. It figures in the map drawn by him as endpaper to *The Small Years*. His quiet, unregarded genius haunts these orchards, hop gardens, copses and meadows. I cannot forget him. I do not want to, though I am saddened that poetry of such quality as his should have appeared during a period when literary fashion has been set against traditional form, locality of theme, and a humble worship of nature and the God who conjured it, through the weather and the works of man, into the English scene dear to our forefathers. At the time of Kendon's death, *The Times* printed a long and benign obituary. On the day it appeared, I overheard a young literary man say to another, at luncheon in The Savile Club, 'Who *is* that person Kendon? How absurd to give him nearly a whole column!'

[5]

I was given such a free hand at Dents that I felt my work there
to be an extension of my home-life at the other end of Covent
Garden market. I walked through the arcade of the covered
market from my chambers in Lincoln's Inn to Aldine House in
Bedford Street, humorously aware of certain historical family
associations with that ducal neighbourhood, and its down-to-
nature odours; the earthiness of vegetables, the tempting
fragrance of the fruits.

I recalled too the youthful intoxication of the hours when my
friend, Bertie Bridge, the bass-player, smuggled me into
rehearsals at the Opera House, and secured tickets for me to
assist, as the French phrase it, at performances of *The Ring*,
Pelléas and Mélisande, and the Puccini love-potions. I did more
than assist; I took the whole occasion under the wing of my
young imagination: the stage and auditorium together. And
when I stumbled out, drunk on the magic, the subsiding reek
of bananas, potatoes, carrots and cabbage rocked me on its warm
midnight tide. Whenever I go, half a century later, as a visitor to
the Garrick Club, on the fringe of the Market, that smell of the
good earth and its products greets my nostrils, evoking the
agonies of Tristan and Isolda, the cold little hand of Mimi, and
the gentle, religious personality of that young contrabass-
player, whose figure in the orchestra below I could barely
distinguish, from my bench in the gallery.

This sense of being at home wherever I worked redoubled
my confidence and my energy. I was mainly concerned with
developing the modern side of Dent's list, and attracting new
authors. For this purpose I set my bait. It was a series of contemporary poetry at half-a-crown a volume. I did this in the
belief that beginners who are destined to stay the course, and to
mature into professional masters of language, usually start
under the discipline of poetry. This belief is the only one which
will persuade publishers to put out books of verse, which with

rare exceptions figure on the debit side of the balance-sheet.

I was fortunate in editing for a House that could afford this little gamble, and that had a tradition of literary idealism, as their catalogue showed. Were they not the publishers of Everyman's Library, that universal benefactor, and also of the more scholarly Temple Classics and Temple Shakespeare?

Hugh Dent and most of his colleagues on the Board were therefore co-operative in this venture into publishing poetry by contemporary writers. My second enthusiasm was also accepted. I believed that as a publisher's mainstay is his catalogue of steadily selling titles, he should constantly review it, to put sales pressure on the books most likely to respond. I saw one such prospective permanent seller in the *History of English Literature* by the two Frenchmen, Legouis and Cazamian. It was very expensive, however. I suggested printing a large, cheap edition at half a guinea (it has some fourteen hundred pages). It has reprinted again and again in that format.

What a catalogue, that contains the complete editions of Joseph Conrad, W. H. Hudson, Hazlitt edited by P. P. Howe! I longed to add some of these riches to Everyman's Library, and to rent other modern classics from rival imprints. Alas, that publishers still must be referred to as rivals to each other; this is one of the penalties of a necessary emphasis on individualism.

I went one day to Methuens, in Essex Street, and bearded the famous old man of letters, E. V. Lucas, then Chairman. I wanted to put W. H. Hudson's *Shepherd's Life* into Everyman, and told him so.

At first he was sly and suspicious, but no doubt my clumsiness and business naïvety mollified him. He had greeted me by saying, 'Now what nefarious game are you up to?' He ended by letting me have the book, one of the masterpieces of English prose.

I great bolder with success.

'And now,' I said, 'Dents have one lot of Charles Lamb's letters, and you have the rest. Why not amalgamate the two in the final, authoritative edition under your editorship and Dent's imprint?'

That started something which ended successfully. Lucas then took me by the arm, and said, 'Now, my boy, having discussed Lamb, let us go together to Simpson's in The Strand and discuss a saddle of mutton!'

One evening at Lascelles Abercrombie's home in Stanley Gardens, his three sons bombarded me with enthusiastic praise for the poetry of a Welsh boy named Dylan Thomas. I looked at a copy of verse called *Eighteen Poems* put out by David Archer, a benevolent amateur bookseller in Red Lion Square, and I appreciated the excitement with which Lascelles's sons urged me to look at a set of manuscripts of twenty-five more poems. I suggested, however, that I would have liked more coherence in the verse, and less telescoping of images. My objections were treated as evidence of my advanced age (I was then forty-two), and I was persuaded to meet the prodigy and read the second set of poems.

This was arranged, and one morning at eleven o'clock, Dylan Thomas, then a youth of twenty, called on me at my office in Aldine House in Bedford Street.

He was short, chubby, dressed in a fisherman's jersey, and gave a general impression of being tousled and unwashed. Further, he appeared to be dazed, or sleepy, as though he had been out all night. laying lobster-pots. His crown of curly hair seemed salt-encrusted; his eyes were large and strained, his full lips bruised, with black lines where they had dried, in contact with each other.

His manner puzzled me. He might have drifted in by chance, and to no purpose. I produced the manuscript of the twenty-five poems, which I had read with increased interest, and told him that Dents proposed to put them out in the Halfcrown Series, printed in Eric Gill's *Perpetua* fount, a bold, clean type.

Thomas accepted this news with half-focussed interest, and showed none at all when I told him that he would be in good company with other poets whose work I was sponsoring: Frank Kendon, W. J. Turner (an erratic, difficult character, who was music critic on the *New Statesman*), Norman Cameron (a friend of Robert Graves, and subject to his technical dis-

P

cipline), Clifford Dyment, Conrad Aiken, Hal Summers, and several other poets, English, Irish and Welsh. I mentioned particularly Edwin Muir, for I believed his poetry to be of rare quality, deeply rooted in a sombre personality enriched by scholarship, and the discipline of a professional life spent in translating.

By this time Dylan Thomas appeared to be about to fall asleep, so I roused him by referring again to his own work, and I told him that his *Twenty-five Poems* would be the fifteenth volume in the series.

I then got up, to usher him from the room. To my embarrassment, he asked me to lend him half-a-crown to buy a drink! This was my first encounter with the new, unceremonious social code of the younger generation, and I did not appreciate it. Nor was I eager to accept the fact that a boy of his age should already be slightly fuddled at eleven o'clock in the morning. I could now account for the sleepy manner, the vague stare, the blackened lips, the slovenly clothes. Those signs of bohemianism and self-indulgence had no relevance to his poetry. His social conduct was, to use his own phrase, 'Groping for matter under the dog's plate,' and I was distressed that he could show so little respect for his own dignity, and for the preservation of health and energy necessary for him to develop his poetry.

The rest of his unhappy life story is well-known. It has been over-publicized by the ghouls who infest the world of the arts. Dylan Thomas was a man of genius, but the genius was debauched and prematurely destroyed by his indulgent habits. Throughout my dealings with him I had the impression that he was deliberately committing suicide, by slow degrees, driven by some strange, Celtic spirit of perversity. There was no real evil in him; no meanness, jealousy, self-conceit. He was infuriating, for he rarely kept appointments or answered letters. He was always cadging small sums of money. He had the social and moral outlook of a tramp, unadult and fundamentally fear-ridden. But he was lovable. The charm emerges in Augustus John's portrait of him. As a speaker of verse he was gifted, like so many Welshmen, and he had a perfect sense of timing. This brought him fame as a broadcaster, a dangerous, bubble reputation, but it took his poetry out with it, to an ever-increasing audience. Finally, his dissolute life and squalid death attracted even wider attention, from a public more interested in melodrama and in conventionalized types as representative of human activities, than in individual identity and the mystery of a personal achievement.

A minor and unworthy literature is gathering round his life-story and his work, inflating both, disproportionately. I am more content to have sponsored Edwin Muir's traditional but subtle muse, and I believe that as time passes my preference will be justified.

[6]

As a man grows older he becomes the victim of his own career. There is no prison so secure as success. It walls us round with reputation, and we tend to lose all possibility of the common touch. If our imagination survives so long, we lament the danger, freedom, anonymity of our years of struggle, when we were accepted, or rejected, on our real value as individuals, and not as legend has petrified us into monuments. Perhaps the sadness so often experienced in later life is a recognition that we are buried before we are dead, and our obituaries prematurely chiselled by a younger generation eager to replace us in this mad quest for finality. There is no guarantee that even the grave ends our voyage home.

I was sitting one evening in my chambers with Laurence Binyon and Robin Flower, older men than me, both of them learned scholars, Binyon an authority on Oriental art, Flower on Gaelic poetry. They worked in the British Museum, and it may have been this daily contact with the past, in all its variety and vastness, that made them so modest about their own contribution to the art of poetry. Binyon's verse is the better known, and his translation of Dante's *Divine Comedy* into *terza-rima* is the most fluent and beautiful that I know. It catches the single wave of rhythm that propels each *canto* of the original Italian, shapely and transparent like those billows rolling in at sunset from the Atlantic to the shore at the Cape of Good Hope, the lowering majesty of light shining through them.

Binyon, a quiet and somewhat melancholy figure, his features drooping like those of a noble old hound, had said something about the last stages of a lifework, and Robin Flower agreed that there could be little self-congratulation in the retrospect. He was a rough-hewn man, with a large round head and face under a thatch of blond hair. His holidays from the Museum were spent in the remote island of the Great Blaskett, collecting folk tales from the few survivors of a civilization fabulous when the snakes left Ireland on the command of St Patrick.

Binyon spoke so sadly that neither I nor Robin Flower could formulate an immediate reply. The spell of dejection silenced us, and while it was working, there came a voice from the Chapel of Lincoln's Inn, outside my study window. It was the bell ringing the curfew at nine o'clock, warning the porters to shut the gates of the Inn. It was a musical baritone, touched a little with time and the mosses of memory, which gave it a faint huskiness.

'There, Laurence,' I said, half playfully because my younger nerves would not accept his mood of resignation, 'there is corroboration of your gloom. That bell was brought home from Cadiz by the poet John Donne, when he went on the piratical expedition under the Earl of Essex. He gave it to the Inn of which he was a member. I'll bet that if we went down into Chancery Lane and inquired of every passerby during the three hours between now and midnight, not one of them would know the name of the donor, or that he had introduced into English poetry the cadences and rhythms of impassioned speech, natural impulses of his own character which afterwards enlivened his sermons when he was dean of St Paul's Cathedral.'

Still half playfully, I quoted the last couplet of Donne's sonnet on Death:

One short sleep past, we wake eternally,
And death shall be no more. Death, thou shalt die!

Then we all sat silent for awhile, until Robin Flower spoke:
'That is the fault of this industrial age. Europe is now
destroyed, as a culture, and so will all civilizations be destroyed
as soon as they become rootless, gathered into factories and the
like. There is something in the soul of a people so long as they
are near the soil, or mastering the sea as a lover masters a
woman: so long as they are subject to the authority and
teaching of solitude. I have met this in the Western Islands, and
found a poetry there: but it is the last.'

We debated this matter as though holding a post-mortem,
all three of us sadly conscious of something rotten in the state of
Europe, whose great culture after two thousand years of
blending, from the promise and riches of Judea, Greece, Rome,
into a utility of compassion through the infusion of Christianity,
was now succumbing between the wars to the invading
African cults, processed by America. We recognized the
power of this primitive cult, but failed to realize what it
nurtured, for the second world war was yet at the threshold; and
we dared not face the significance of the revival of deliberate
savagery in the Western World, threatening the freedom of individuals, under the benevolence of laws so painfully, slowly
established on foundations of suffering, courage, and faith.

I went down the eighty-two stone stairs with my friends, to
see them across the two squares, to the gate into Lincoln's Inn
Fields. The night was bright under a clear moon, and the
windows of the offices of the *New Statesman* flashed like
mercury. One of them was lighted from within. Ah! I thought,
it is press-night, and Kingsley Martin is composing a last-
minute leader about the latest threat to the forces of reason.
That was the only lighted window I could see from the gateway
of the Inn. Such was my mood that I imagined this window to be
the only light in the world.

I said good night to Binyon and Flower, and stood outside
the gate, to watch them walking slowly along, under the old

brick wall of the Inn Gardens, towards Great Turnstile, High Holborn and the self-assured traffic of the twentieth century. They looked fragile under the night, and Binyon's character conditioned even his manner of walking: slow, grave, resigned. He was a quietly impressive man, and his poetry reflected his virtue.

I walked round New Square before climbing up to my rooms, and my old Aberdeen terrier welcomed the excursion. He disappeared into the shadows of the trees overhanging the railings of the garden, but I could distinguish by sound, and an occasional blackness in the dark, his progress rail by odorous rail, not lagging far behind my strolling figure, with which he was in silent communication.

As I moved round the Square, I saw through the trees another light. It came from the rooms beside the gate, where Ellis Roberts lived. He was at that time Literary Editor of the *New Statesman*, following Desmond MacCarthy. He was a gothic figure, with protruding eyes, long 'dacked' hair, a flat parsonic hat with wide brim, and a pendulous double chin that swung as he talked.

My wife and I had been to luncheon with him that same day, for he was entertaining Max Beerbohm and his first wife. They were on a visit from Rapallo. I chuckled as I walked on, recollecting the amusing debate between my wife and Max Beerbohm. She, an enthusiast for abstract art, was praising the work of Ben Nicholson, son of the painter William Nicholson whose traditional skill was more comprehensible to me. Evidently Max shared my prejudice, for with a theatrical gesture he plunged a hand into the pocket of his salt-and-pepper trousers, produced several silver coins, and laid them out, with a nice mockery of deliberation, on the palm of his hand, then to exclaim, 'There! A composition by Ben Nicholson!'

I was joined by Hamish, my terrier, who had mistaken my quiet chuckle for a summons, and we walked together past the pillars of the arcade under Inigo Jones's chapel, paused again at the bole of the plane-tree in Old Square, and entered Number

Thirteen, leaving the moonlit serenity of the night, and the problems of a dissolving Europe: its arts, its international politics, its morals. A personal career, an individual achievement, loomed large or small, against the background, according to the mood one was in, and there was no other criterion. Such was my conclusion as I went to bed; but I knew this was only a postponement of the real and final answer.

[7]

Pethick-Lawrence, our next-door neighbour, lived for half a century in his chambers in Old Square. We were there for only five years, but they were crowded with activity and hospitality, for no home could be more central to every facet of civilized life. Writers, lawyers, publishers, newspaper men (a lively and generous sodality) used our rooms as a clearing house for companionate relaxation, and on Wednesday nights we welcomed all comers.

James Stephens, the Irish leprechaun, was a regular attendant at our mid-week open house. One night he brought a young woman whose remarkable beauty of person silenced the hubbub of voices as she entered, rather shyly and demurely. She was dressed in mourning. Her name was Dilys Powell; unknown then, but later to become familiar to the public when she established herself in her profession as a journalist. Years afterwards she wrote a book that explained the sad beauty of our first meeting with her. It is called *An Affair of the Heart*, the account of her post-war return to Greece, where her first husband had died while in command of the British School of Archaeology. I know of no book more poignant in its tribute to the 'glory that was Greece', offered with a dignity partly born of remembered grief, partly of her own innate character.

Younger writers, including the politically minded poets of the nineteen-thirties, came to 13 Old Square, buzzing like angry bees under the provocation of the Spanish Civil War, all of them, with the exception of Roy Campbell, partisan of the Republicans, as might be expected of young idealists determined to remove the rule of Superstition and to establish Utopia.

The younger the poets, the more savagely they rejected traditional forms and melodic line. They proposed to command attention by means of violent, incongruous imagery, and plebeian idiom. This was intended as a service to democracy, though most of them were acquainted with the masses of the industrial proletariat only by glimpsing them from the playing-fields of the public schools. Their anti-romanticism was highly romantic, as most of them must have discovered, since another world war has swept away still more of the barriers of Privilege, and the comfort of the Welfare State has proved all mankind to be much alike in the use of its leisure and affluence.

I suspect that leisure, like happiness, is a by-product of individual personality, and the ordering of one's life. A tyrannical old dowager, leading a rich, idle dotage in Bournemouth, is likely never to find a moment's leisure during her ineffectual day; nor might a harassed unmethodical mother of a young family. But a change of emphasis in their characters would re-orientate the twenty-four hours in both the over-idle day of the one and the over-worked day of the other.

Perhaps leisure is a condition of mind also like happiness, both being rewards dependent on humility, that intellectual patience which knows the value of waiting, of the easy gesture, and the grace of unselfconsciousness. These are cognates of the machinery by which we master time, that immemorial tyrant over man's days and the destiny of nations.

The individual who by faith, or by natal luck, is master of an art, or indeed of any activity of body and mind, achieves thereby this mastery over time, and his command shows itself in the grace and ease of his working gesture. His memory, his judgment, his manipulative power, all are enriched and released by this single control of the time factor. Watch a great pianist at work, or an actor; their authority and their magic depend upon timing. In creative work the same rule holds good.

I suppose Mozart is the supreme example. He lived for thirty-five years. At the age of five he already showed that mastery over time, in compositions lucid with melodic line, perfectly phrased through every fraction of a second. I believe that in consequence (and consequence is literally the right word), his short life, crowded with tours, public performances and the vast output of superhuman composition, was one long process of leisure. Even an indifferently successful marriage could not spoil that gesture or make it convulsive. He may have been buried in a pauper's grave, but he died as he had been born, rich beyond the dreams of Croesus.

These matters are more important than the interplay of social conditions, the accidents of family inheritance, the justice and injustice of economic environment, and all the other external considerations with which politicians and trade union officials concern themselves. This is being proved again and again by individuals whose lives and achievements appear to bear no relation to the circumstances and heredity into which they are born. It is a mystery, and it tempts one to believe that anarchy is the only real system by which mankind's society and history are regulated.

That will not do, however, for there are tigers and wolves among us. In consequence, there must be systems of control: religious creeds, dogmas, policings, political parties. But how clumsy they are, in comparison with the internal government of which the individual genius is capable, so long as that genius in everyman is recognized and sanctified. That recognition was Christ's unique achievement, and it marks the supremacy of his un-doctrine.

Learning thus as the years moved on, I discovered that professional activity is like a snowball, gathering in size as it rolls along. Work flowed in, and as editor in Aldine House, free-lance literary journalist, poet and novelist, I might have found myself in the condition of nervous prostration that nearly wrecked me during the year of my brother's death. I was working harder than in the days when I tried, and failed, to balance two careers, one in Whitehall, the other in Fleet Street. But now, all was serenely ordered in a home that appeared to have no enclosure; that was maintained by a person of infinite enterprise and resource. The silverwork and jewellery which appeared as accompaniment to this control were a true signature of that dear authority.

Among the friendships that I made outside the circle of our home-life in Lincoln's Inn, was one which I valued most of all. It is strange that I cannot recollect my first meeting with Walter de la Mare, but I know it was after I reviewed one of his volumes of verse. We approached each other gradually, by means of formal and then less formal letters, so that by the time we met an intimacy had already been established.

I have written about him so much since his death in 1956 that I can say little more. I have lectured about him and given readings of his poetry in the most unlikely places, and always have found large and enthusiastic audiences. Once in Geneva University I talked about his long poem *The Traveller* and its relation as epilogue to the whole of his lifework. The effect was almost frightening. As I finished reading, I saw people in tears, and a funereal silence followed before the outburst of almost hysterical, reactionary applause.

De la Mare's personality and poetry, as I tried to present them, were similarly received when I gave an informal address one morning to the whole of the English Faculty at Mysore University in South India. I have never lectured in so opulent and fairylike a setting. But even in that foreign world, to a large crowd of people who could not possibly conceive what soil and roots had bred this poetry, its magic was immediately apparent. The poet was at home wherever his work revealed him. I took it into Europe, to Germany, Denmark, Sweden, Holland, Italy. The magic always worked.

It dominated his personal contacts also. He was possessed by a kind of diagonal magnetism that drew all *vis-à-vis* conversations athwart the usual trends of social give and take. There was no perversity or affectation in this. Indeed, his sincerity was intense; it concentrated into eagerness; and that was infectious.

One could not be frivolous when talking with him, though humour played over the tête-à-tête, like summer lightning. His mouth, a dominant feature in that severely Roman head, was mobile under this influence of humour. This relieved the severity, the depths of fear and even agony, that set the character of his dark eyes. It prevented his general expression, the whole countenance, from being one of desperation and despair.

He was a questioner. He drew people out, but with a deference that gave them the illusion of being knowledgeable. And what he wanted to know was usually something that could not be defined, though this fact had hitherto been hidden under a cover of ordinariness. Thus, one afternoon at tea in his flat in South End House, Montpelier Row, Twickenham, he suddenly broke the run of talk because I said, 'Oh! let us leave that problem until tomorrow!' It was no more than a pause, a mere comma, while I introduced some other image, or facet, to the discussion. But his powerful face set into a mask of apprehension, and alarming doubt.

'How can you be certain,' he asked, tensely, his voice trembling, 'how can you be sure there will be a tomorrow?'

And of course, the passion of uncertainty behind what would seem to be a ridiculous query gave it a dreadful validity. I stared back at him, into the threat of nothingness, of *Finis*.

The other persons present were Sir Stephen Tallents, like myself an ex-civil servant, and the North Country poet Wilfred Gibson. Tallents, the elusive trouble-dodging official, froze into utter stillness, cunningly avoiding the killer. Gibson was a simple soul, who had spent his whole life writing nothing but matter-of-fact verse in sub-Wordsworthian vein. In old age he was sinking into that congenital simplicity. de La Mare's doubt immediately found a lodgment in Gibson's innocent and timid mind. He started up, wide-eyed, and said with childish emphasis, 'Why yes! There will be no tomorrow!'

Tallents's shrewd and wary eye angled in my direction. He did not believe in this. He thought it was a literary ploy, irrelevant to the agenda before the committee. But I was not willing to be drawn to his side. I had long since left Whitehall and its lifeless certainties.

'Never mind,' I replied to De la Mare. 'Between now and tomorrow there is always eternity, and we have infinite time.'

The discussion was resumed after this reassurance, and once again we conjured up the procession of people, in their costumes of the period, who had lived in those panelled rooms over the past two hundred years. The rooms themselves seemed animated to share the inquiry, and were more eloquent than the humans gathered there that summer afternoon. I felt presences, bewigged and powdered. Perhaps the skill of Professor Reilly, the architect who owned this end house of Montpelier Row, and had restored it with such historical insight, was responsible for my imaginary panorama.

A huge plane-tree dominating the riverside gardens, outside the deep-set windows, slept in the sunshine, adding to the mood of timelessness, in which the paradox of motionless flux was normal and acceptable. But the whole bizarre situation was an internal drama, spun out of the imagination of our host, whose everyday life was conducted under that scrupulous but supra-rational baton.

[8]

Looking back over the story of mankind, in all continents, I think that the most general observation is that man in the mass has always lagged behind the development of the individual. The part has been larger than the whole, and, in so being, has demonstrated that this quality, something other than a con-formation to material laws of time and space, quantity and mass, is our certain promise of emergence, even though the mob-spirit in us, which Tolstoy believed was never under control by statesman or political system, may plunge us yet again into near-annihilation. It has been doing so consistently since history began. The archaeologists find that the prologue to history, long, dreary and cruel, was a synopsis of the story of blind destruction.

Outstanding in that story is the seeming hatred of home. Man no sooner goes out into the market-place, the forum, the stadium, the arena, than he merges his individuality into a kind of brute force, blind, backward and ferocious, that takes on a separate authority for mischief, wantonness, indifferent as the ocean that rages first, then turns playful, 'Smashing the rocks with a dead child.'

This is the headless, heartless monster which no machinery of government, divine or human, has yet been able to tame. We had believed, during the nineteenth century, that it could do so, at least among the communities of Western man. But the twentieth century has blown that belief away under the explosives of two world wars. We have seen houses, villages, great cities, consumed, as in the days of the anarchic past. So complete has been this latest outbreak, that the very idea of stability, moral as well as material, has been debased.

I remember how I sat here in my Kentish home, on our hill-top under the shelter of a large cherry orchard, while the Battle of Britain raged overhead during the autumn of 1940. I found myself concerned not only for physical safety but also the spiritual. A kind of contempt, as toward a traitor, shook my mind as I felt the fabric of the building heave and settle under the force of the explosions. Home itself, in all its gradual and exquisitely intimate growth over the years, in the soil of love, service, sacrifice and private triumph, appeared to be a cheat.

Lust, a passion for action, any action so long as it was revengeful, came down in a curtain of fire over my mind, blinding me to all my possessions, all affiliations with persons and significant things sanctified by usage and familiarity. And I knew that this was the worst that can happen to the Holy Ghost in everyman, his only guide to fulfilment of the promises made by our religions, our sciences, our superb arts, since consciousness and memory awoke us to our distinction from our illimitable, and otherwise unconquerable, environment.

I believe that in the terror of this wartime recognition, my conception of what home really means was established as a cornerstone to my structure of belief. It was not new, not an encounter on the road to Damascus. I had believed it instinctively since childhood, as most human beings do, unless their nativity is disastrous, in slums or of brutal parentage.

But the signalman of our later hopes, the symbol compounded of all mythologies that have flowered out of the plant of our human nature, this Christ who is our crowned scientist, philosopher, artist was born under the accident of homelessness. His conquest of that disability may be one of the most valuable elements in the story of his life, which is a picture-writing of the evolution of human consciousness, and the parallel recognition of the function and value of home, its place and its indestructibility.

So we carry our home within us, and as we battle our way through the years, goaded by experience, we learn sooner or later that the thing we have been searching for has remained out of reach because we hoped to find it elsewhere. The error has taken many forms, most of them social: the political creed, the religious dogma, the mythology and the Utopia. But these external machineries always fail us in the end of our lives, leaving us to loneliness and despair. Once we have discovered that home is nothing more, and nothing less, than the house within the mind, then the voyage is over.

How can that be possible, in a world which again and again relapses into barbarism? The establishment of a home demands a disciplined employment of science, the arts, the affections of sacrifice and tolerance. It has its own intimate language. The very word 'barbarism', meaning unintelligibility, stands for the destruction of all these qualities; and our experience in the twentieth century has taught us that this barbarism is the ground base of existence, into which we lapse at the pull of the vile gravitation of cruelty and fear.

I saw this horror at work in Africa and India, fecundating as a monstrous disease in the poverty, the teeming over-population, the religious fanaticism, and the clash of racial prejudices. During the voyage home I faced the despair which followed my confrontation with these destroyers of the chances for individual dignity. I recalled the sadness with which that great man, Radhakrishnan, had spoken to me of these adversaries to a sane, constructive government in India.

But in a community at the other extreme of social well-being, the United States of America, at least a quarter of the population is badly housed and precariously nourished. When these inequalities of material welfare are mastered, in a future world-society where the two explosive threats of nuclear war and over-population have been neutralized, what will be the certainties of a homecoming for the individuals in that ever-postponed Utopia?

I see the answer in a small glass aquarium, which my brother was carrying over Battersea Bridge, while the lurid sunset of the first day of the twentieth century filled the River Thames below his feet with the simulacrum of blood and fiery disaster. I see myself clinging to his coat, terror-stricken because of the certainty that the precious gift, the aquarium, would never be brought safely home. The gangs of Battersea urchins prowled the streets on the south side of the river. My brother's sensitive hands were numb with cold. The pavements were harsh with frost, and night was closing down over us.

But we brought the aquarium home. My brother's character had won: the quiet determination, the faith in an idea. That journey over the bridge between Chelsea and Battersea, interminable and terrible to two infants, set the theme whose variations have fulfilled my life, the theme of a faith maintained and embodied in work, through the long voyage home.